Stories in Season

OTHER TITLES BY BRUCE TAYLOR

The Word in the Wind
No Business as Usual
Looking Up at Love
Life Woven into God
Between Advents
Christ's New Address
Love Walks on Wounded Feet
God at Work
What Happens Next?
Truth Be Told
Practicing the Promise
To Be a Disciple

Stories in Season

Narrative Sermons for the Christian Year

BRUCE L. TAYLOR

RESOURCE *Publications* • Eugene, Oregon

STORIES IN SEASON
Narrative Sermons for the Christian Year

Copyright © 2025 Bruce L. Taylor. All rights reserved. Except for brief quotations in critical publications or reviews, no part of this book may be reproduced in any manner without prior written permission from the publisher. Write: Permissions, Wipf and Stock Publishers, 199 W. 8th Ave., Suite 3, Eugene, OR 97401.

Resource Publications
An Imprint of Wipf and Stock Publishers
199 W. 8th Ave., Suite 3
Eugene, OR 97401

www.wipfandstock.com

PAPERBACK ISBN: 979-8-3852-5265-7
HARDCOVER ISBN: 979-8-3852-5266-4
EBOOK ISBN: 979-8-3852-5267-1

07/28/25

Scripture quotations marked (NRSV) are from Common Bible: New Revised Standard Version Bible, copyright © 1989 National Council of the Churches of Christ in the United States of America. Used by permission. All rights reserved worldwide. Emphasis added.

Scripture quotations marked (RSV) are from Revised Standard Version of the Bible, copyright © 1946, 1952, and 1971 National Council of the Churches of Christ in the United States of America. Used by permission. All rights reserved.

Scripture quotations marked (KJV) are from the King James Version of the Bible.

In memory of
Grandmother Iva Mae Ward,
who told me stories

Contents

Introduction	xi
FIRST SUNDAY OF ADVENT Jeremiah 33:14–16, 1 Thessalonians 3:9–13, Luke 21:25–36 **"Tomorrow, God"**	3
SECOND SUNDAY OF ADVENT Isaiah 40:1–11, 2 Peter 3:8–15a, Mark 1:1–8 **"Accepting Salvation"**	9
THIRD SUNDAY OF ADVENT Isaiah 35:1–10, James 5:7–10, Matthew 11:2–11 **"Waiting for the 9:01"**	16
CHRISTMAS EVE (EARLY) Isaiah 9:2–7, Titus 2:11–14, Luke 2:1–20 **"The Littlest Shepherd"**	25
CHRISTMAS EVE (LATE) Isaiah 9:2–7, Titus 2:11–14, Luke 2:1–20 **"Salvation in the Subway"**	32
NATIVITY OF JESUS CHRIST/CHRISTMAS DAY Isaiah 57:7–10, Hebrews 1:1–4, John 1:1–14 **"A Christmas Carol—Epilogue"**	37
FIRST SUNDAY AFTER CHRISTMAS Isaiah 61:10—62:3, Galatians 4:4–7, Luke 2:22–40 **"The Gift We Got"**	43
EPIPHANY OF THE LORD Isaiah 60:1–6, Ephesians 3:1–12, Matthew 2:1–12 **"Epiphany"**	51

SECOND SUNDAY AFTER EPIPHANY
Isaiah 62:1–5, 1 Corinthians 12:1–11, John 2:1–11
"From Water to Wine"   61

FOURTH SUNDAY IN ORDINARY TIME
Micah 6:1–8, 1 Corinthians 1:18–31, Matthew 5:1–12
"Beatitude"   68

TRANSFIGURATION OF THE LORD
Exodus 24:12–18, 2 Peter 1:16–21, Matthew 17:1–9
"Eyewitness to Glory"   77

ASH WEDNESDAY
Isaiah 58:1–12, 2 Corinthians 5:20b—6:10, Matthew 6:1–6, 16–21
"The Committee"   85

FIFTH SUNDAY IN LENT
Ezekiel 37:1–14, Romans 8:6–11, John 11:1–45
"To Live Again"   91

PALM/PASSION SUNDAY
Isaiah 50:4–9a, Philippians 2:5–11, Luke 19:28–40
"Conversation in a Workshop"   96

GOOD FRIDAY
Isaiah 52:13—53:12, Hebrews 4:14–16; 5:7–9, John 18:1—19:42
  100

THIRD SUNDAY OF EASTER
Acts 2:14a, 36–41, 1 Peter 1:17–23, Luke 24:13–35
"Word and Sacrament"   111

FIFTH SUNDAY OF EASTER
Acts 11:1–18, Revelation 21:1–6, John 13:31–35
"Revelation"   118

ASCENSION OF THE LORD
Acts 1:1–11, Ephesians 1:15–23, Luke 24:44–53
"Witness to the Power"   124

THE DAY OF PENTECOST
Acts 2:1–21, Romans 8:14–17, John 14:8–17, 25–27
"When the Spirit Moves You"   131

TRINITY SUNDAY
Isaiah 6:1–8, Romans 8:12–17, John 3:1–17
"Nicodemus' Diary"   141

NINTH SUNDAY IN ORDINARY TIME
1 Samuel 3:1–10 (11–20), 2 Corinthians 4:5–12, Mark 2:23—3:6
"Out of the Mouths . . ."   148

TWELFTH SUNDAY IN ORDINARY TIME
1 Kings 19:1–15a, Galatians 3:23–29, Luke 8:26–39
"Found"   156

FOURTEENTH SUNDAY IN ORDINARY TIME
2 Samuel 5:1–5, 9–10, 2 Corinthians 12:2–10, Mark 6:1–13
"Talk of the Town"   162

SEVENTEENTH SUNDAY IN ORDINARY TIME
2 Samuel 11:1–15, Ephesians 3:14–21, John 6:1–21
"Fish, Loaves, and Faith"   168

TWENTY-FIRST SUNDAY IN ORDINARY TIME
Jeremiah 1:4–10, Hebrews 12:18–29, Luke 13:22–30
"A Pilgrimage Tale: Going to the Banquet"   173

TWENTY-SECOND SUNDAY IN ORDINARY TIME
Jeremiah 2:4–13, Hebrews 13:1–8, 15–16, Luke 14:1, 7–14
"Angel in Our Midst"   179

TWENTY-FIFTH SUNDAY IN ORDINARY TIME
Proverbs 31:10–31, James 3:13—4:3, 7–8a, Mark 9:30–37
"First Things First"   187

THIRTIETH SUNDAY IN ORDINARY TIME
Joel 2:23–32, 2 Timothy 4:6–8, 16–18, Luke 18:9–14
"Not Like These Sinners"   194

THIRTY-SECOND SUNDAY IN ORDINARY TIME
Haggai 1:15b—2:9, 2 Thessalonians 2:1–5, 13–17, Luke 20:27–38
"The God of the Living"   200

THIRTY-THIRD SUNDAY IN ORDINARY TIME
Judges 4:1–7, 1 Thessalonians 5:1–11, Matthew 25:14–30
"The Memories in the Closet"   205

CHRIST THE KING
Ezekiel 34:11–16, 20–24, Ephesians 1:15–23, Matthew 25:31–46
"Faces of the King"   213

THANKSGIVING
Deuteronomy 26:1–11, 1 Timothy 2:1–4, Matthew 6:25–33
"Paradise"   223

Introduction

Storytelling is as old as humanity. Indeed, one feature that distinguishes human beings from other species is the ability to tell stories, whether an account of some historically factual event or a tale completely imaginary, whether orally or by gesture or by drawing on the wall of a cave or by writing on parchment or paper. And the ability to communicate truth, trivial or profound, may be accomplished as well or even better by way of fictional accounts rather than with verifiable reports of things that have actually occurred in real times and places. So, Aesop and Hardy are as "true" as Herodotus and Gibbon, and the liturgically poetic first chapter of Genesis, for instance, may be treasured as an explanation of creation without absurdly insisting that science is "ungodly" or the product of the devil.

All forms of communication share some goals and characteristics. Presumably, the object is, in the first place, to hold another's interest; if the "telling" fails to do that, the effort will have been pointless. So, to some degree, it must be entertaining, or at least pleasurable. Over time, whether by intuition or by prescription, storytelling has come to incorporate techniques not only to assure comprehension, but to evoke curiosity—techniques such as humor, irony, suspense, pace, and familiar connections with the subject matter, that is, referencing touchstones of common experience.

All children, I think, like to be told stories. I especially remember an older church couple in Salt Lake City who babysat me as a young child, delighting me by reading to me the children's story on the inside back cover of each month's *Presbyterian Life* before or after a lunch or dinner of ebelskivers, and my maternal grandmother in Manhattan, Kansas, blind for most of her life, telling me stories from memory or reading them to me from a Braille storybook. Wanting to be told a story is something that most of us never outgrow. "Hollywood" is an entire industry based on that reality—ironically, by creating visual illusion. As pleasurable as reading is for most of us, including reading fiction, a large number of adults also like to have stories told to them, usually more complex than children's books but still nurturing the imagination. I was introduced to audiobooks (mainly, mysteries) about the time that, as moderator of the trustees of one of the presbyteries I served, we discovered that our bookkeeper had been embezzling presbytery funds, and I was suddenly having to attend weekly meetings that necessitated a three-hour drive each way to and from the presbytery office one hundred fifty miles away. Dealing with the embezzlement and its direct and indirect fallout lasted three years. The audiobooks made the daylight journey to the Friday meetings a lot more enjoyable and kept me alert as midnight came and went on my way back home. Eventually, I wrote a couple of mysteries of my own to tape-record and supplement the books that I had heard multiple times. It was also during this time that I developed the practice of writing and delivering a story sermon about once a quarter.

One aspect of gaining and holding attention in the process of communication is variation. I had been writing all my sermons more or less in the traditional form by the time that something first prompted me to write a story as a way of communicating the "truth" of the scripture passages from the lectionary for Palm and Passion Sunday, 1992. In childhood and adolescence, I enjoyed writing stories and short plays, and was encouraged in my creative efforts by my parents and teachers. I certainly produced no great literature, or even mediocre, but it was always an enjoyable pastime. Although I had occasionally included a brief excerpt from a book or short story or poem in my sermons, it was not until six years into the parish ministry that I decided to write a story myself to use as a sermon. I had noticed that most Palm Sunday sermons I had heard rather encouraged congregations to interpret the day as a practice Easter celebration rather than a paradoxical prelude to Christ's passion, and perhaps even tended to excuse skipping the Maundy Thursday and Good Friday worship services (and even excuse avoidance of thinking about the uncomfortable events of Holy Week, detouring instead directly to the triumph of the empty tomb). "Conversation in a Workshop" was such a radical departure from my customary preaching that it seems to have made a special impression on the worshipers that day, aided perhaps by my dressing the part of the character in the story and acting out appropriate movements and gestures in the telling. Comments suggested that it had all communicated a new understanding of the passion and the irony of the Palm Sunday parade. There were similar responses when I ventured to repeat the sermon in a subsequent pastorate. Surely, the novelty of the technique had something to do with the congregations' reactions.

Once a story idea formed, each of the stories I have preached over the years fairly wrote themselves. But I have never found myself able to "force" a story. Not every set of lectionary readings prompts a story for me (indeed,

I may have preached on a passage several times before a relevant story ever occurred to me), and, in the case of parables and other vivid biblical narratives, I find it difficult to "gild the lily" and would not want to do so anyway, other than a few stories that have focused on what the characters in that biblical episode were thinking and feeling. At any rate, I fear that preaching in this style too frequently would dilute its effectiveness and hazard rendering the sermon more "entertainment" and less an unanticipated fresh encounter with the gospel. The evangelistic opportunity offered by Easter church attendance, including many once-a-year or first-time worshipers, I judge, means that highest of all Christian feast days calls for the clearest, even if prosaic, proclamation of the word and transparent administration of the eucharist; I never ventured to invent a story for the Easter sermon.

This collection includes many of the story sermons that have appeared in the published volumes of my sermons for each Sunday and major feast day of the Protestant Christian calendar, plus a dozen that have not previously appeared in print. One of the story sermons included here was written specifically for this book, and has never (yet) been preached. They are all arranged here according to the church season rather than by the specific lectionary year—sermons preached during lectionary years A, B, and C appear together successively according to the church calendar. Nevertheless, the three lectionary cycles share a similar sequence of Jesus' life and theological emphases that the arrangement of the stories here reflects.

I was always eager to share these stories with congregations. I have looked forward to preaching every sermon that I have written—including the very few in these volumes that have never been presented from a pulpit—but the time between finishing a story sermon and preaching it was usually one of special anticipation for me, and I hope that the sermons in this book will prompt the reader to seek out and read the other stories that appear in my other volumes. And, for those ministers who may read this book, I encourage you to experiment with this approach if the Spirit prompts you to do so. The Bible itself, the grist for whatever bread we offer from the pulpit, is the truth of God presented largely in story form, communicated from believer to prospective or veteran believer, shaped by the experience and conviction of generation after generation, around the campfire, around the table, around the altar, at times of joy, at times of fear, at times of crisis, at times of dedication.

Each of us loves a good story. Each of us is capable of telling a story. And what more important story is there to tell, inspired by the Holy Spirit, than the continuing story of God, and God's Son, in the lives of God's faithful people? It is never out of season.

Advent

First Sunday of Advent

Jeremiah 33:14–16
1 Thessalonians 3:9–13
Luke 21:25–36

"Tomorrow, God"

"So what has it gotten you, this 'good news'?" The voice came from the next cell. Raspy and mocking, it issued between fits of coughing and wheezing.

The old man lifted his head slightly and drew his legs up close to his chest to preserve his warmth, which the cold stone floor had been sapping from his outstretched limbs. Somewhere, there was the sound of slowly dripping water. The jail was dank and smelled of human waste.

"He will not abandon me," the old man replied to the taunt from behind the stone wall.

A raspy laugh answered his statement, but it quickly disappeared into another fit of coughing.

"Nor *anyone* who turns to him in faith," the old man added.

To this, there came a snort from the next cell. "I heard him," the raspy voice said after a few seconds. "That Jew who spoke down by their meeting place. What do they call it? 'Synagogue,' that's it. I heard him. A lot of rubbish about the cross proving his point." Another snort, which led to more coughing. When he recovered, he added, "They sent him packing, fair enough—talking about a king on a cross, indeed." There was a thud. The man to whom the voice belonged had apparently been standing at the bars of his cell, and now had sat down on the hard floor. "Good news. Ha!" There was silence again, broken only by the sound of dripping water. Eventually, he asked, "What are you called?"

"Jason," the old man replied, his chin resting on his knees and his arms wrapped around his legs. "Some know me now as a follower of Jesus."

"Jesus, yes, that's the name that little Jew called him," the other man said with a slight chuckle. "The Christ, he said he was—the anointed one, whatever that means."

"It has to do with the Hebrew scriptures," the old man informed him. "He's the one the prophets of the Jews said would come."

"Bah," the voice from the other cell uttered.

"The Lord," the old man added.

"Have a care," the raspy voice replied. "Talk like *that's* what got you *in* here. So the guard told me. And not the first time."

"Friends put up my bail the first time," the old man admitted. "Then I was arrested again after some ruffians disrupted our worship."

"Worship of what? The Jewish God?"

"Yes, Jesus' Father—the God to whom Jesus prayed."

"You people are daft," the other man said. "Didn't learn your lesson the first time?"

"The truth is the truth," the old man responded. "My being threatened with arrest or not doesn't change that."

"The *truth* is that the world belongs to the emperor, and he's not interested in sharing it with your 'king.'" Now that the man had a theme, his cough was less persistent. "And what kind of a king wastes his time in a place like Palestine? And dies on a cross? From what I heard, he died like a criminal. *Gods* don't *die*. And *kings* don't die on a *cross*."

"Oh, he's not dead," the old man answered. "He's alive. He's here with me now."

"With you *now*? Sharing a *jail cell* with you? *I* hear no other voice. I saw you when they brought you in here. You're alone, my insane friend, you're quite alone."

Now the old man laughed softly. "Quite the contrary," he said in a low voice, not to convince the other man, and with a smile that the other man could not see. "And it's not the *first* time he's been in a jail cell."

"If someone bailed *me* out of here, *I* wouldn't go looking to be thrown back in again. That just *proves* how insane you are!"

"One day," the old man said, "none of this will be regarded as the disgrace the authorities intend. Even now, I count it a privilege."

There was an immediate burst of incredulous laughter that quickly gave way to another fit of coughing, then more laughter. "Rotting in jail a *privilege*? Being arrested '*good news*'? What has this God of yours done to your sense of values? Surely no one *else* in Thessalonica would think being in this stinking hole is an *honor*!"

"Being in *jail, no*. Being in jail because of *him, yes*. And his being *with* me here, *definitely*."

"You'd do better with a god who's strong enough to break these bars and show you the privilege of breathing clean air again, and not worrying about rats nibbling at your toes in the night."

"Whether out *there* or in *here*, I am *equally* free," the old man said. "And the fact that these things are happening only means that the day of his final triumph is drawing near."

"Bah," was the only response.

After a time, the old man began to hum to himself, and then to sing softly.

"What's that you're doing?" the raspy voice asked.

"What? Oh, I'm just singing."

"I *know* you're singing. What is the *song*?"

"It's a hymn. Something that we sing to the Lord in worship."

The other man snorted. The old man resumed his song, still singing softly, barely audibly, but still loudly enough that the song could be identified as a cheerful tune, not a sorrowful one.

"How can you do that?" the other man asked, his voice now angry. "How can you do that? I want you to stop. You're insane."

"I don't mean to distress you. But I assure you, I'm quite sane."

"How *can* you be? Singing like *that* in a place like *this*. Don't you know they could find you guilty of *treason*? Don't you know they could *kill* you?"

"What they do to me is of little account. They cannot do to me what they most *wish* to do. They cannot separate me from my Lord. And they certainly cannot do worse to *me* than they did to *him*. And he *lives*. And *I* shall live *with* him. Besides, it is little time now until he comes again and all this will be changed."

"I thought you claimed he was with you in your cell?"

"He is. In his Spirit. But he will return in a way that *all* people will recognize, and then every prison will be opened, as all eyes will see him."

"When?" the other man demanded.

"Soon," the old man replied. "When the time is right. When everything is ready."

"Dreams. Just dreams. Silly, stupid dreams. Nothing ever changes. If you're on the bottom, you *stay* on the bottom. The rich and the powerful make sure of that. They have the law in their pockets. Nothing ever changes."

There was more coughing, loud this time.

When the coughing subsided, the old man said, "I think things changed quite a *bit* when Jesus was raised from the *dead*."

This time, the old man's words were met only with silence—no rebuke, no challenge. After a few moments, he asked, "Would you mind if I finished my song?"

"Go ahead," the other man answered weakly.

"I could teach you the words," the old man ventured. "Then we could sing it together."

"I don't want to sing," the raspy voice replied, now gruff again. "I don't feel like singing. Singing in here . . . that *is* insane!"

The old man started again where he had left off, and when he had finished, he started praying for his neighbor, out loud.

"What are you doing now?" the raspy voice demanded to know. "What are you saying?"

The old man continued with his prayer, abbreviating it from what he had intended, and then turned his address from God to the man in the next cell. "I was praying for you, asking God to comfort you and to open your mind to him and welcome you into his kingdom."

"Don't," the man barked. "I don't like it."

"I'm sorry," the old man said. "I didn't mean to upset you. I've *been* praying for you ever since I came *in* here."

"Why?"

"I've been praying for *all* who are here, and for all who have *ever* been here and all who ever *will* be here."

"Why?"

"Because *Jesus* would. And I think *Paul* would."

"Paul. That's the one who was forced out of town, along with some of his friends."

"Yes."

"You're insane!" the other man responded.

"Would you like to learn to pray?"

"What? To someone who was executed on a *cross*?"

"To God. To his Father."

"To the god who *allowed* him to be executed on a cross?"

"Yes. The God who may allow *me* to be executed on a cross."

"So he *will* abandon you?"

"No. He will not abandon me. Just as he did not abandon Jesus, but raised him from the dead."

"You're insane," the other man sneered, and then coughed again.

"Jesus told his followers that they would undergo all sorts of trials. Nations will be in turmoil. Even the forces of nature will seem to be at war. But the Son of man will come with power and great glory. Then our salvation will be near its completion, *and* the salvation of the world. Now is the time to repent and to make ready."

"You're definitely insane," the other man said.

"No," the old man said. "It is the *world* that is insane, until it acknowledges that Jesus is Lord."

"And then what?" the other man asked, sarcastically.

"Then hatred will end. There will be no more prisons. There will be no more war. Idolatry will end. Everything that the prophets promised will come to pass."

"And when will this be? In time for me to be home for supper, perhaps?"

"Soon," the old man repeated. "When Christ returns. When the time is right. When everything is ready."

There was now silence for several minutes. The old man again became aware of the sound of dripping water. He began humming again, and eventually the hum gave way to words, as before, and shortly after he concluded his hymn, the raspy voice came again, this time without anger, without sarcasm, without pride.

"Teach me to pray."

The old man smiled. "Of course," he said. "When his disciples asked how *they* should pray, our Lord taught them these words . . ." The old man spoke them phrase by phrase, with the other man repeating, coughing occasionally. "Do you think we can say them together now? Let's try it." The old man patiently voiced the prayer he knew so well, and the other, in a voice less confident but determined, joined in.

After a few moments of silence, the raspy voice asked, not with any trace of anger or impatience, "What happens now?"

"Now, we live in faith and act in hope."

"'Thy will be done.' Is he going to have us released?"

"If we are living in faith and acting in hope, he has *already* released us—has released us from fear, has released us from anger, has released us from hatred. Do you see how he has already released us from loneliness?"

The other man coughed quietly.

"Jesus is here with us. And God has also given us each other."

"I'm not sure I can have faith in something I can't see," the other man said softly from the other side of the stone wall, more in the way of a confession than an accusation.

"Can you see *me*?" the old man asked. "For me, faith is reflecting back on yesterday and understanding that God was faithfully caring for me then, experiencing whatever today has to offer and trusting that God is working his will through it, and knowing that tomorrow, God will be faithful to his promise of salvation, despite what I see or can't see. Every moment of life is a blessing, a gift. I can demand no more, have done nothing to deserve the good things that I have already received."

"And you never have doubts about your God?" the raspy voice asked in a tone that suggested a quest for understanding.

"Oh, yes. Well, not 'doubts' so much as impatience, wondering why things don't happen faster. But then, something happens that causes me to look back on events and see that God's timing was right after all. Over these months that I have been walking in the way of Jesus, his Spirit has helped me to be more patient, to be more trusting, to be more confident that God's will shall be done, that God will take care of tomorrow. I think of how bleak it must have seemed for the disciples when Jesus was crucified. And then I think of their joy when he was standing among them, talking with them, even eating with them after he was raised from the dead. And I know that tomorrow is secure in God's hands. And then, you know, the waiting becomes much easier."

It was quiet again for several minutes, except for the sound of the dripping water and the occasional muffled cough from the other jail cell. Finally, the other man asked in his raspy voice, "Perhaps you could teach me what you were singing."

Second Sunday of Advent

Isaiah 40:1–11
2 Peter 3:8–15a
Mark 1:1–8

"Accepting Salvation"[1]

Paul Sandoval leaned back in his chair and scratched his scalp of thick, black hair after hanging up the receiver of his office telephone and glanced out the window at the few flakes of an early December snowsquall. The call had come directly from Santa Fe within an hour of the governor's signing the clemency order. A letter would be arriving via facsimile transmission within a few minutes; he should wait for that before walking through the security station and opening the iron gate that would give access to the cell block and eventually the eight-foot-square cubicle where Billie Yellowhorse had been jailed for nearly two years. Billie would have been transferred to the state penitentiary on Thursday, but he had already been an inmate of the McKinley County Jail for longer than any other prisoner in recent history—ever since the night of the accident that had taken the lives of Joseph Sam and his little daughter Martha. The trial had been postponed three times—once due to the resignation of the public defender assigned to the case, who had departed Gallup for greener pastures, then the prolonged illness of the second public defender who had been assigned to the case, then the illness of the judge. Finally, trial was made to a jury, which had found Billie Yellowhorse guilty on all counts.

---

1. The story was suggested by an incident in Tony Hillerman, *Coyote Waits* (New York: Harper & Row, 1990).

Deputy Sandoval had been on duty on the night of the accident, back in the days when he was on patrol, and he had been the first sheriff's deputy to respond to the grisly scene on State Highway 197 eight and a half miles east of the junction with Highway 371. Joseph Sam and his daughter had been turning right out of a dirt road onto Highway 197 when Billie Yellowhorse's pickup truck jerked out of the westbound lane at a high rate of speed to pass another vehicle headed west on the highway. The pickup had struck Joseph Sam's blue Ford sedan essentially head-on. It was a miracle that Billie wasn't killed, in fact, wasn't even injured. But the roadside Breathalyzer test had been confirmed by a blood alcohol reading that Billie was well beyond the legal limit of intoxication.

Tragic as the accident was, it seemed even worse because of the fact, as reported in *The Gallup Times*, that Joseph Sam and his daughter were on their way home from a revival meeting, one of many held frequently on and around the edges of the vast Navajo reservation. The circumstances of the accident resulted in multiple charges against Billie, a man then seventy-two years old with a face wrinkled by sun and wind and whiskey, his hair long and gray. His family had complained to him of his drinking, had even called the Navajo Tribal Police one night when he had driven off from his home near Standing Rock to ask them to intercept him on the highway before he hurt himself or someone else. His New Mexico driver's license had been suspended, and then eventually revoked, but then he started driving again, frequently into Gallup where, inevitably, he would find a bottle.

"Jim Nakai," Paul Sandoval had finally written down on his notepad that night. It took some time to untangle the slurred utterance that Billie Yellowhorse had kept repeating as he swayed back and forth in the patrol car's headlights.

"What *about* Jim Nakai?" Sandoval had asked. "What *about* him?"

"Jim Nakai," Billie had repeated, and then he had passed out and collapsed on the narrow shoulder of the highway.

After a brief examination at the clinic in Crownpoint, Billie had been driven to the jail, and had been there ever since, except for the arraignment and the trial. The name "Jim Nakai" meant nothing to Billie's family, they told the sheriff's investigator, and Billie had never again said anything about a Jim Nakai, whether to Deputy Sandoval, either of his public defenders— who both seemed rather uninterested in the comment—or the jury. When asked directly by Deputy Sandoval the day after the accident who Jim Nakai was, Billie had just returned a blank stare. Without some help from Billie or his family, it would have been an impossible job, anyway—there were probably hundreds of "Jim Nakais" on and off the reservation, common as the name was among the Navajos.

But about two weeks ago, on the second day after the trial had ended, and a day after the news of Billie's conviction had been disseminated through both *The Gallup Times* and *The Navajo Times*, as well as *The Albuquerque Journal*, one Alice Nez had called the sheriff's office inquiring if the police had ever questioned the man who ran away from the accident. Her husband, it seems, had been the driver of the car that Billie's pickup was passing when it collided with Joseph Sam's car, and Hosteen Nez had immediately pulled off of the pavement and started on foot back toward the accident. While jogging eastward on the highway, he had seen the figure of a man running off down the dirt road that led to the church and, beyond, to a little cluster of hogans. It was pointless asking Alice Nez why she or her husband had not come forward with the information at the time, and it was two days before a deputy was sent out to inquire of the residents and church attenders whether they had seen anyone running down their road that night.

It turned out that the hogans belonged to various members of one branch of the Nakai family, and while, predictably, no one acknowledged seeing anyone running down the road toward them that night, they did admit to having a Jim Nakai among the relatives; he was now sitting in the San Juan County Jail awaiting trial on charges of petty theft and assault and battery in the purloining of a CD player from a store in Farmington. In an altercation over the theft, the store owner had received a blow from Jim Nakai's right fist. In exchange for dropping the petty theft charge, which would have been Nakai's "third strike" under a new state statute, Nakai had admitted to the district attorney in Aztec that *he* had been the driver of the Yellowhorse pickup the night of the accident. Billie had picked him up, a hitchhiking stranger, and Nakai, becoming nervous about Billie's intoxicated state, had persuaded the older man to let *him* drive. That disclosure led to a quick review of the case, and the decision to release Billie Yellowhorse and expunge his conviction.

At length, a young woman in a sheriff's department uniform entered Paul Sandoval's small office with a piece of paper in her hand. "This just came by fax," she explained, and laid it on his desk. Deputy Sandoval, who already knew what the letter said, read the instructions in cursory fashion, and rose from his chair, document in hand, and started his walk to cell number six. When he reached the cell, he unlocked the frame of iron bars that was its door. Billie, sitting on his bunk, looked up as the deputy announced, "You're a free man, Billie. The governor has issued a pardon on the basis of new evidence in your case, and has directed me to apologize to you on behalf of the people of the State of New Mexico."

Billie looked more *bewildered* than *grateful*. In fact, he did not look *happy* at *all*. Paul Sandoval wondered whether he had heard him correctly.

The man *did* speak English, he knew, but he looked so pathetic, sitting there in his jail-issued blue denim shirt and jeans and much older than his seventy-four years, that Sandoval wondered whether he comprehended what he had just been told.

"Jim Nakai confessed to being the driver. You're free to leave. Do you want me to call someone to come get you?"

The man in the jail cell lowered his head and looked at his hands.

"Did you hear me, Billie? You're free."

After a few seconds, still looking at his hands, Billie Yellowhorse said slowly, "I belong in jail."

"Jim Nakai—the man you picked up that night. He says you weren't driving. *He* was. Are you telling me that isn't *so*?"

"I don't know," Billie said, still looking at his hands. "I don't remember. I don't remember any of it." He paused, but Paul Sandoval did not break the silence. Eventually, Billie added, "I was too drunk." After another pause, he said, "I am ashamed. I belong in jail. I am a sinner."

"Well, sinner or not, the people of McKinley County aren't going to pay for me to feed you any longer. You're going to have to leave."

"I'm a sinner," Billie repeated, shaking his head slowly, his long gray hair, loose and disheveled when Paul Sandoval first saw him at the accident scene, now neatly pulled back in a ponytail. "I belong in jail."

"Now, listen," Paul tried to reason with him. "Your family has been without you helping them for two years now. You may think you belong in here, but there are people somewhere who are depending upon you," though, in truth, he didn't know who that would be. The man had family, yes, but none of them had ever come to visit him in jail, so far as he knew. "Don't you have sheep?" the deputy asked, and immediately thought that that was a rather stupid thing to say, as if sheep were more important than a wife and children and grandchildren and perhaps great-grandchildren.

"Had to sell them all," the man said slowly. "Too much liquor." Then, after a few seconds, he said, "That preacher told me, 'Whiskey is the devil's drink.' He was right. And now two people are dead. I belong in jail."

In his eighteen months of being assigned to supervise the county jail, Deputy Sandoval had never been faced with a prisoner who didn't want to leave. But the reference to a preacher and the devil gave him the idea that Billie Yellowhorse needed to talk to a minister. He went back to his office, leaving the door to Billie's cell open, and pulled out a list of telephone numbers from his desk drawer. He studied the names under the title "Chaplain," and put his left forefinger under the one opposite the name "Rev. Mark Johnson," then reached for the telephone and dialed. A few seconds later, he said into the receiver, "Reverend Johnson? This is Deputy Sandoval down at the jail. We've got a situation here . . ."

"Hello, Billie," Reverend Johnson said to the old Navajo who was still sitting on his bunk, looking at his hands folded in his lap. "Yah-teh."

Billie looked up at him with mournful eyes. "Yah-teh," he returned the greeting without any enthusiasm in his voice. "Hello, Rev'ren," he added.

"May I come in?" the minister asked, sounding unsure of himself.

"Yeah."

"May I sit down?"

The Navajo looked up again, and scooted a couple of inches toward the far end of the bunk to accommodate the minister.

"Well, Billie, I understand that you're free to leave and go home. I regret very much that you've been kept here unjustly." Billie Yellowhorse was silent, still looking at his hands. Eventually, the minister ventured, "But I understand from Deputy Sandoval that you don't think you should leave."

"I'm a sinner," Billie said without moving his head. "I got drunk. I killed two people."

"No, Billie, *you* didn't kill them. You weren't *driving*. That's what they've found out. That *other* man, Jim Nakai, the one you picked up—*he* was driving. And then he ran away from the accident, but they found him."

"Why was he driving my truck?"

Reverend Johnson didn't know whether Billie had forgotten the circumstances or was trying to drive home a point. The minister began slowly. "Well, according to Deputy Sandoval, the man said that he had offered to drive. He, um, he thought you shouldn't be driving."

Billie turned his head to look at the minister sitting beside him. "You know that man, Brother Wilson, up there at Tohatchi? He told me, 'Liquor is the devil's drink.' Up there, at that revival he had up there one night. 'The devil's drink,' he said. 'You wanna be a friend of the *devil*, drinking what *he* drinks?'" Billie turned his gaze back at his hands, still folded in his lap. "I've been drinkin' with the devil. I'm a sinner. And so that man, that Jim Nakai, he started driving, because I was drunk, and two people are dead. I belong in jail."

Reverend Johnson cleared his throat with a little cough. "When I've been here before," he started tentatively, "we've talked about how God forgives sinners. We've talked about how everyone needs to repent—change their ways, change their habits, change their way of thinking—and that when we do that, and have faith in God's forgiveness, then God does what he promises—forgives us—and lets us start over again."

"I believe in God. I believe in Jesus," Billie said matter-of-factly. "And I know there's a devil," he added, and then said, conclusively, "And I know there's a hell."

"Billie," the minister said, more earnestly now, with urgent conviction in his voice, "then you must believe God has forgiven you. You must believe that God does not want you to sit in this jail cell the rest of your life. For two years, you haven't had any alcohol. You know now that you can live without it, even when things look the most discouraging."

"I don't want to drink anymore," said Billie. "I don't want anybody else to die."

The minister refrained from putting his hand on Billie's shoulder, aware that such personal contact was considered impudent by many older Navajos. "Billie, God has *heard* you. Now, *you* need to hear *God*. He sent his own Son to take on the punishment for our sins, so we could be free. Do you believe that? Are you grateful for that?"

"Yes," the man nodded, still looking at his hands, but the minister could see a tear trickling down his face.

"Are you grateful enough to quit drinking?"

"Yes," Billie nodded again. "I don't want anyone ever to be hurt again."

"Are you grateful enough to leave this jail?"

Billie was silent.

"You believe in God," the minister said. "You believe in Jesus. Then you need to believe that you are forgiven, and you can go home."

Reverend Johnson's gray Toyota bumped to a halt at the end of the long, rutted dirt road a few miles southwest of Standing Rock. The old Navajo man's eyes had taken in every piece of the landscape on the drive from Gallup, and now were misty with tears welling up but not quite spilling down his cheeks. The two men sat in the car in front of the tiny frame house surrounded by little skiffs of snow, giving time, in the traditional way, for whoever might be inside the house to come into harmony with the idea of receiving visitors. But, of course, Billie Yellowhorse wasn't a visitor. This was his home. Or was it still? It was the *house* he had lived in. But how would his wife and whatever relatives might be there that day receive him?—he who had disgraced them, he who had abandoned them, he who had surrendered his will and his freedom to a bottle of whiskey one night two years ago and had been an exile in the white man's world of laws and courts and jails ever since?

"I think it's time to get out," Reverend Johnson said at length. He opened the driver's side door as, with a shaky hand, his companion opened the passenger door, got out, and closed it. The minister moved around the front of the car to stand alongside the gray-haired Navajo, and they both looked at the door of the house with anxious uncertainty. It took only a few seconds for the door to be opened, and Agnes Yellowhorse to emerge.

At first, the husband and wife stood where they were, looking at each other. Then, slowly, because of age, not because of dampened affection, they walked toward each other and met halfway between the car and the house. They looked deeply into each other's eyes. At length, Billie said, "No more whiskey. I'm home." Agnes Yellowhorse put her hand around her husband's arm, and they walked together toward the open door. Reverend Johnson thought to himself, "Just in time for Kishmus"—the Navajo name for "Christmas."

Third Sunday of Advent

Isaiah 35:1–10
James 5:7–10
Matthew 11:2–11

"Waiting for the 9:01"

The morning sun had just climbed over the hill on the south side of the river—the hill on which the university was nestled among a forest of bare branches—and now it illuminated the taller hill that dominated the center of town, crowned by the great cathedral that towered above the shops and offices and apartments, and the railroad platform on which a lone figure stood. Dressed in a gray wool coat, checkered blue scarf, and dark gray hat, the man began pacing back and forth, perhaps in anticipation, perhaps to stay warm, but he paused every few steps to glance eastward up the tracks. Occasionally, he grasped the collar of his coat against the cold December air that turned his breath into little white puffs. The train from the city was not due for another twenty minutes yet, but the man showed no interest, whenever he passed the door to the waiting room, of seeking refuge from the chill.

    As he came back into the shadow of the station, a heavy wooden door on the side of the depot noisily slid open, and a porter dressed in the railroad's winter uniform pulled out onto the platform a cart bearing half a dozen suitcases and boxes. "Just left Brampton eight minutes late," the porter said as she passed the man. The man nodded vaguely in acknowledgment of the information. The porter dropped the handle of the cart and stood for a moment watching the man walking away from her toward the east end of the platform. She judged him to be well into his seventies, though his gray beard might have made him look older than his age. The porter had only worked at the station for a couple of weeks, but every morning since she began, the man in the wool coat had shown up about this time, pacing back and forth until the train arrived, and again later in the day when it was time for the evening train to arrive. Then he would walk up to the door of the silver and blue and yellow coach, looking intently into the faces of the passengers who stepped off onto the platform, and when they had all passed him by and the departing passengers had climbed up the steps into the coach and the conductor had closed the door, he would shake his head a little sadly, and watch the train as it pulled out on its westward journey far down the track until the red rear light disappeared from view around the curve toward Kitchener. Then the man would descend the stairs to the street level below and disappear into the morning traffic or into the evening darkness.

After her first few days on duty, the porter had asked the station manager about the man. "Been coming for as many years as I've been working here," the station manager had told her. "Meets every westbound train. Don't know who he is—never asked. He's got nothing better to do, I suppose. Maybe he just likes trains. Or maybe he's not quite right in the head. He hasn't been harassing you, has he?"

"Oh, no, sir, no," the porter assured him. "I just wondered. It seems so strange."

"Just humor him," the station manager had replied, swiveling his chair back to his desk and continuing with his paperwork.

But all those *other* days she had noticed the man, the weather had been *warmer*. Cardinals had flitted from tree to tree along the street below the tracks, children had laughed as they ran along the sidewalk to school, passengers had sat on the outdoor benches reading the morning newspaper. It had been a mild December so far, but now a cold east wind was blowing in off of the lake, and as she watched the man, low clouds pushed by the wind suddenly blotted out the sunshine and blanketed the town with a pall of somber hues. The sudden gloom moved her to concern for the pacing figure. Her friends often called her inquisitive and rather impetuous. For days now, the mystery of the old man on the platform had been growing. It had finally become too much for her. As he walked back in her direction, she resolved to satisfy her curiosity. "Are you waiting for someone, then?" she asked when he was still a ways off from her.

"What?" he looked up and around vaguely, then noticed her as for the first time. "I beg your pardon," he said in a soft brogue.

"I'm sorry, I didn't mean to startle you. I just asked if you are waiting for someone on the train."

"Yes. That is, I think so. I mean, I am hoping." He turned away from her to look back up the track, then he began his slow walk to the east end of the platform again.

"Cold, eh?" she called after him, but he apparently did not hear her.

As the man approached the porter on his return trip along the platform, he started to turn around before reaching her, but she called over to him, "Someone you know, then? A friend or a relative?"

He stopped and turned back toward her. "Someone I know? Yes. That is, we've only met once, long ago, but I know him, yes. I have followed his career very closely."

"Well," said the porter, "it will still be several minutes yet. Why not wait inside where it's warm?"

"No, no," said the man. "I must be here when he arrives. I must be ready."

The porter thought a few seconds. "I could let you know when I see the headlamp."

The man smiled a bit, raising his hand and waving it slightly. "Thank you, but . . . I'll stay here waiting."

As he started walking back east along the platform, the porter strode over to walk alongside him. "I know it's not my business—" she said, bracing herself for an affirmative gesture from the man; when it did not come, she continued. "I couldn't help but notice that you've been here every day since I've been working. And when I asked about it, I heard that you've been here to meet the westbound trains every day for several years."

"Yes, well, you see," said the man, stopping now, "I don't know exactly when he's coming. I only know that he *is* coming, and I need to be here when he arrives."

"He's coming out from the city, then?"

"He's been in the city recently, yes. And other places. I hear of him working all around—Kingston, Barrie, Peterborough."

"Perhaps you could go to meet *him*?"

"Oh, it would be hard to know where he is from day to day. And his work is too important for me to presume so much. *He* knows what has to be done, and when, and where. He'll come," said the man smiling more broadly now at the young woman and nodding. "He'll come. He *said* he would come." He looked back up the track and nodded to himself. "He'll come."

"He must be quite important to you," she said.

"Important?" the man responded as they began walking, his voice hinting some surprise at her lack of perception. "He has carried on the vision of my own work, and that of my predecessors, and made it his own. Very important work, not appreciated by everyone. But he has taken it to such new heights, has revealed its profound implications for all people. I thought I knew what it was all about, but now I know that I really understood so little." He looked at his young companion and saw that she did not at all comprehend what he was saying. He explained more simply, as in summary, "Everything will be fine when he arrives. Everything will be just fine."

"Then maybe I should be waiting for this person to come, too," the young woman said with a chuckle.

She had expected the man to laugh with her, but instead, he looked at her quite intently now. "Yes, indeed you should."

The young woman's mood of gentle mirth disappeared, and she became all sober. There was such an earnestness in the man's voice, a sense of urgency, almost, of pleading.

"But you've been waiting for him for *years*," she finally said.

"Yes," said the man. "I've waited a long while. There have been times when I almost gave up hope, but then I would receive his assurances through a trusted messenger, I would remember the promise that he made me long ago, and my hope would be restored."

The young woman looked at him, but she remained silent. He glanced up the track, and then turned toward her and spoke in a tone of close confidence. "You see, I know he will come, because I know *him*. It's not that we've conversed face to face in all these years, but I have spoken with others who have been with him recently, friends who assist him in his work, and they have told me that it is well worth the wait, not to give up hope. For a time, I doubted whether I *should* wait—the reports of his comings and goings seemed so different from what I had hoped, disappointing at first. I had expected that he would perpetuate my *own* work, continue in the paths that *I* had pioneered, adhere to the plans that *I* had made. But that was before I understood the true importance of it all, saw the real meaning—when I was younger, thinking mainly of myself, my own desires, my own ambitions; I thought that I might be able to use him to advance my own agenda. But the things that I heard *he* was interested in, the things he was *doing*, didn't seem to fulfill my plans, my expectations. He heard of my disenchantment, my disappointment, even, and sent word to me. 'Can't you understand what my work is all about?' he said. 'See how people's lives are changed, made more complete, less concerned with selfish ambitions. If you want something different, if you don't think that's important, you should quit waiting for *me* and look for someone else who is more in tune with *your* desires. But if what *I* have to offer—what you hear that I am doing everywhere I go—if *that* is what you want, be patient and be ready to meet me—I am coming.' And

I grew to understand over the years that I had only scratched the surface, you see, only glimpsed through my own poor efforts and understandings the enormous scope of it all, had such a narrow conception of the work. I thought *I* was the teacher, but now I realize that *he* is the master. So," said the man, "here I am, ready and waiting to meet my master. And I fully expect him to step off of that train this morning. And should he not, then I will be here tonight, after spending the day trying to be faithful to his vision, fully expecting him to step off of *that* train. I trust his judgment about when it will be right."

The young woman looked into the man's blue-gray eyes, aged and filled with longing, and then she looked up the track. She still did not understand exactly what or whom the man was waiting for, but she had a sense that she, too, should be expectant and hopeful, though she didn't know what it was she was expecting. She *did* have hopes in her life, of course, or did *once*—her homelife had not been perfect, and now her parents were divorced and her mother was sick and she seldom heard from her father. There had been bigger dreams after university, but she had to take any job that would support her, even lugging baggage carts on a cold and windy railroad platform. There had been a young man, and he had made fine-sounding promises, but, after she had given her heart and her body, he was gone. Her hope had seemed to dissolve even as her yearning had become more acute. She had been interested in banning land mines and saving the old growth forests and promoting a local rock group, but none of those things seemed ultimately satisfying. She had wanted to be a part of something bigger than her own life that would give it meaning, had wanted to surrender herself completely to something worthy of her devotion, but everything had disappointed her in one way or another. She had high hopes when her political party won the election, but now that it was in power, nothing had really changed—more economic muddle and continuing constitutional crisis punctuated every few weeks by a whiff of scandal, and, more immediately worrisome, talk from her own party about accelerating the payments due on her student loans. She wished that something could stir in her the hope and devotion that this man had.

"You really think this could be the day, then—he could really be on this train?" she asked the man.

"I fully expect it," the man said, looking east up the track and nodding. Then he added, "That is what I live for."

The young woman followed the man's gaze, and she felt an anticipation rise in her breast. Exactly *what* was about to happen, she didn't know, and she realized that this event, she had no part in arranging, had no way to make happen. For the *old man's* sake, she *hoped*, though, that *this* was the day. But no, that wasn't all of it. For some reason that she could not pinpoint, she realized that it was not for the old man's sake alone—she found herself hoping that this was the day for *her own* sake.

    They stood together waiting in silence, a man nearing the end of his life and a woman just turned an adult, watching, watching. She had looked up that track many times over the past couple of weeks, but never with the same emotion that she had now. Then, there it was—just a faint, tiny pinprick at first, but then growing in brightness as the young woman's certainty grew that it was real—the headlamp of the 9:01. She grinned and turned toward the man, and could just make out the trickle of a tear down his cheek through the blur of her own tears of joyful hope.

CHRISTMASTIDE

Christmas Eve (early)

Isaiah 9:2–7
Titus 2:11–14
Luke 2:1–20

"The Littlest Shepherd"

"Aw, gee," Tobias had grumbled, kicking at the dirt with the toe of his sandal. "Why do *I* always hafta?"

"You don't 'always hafta,'" his mother responded, doing her best to look stern despite the comical aspect of her youngest son acting the part of the youngest son. "Your brothers Elias and Jacob take turns with you."

"But *I* do it more than *they* do," Tobias continued to whine. "It'll be cold."

"They do it when their studies permit. Now that they are in the synagogue school, they can't be spending every night out with the sheep."

"Why did *I* have to be born last?" the young boy said with a groan.

"Because you're *special*," said his mother, "just like *David* was born last in *his* family and God chose *him* to be *king*, didn't he? Because he was special and his older brothers wouldn't do."

This answer broke the cadence of the conversation outside the front door of their modest little house on the outskirts of Bethlehem, which was the town where King David himself had been raised and where Samuel had anointed him king to replace Saul those many years ago. Tobias had to consider how to respond to his mother's case that he go out to tend the sheep through the night. Saying that he was afraid of the dark—which was partly true—had never worked. Needing his rest so that he could grow big and strong had never worked—his *brothers*, who had each had the task before him, were bigger and stronger than *he* was. And, it looked like the coldness of the night wasn't going to work, either; he knew that his brothers before him had spent winter nights out on the hillsides, too, and had obviously survived. He thought of something new.

He coughed. "I . . . I think I must be getting sick."

"Then you had better stay in bed all day tomorrow when you get home and not go to the market with me or go out with your father on his rounds."

Well, that one didn't work. And Tobias could think of nothing worse than staying indoors all day long, missing out on a trip to the sights and smells and bustle of the market, or missing out on accompanying his father, who was the town's recognized doctor of horses and cows and goats and sheep, and who allowed his son to accompany him on his visits to farms and houses where some prized specimen of livestock or other was ailing. "Aw, gee," he repeated.

"Now, take some blankets and your water and run along to the flock." He would be replacing Mordecai, and would be joined by Simeon, who was replacing Enoch. Four families pastured their flocks together, and had worked out a system of trading off responsibilities so that there were always two shepherds on duty. Each family also had a dog to help keep the flocks together and ward off predators. Tonight, Tobias and Simeon would take turns sleeping while their dogs would patrol the perimeter of the flock and stay alert for any wolves that might be plotting mischief. Simeon was two years older than Tobias, and considered himself two years *smarter* than Tobias, and wasn't interested in befriending his younger counterpart. In fact, Tobias was the youngest of all the boys who shared the shepherding duties, and was bossed about by all of the others, which is what made spending the night on the hillside so unbearable. It wasn't so much the lumpy ground, which was no harder to sleep on than the mat on the floor of his house. It wasn't really the dark or even the cold—it was still something of a bit of adventure to be out all night long in the country. It was being the *youngest*, and the *littlest*, and the easiest to order *around*. That is what made Tobias object every time it was *his* turn to tend the sheep, night or day.

There had been a time, of course, when he had *pleaded* to be able to do what his older brothers were privileged to do. Finally, as he grew older, he had been allowed to accompany them on their sheepherding shifts to learn what was going to be required of him. But when he had come to be considered old enough for the responsibility of staying with the sheep by himself, it had taken only a couple of outings before he decided he would rather be doing *other* things.

"Aw, gee," he said again as he entered the house. He put the roll of blankets under his arm and reached for his canteen, a pottery jug on a leather thong that he would lower into the community well as he passed by on his way to where the flocks were being pastured. As he shuffled past his mother, she bent over and kissed him on the cheek. "There's a good boy," she said, just loudly enough for him to hear, as he plodded down the street toward the well.

The days were short now, and the air chilled noticeably as soon as the sun set. Tobias wore two tunics under his cloak to stay warm. He lowered his canteen into the well, and had to lean over the side before hearing the echoed splash and the gurgling of the air escaping as water flowed into the jug. The water level was lower than usual for winter because more people had been drawing from the wells around the town. There were a lot of travelers visiting Bethlehem—something to do with a *census*. He didn't know what that was, except that it had something to do with *taxes*, and his father always grumbled about taxes, and *they* had something to do with *Rome*, and his father always grumbled about Rome, *too*. From some of the people he passed on the streets the past few days, he had heard different accents and dialects from the one he was used to. His parents had been talking about how people were coming to Bethlehem from all over the country, and how some of their friends and acquaintances in Bethlehem had had to travel to *other* places because of the census.

Tobias had been to Jerusalem, which was not very far away, on festival days, but he had never been anywhere else away from Bethlehem, and it was a little difficult for him to understand why people needed to travel, or why they would *want* to, or where they went when they *did* travel. But there were a lot of strangers in town, and the businesses that served visitors, like taverns and the inn, were crowded, as well as the streets. In fact, as he was walking out of town toward the field where the flock was, he passed several travelers headed toward the city, including entire families, apparently, some on horseback, but not many, some on donkeys, some just walking, even a pregnant woman on a donkey being led by a man on foot. He remembered this especially, because the woman groaned a little as he passed them.

"It's about time," said Mordecai as Tobias slowly trudged up the hill to where the flock was grazing. "Simeon's been here for a long time already." Simeon threw a glance in Tobias' direction, a look full of contempt and disapproval. "I'm going to be late for supper," Mordecai huffed as he brushed past Tobias, his own canteen, now empty, slung on his shoulder.

"Sorry," Tobias mumbled, almost inaudibly.

"You sleep now," Simeon barked at Tobias. "I'll take the first watch, until midnight."

This meant that Tobias, as usual, would have to be up and awake during the coldest part of the night. Now, it wasn't yet dark and he wasn't a bit sleepy, so he would be lying on the ground unable to fall asleep for a couple of hours yet, and then be shaken awake just as he had finally drifted off to slumber, to sit up and shiver the rest of the night until dawn. But it was useless to protest this injustice, and he spread out his blankets and laid down without a word in answer to Simeon. His dreams, when they came, were of a place that was warm and lighted, where he was eating his fill of his favorite foods and nobody was ordering him around. But the pleasurable scenes were cut short by a violent nudge to his shoulder. "Your turn," Simeon's voice thundered in his ear out of the darkness.

Simeon's face was indistinct in the darkness, just a blur through Tobias' sleepy eyes.

"Get up."

Tobias sat up with a yawn and started shivering as the blankets fell from his shoulders.

"Nothing's going on," Simeon said, already lying down and covering himself with his blankets, curled up under them to ward off the chill.

"Nothing *ever* goes on," Tobias thought to himself. And, in all of his turns at watch over the flocks, nothing ever *had* gone on—no danger had ever befallen them, no threat had ever even presented itself, certainly not in the form of thieves or wolves or anything else that the boys were out in the fields to protect against.

Tobias stood up, clutching his blankets around him, and walked gingerly to where he could see the flock, and sat down again, his back against a boulder, cold and hard. He was hungry, but he didn't want to expose his hands to the cold air to retrieve the bread that he had wrapped up in a cloth and had stuck inside the roll of blankets when he left home that afternoon.

He counted the sheep, which were all visible from where he was sitting—and he came up one short. He counted again. And, again, he was one short. He stood up, and counted a third time. Still the same result. His heart started beating faster as a chill went through him that wasn't caused by the cold air. "Oh, no. No, it can't be," he said to himself. He walked forward toward the flock, and through it, and still he could not see the missing animal. But he heard one of the dogs barking over the brow of the hill. Now he ran in the direction of the barking, and began to hear the panicked bleating of a lone sheep off in the same direction. Eventually, he came upon the missing animal, wedged between two rocks, the dog standing guard just a few feet away. It stopped its barking when Tobias appeared, now wagging its tail as Tobias petted it and said, "Good boy, good boy." The sheep was heavier than he was, but with a gentle lifting tug under its belly, the animal scrambled free from the rocks and ran off toward the rest of the flock, the dog proudly trotting along after it.

As Tobias plodded back toward his sentinel post, he became conscious again of the cold. But now his hunger was greater than his discomfort from the cold, and he paused to bend over and unwrap the cloth in which he had placed his bread. He was surprised to see three dark round objects alongside it—figs. His mother had put figs in as a treat for her little shepherd boy. He ate them with relish, and the bread, too, and sat down again, drawing the blankets around him.

And just then, he heard a noise. It was a noise of wind, like the fluttering of a bird's wings, but louder. And there was suddenly a bright light behind him, like the sun, but brighter even. And he jumped up in surprise, and his surprise suddenly turned to fear as he saw a man bathed in the light. "Who . . . who are you? And what do you want? Simeon! Simeon!"

Simeon was already sitting up in his bedroll, and, though quite a distance away from him, Tobias could see that his face was ashen and his eyes were full of terror.

"Don't be afraid," the man said. "I'm here to tell you about something wonderful, something that everyone is going to rejoice in. You, too," the man said, turning slightly and looking toward Simeon.

Simeon slowly propped himself up on his hands and knees, and crawled across the hillside, too weak from fright to stand up.

"Listen," said the man, turning back toward Tobias as Simeon neared. "You've heard about the Messiah. The Messiah, the Lord, is being born this very night in the city yonder. Go and see for yourselves, and you'll know that you've found him when you find a baby wrapped up in swaddling clothes and lying in an animal's feeding trough."

Simeon was beside Tobias now, still on his hands and knees. As soon as the man finished saying this, there was a great wind sound again, louder than the first, and they heard voices singing down from the skies, "Give glory to God in the heights of heaven, and on earth, let there be peace and good feeling among everyone." Simeon had closed his eyes by now, still shaking on all fours alongside Tobias, but Tobias stood still, open-mouthed and wide-eyed. And then, as quickly as the man had appeared, he was gone, and the light and the sound and the singing had departed with him.

Tobias stood still a moment, trying to understand what had just happened. "Come on," he shouted suddenly, and started running across the hill through the field. "Come on," he shouted again, not even looking back, but racing toward Bethlehem, the collection of buildings just visible on the horizon, dimly outlined by the light of the stars.

Bethlehem was asleep now, or most of it. There were some dogs barking in the distance, and now and then the sound of a cat searching through the garbage left outside an occasional door, but very few lamps lit at this time of night. All the way over the hillside and across the fields, Tobias had been thinking about the woman on the donkey and the man leading it. Surely they would be at the inn. But what was this about a feeding trough? No one would put a baby in a *manger*! He raced through the streets to the inn, and saw that it was all dark inside, but he was feeling emboldened by what had happened in the field, and he pounded his fist on the locked door.

"What?" came a grumble from inside. "Who is it? What do you want?"

He pounded again.

"Stop, stop, you'll wake the guests." After about a minute, Tobias heard the door being unbolted and the proprietor, in his nightclothes, cracked the door open and peered out. "What is it?"

"Is there a woman here?" Tobias asked breathlessly. "A woman about to give birth to a baby? She would have arrived just this evening."

"What? Who are you? Why did you wake me up in the middle of the night?"

"Is she here? Please tell me!"

The proprietor snorted, and grumbled, "She's out in back, in the barn." And he slammed the door shut. Tobias could hear him slide the bolt back into place as he turned to sprint around the corner of the inn. By now, Simeon had just caught up with him, panting too hard to ask any questions, and he followed the younger boy by a few paces back toward the barn.

A light peeked out from the crack of the barn door, and it grew larger and brighter as Tobias shoved the door open wide enough to squeeze inside, Simeon just behind him. The barn was surprisingly warm from the presence of an ox and a couple of donkeys. At first, Tobias couldn't see any people, but he heard a rustling of straw from one of the stalls. "Hello," he said softly, tiptoeing toward the noise. "Is anyone here?"

"Yes," came the voice of a man from the stall. "Who is it?" And as the man stood up, Tobias could see his head and his shoulders over the edge of the middle stall.

"My name is Tobias, and this is Simeon," Tobias said as he inched forward. "We . . . we live here—in Bethlehem, I mean—and we were out with the sheep, and a man told us to come here." It sounded sort of silly in his ears as he heard himself tell the story.

Just then, he heard a woman's voice. "What is it, Joseph? Who is there?" And there came the muffled whimper of an infant from within the stall.

"It's all right, Mary. It's some shepherds. A man told them about us—about the baby." He turned toward the boys who were now rounding the side of the stall. "Come over here, boys, and see a miracle."

"The tomb was empty, I tell you. I heard them say so. And then his disciples saw him, talked with him, *ate* with him! He *is* the Messiah, just like I told you when he was healing all of those people and feeding them and when he was telling off the Pharisees." Matthias sat back in his chair and crossed his arms, looking justified but waiting for a response from Micah. The two men had just returned from Jerusalem, where they had gone for the Passover. Matthias had heard all about the strange events from a cousin of one of the dead man's disciples.

Micah turned to a third man sitting in the shade, and who was watching his son far out on the hillside, just a speck among the sheep. "What do you think? Is such a thing to be believed, Tobias?"

"Oh, yes," the third man answered after a long pause, nodding to himself, his eyes misty with some long-ago memory. "Oh, yes."

Christmas Eve (late)

Isaiah 9:2–7
Titus 2:11–14
Luke 2:1–20

"Salvation in the Subway"

Carol glanced up from her computer screen to look at the clock on the wall of her tiny, spartan office: 4:35. She had been at her desk all afternoon studying the recent history of soybean futures for one of her company's wealthiest clients, a man nationally known as a financial genius. It had once occurred to Carol that the man's fame was based solely on his fortune, and that his fortune was based solely upon reports such as the ones that she routinely cranked out for her superior to review and then for a senior partner in the firm to sign and deliver to the client. Did he have any idea of the hours of tedium that she put into making him millions? she wondered. The futures king lived behind a gated drive in an elegant home in a fashionable part of the city. She had driven by the place once or twice; the address was well known in social circles to which she could never aspire, but a friend had once pointed the house out to her. She did not resent his wealth or his fame, but in a way that she could not quite identify in the abstract terms of justice and equity, she did sometimes think about how the snap of his fingers translated into long hours of boredom at her computer.

Carol was running behind on the report. A lot of people had already left the office to have an early start on the holiday, but she had no particular reason to exchange the bright fluorescent world of her peopled high-rise office building for the dimmer loneliness of her high-rise apartment or the cold dark in between. She got up from her desk, rubbed her eyes, and walked down the hall looking for some office with windows whose occupant had left the door open. Light flooded out from Les Goldberg's doorway; she didn't know him very well, but perhaps he wouldn't mind the interruption. She leaned through the doorway. "Could I look out your window to see what it's doing?" she asked the young man who was thumbing through his desk calendar.

"'Course," he glanced up at her. "Not snowing yet, if that's what you mean."

She walked over to the window and looked up toward the sky. It was already dark outside, but heavy clouds hung low over the city, reflecting the light from a hundred office buildings. Far below the thirty-fourth floor window, the Bay Street traffic was lighter than usual; many people must have left work early. "Any special Christmas plans, Ms. Shepherd?" Les asked.

It impressed Carol as a little unusual that a man she hardly knew—and a Jew, at that—would be interested in her Christmas plans. But, she decided, it was probably only a matter of politeness, not genuine interest. "Oh, not much," she answered. She would like to have been able to tell the truth—that she would spend the holiday alone in her apartment with a dinner of microwaved leftover pizza; that her daughter was spending Christmas and the rest of the school holiday with her ex-husband and his new wife across town by court decree; that she didn't have the time or the money to fly back home to be with her parents and that her father was too infirm for them to be able to undertake a trip to spend the holiday with her; and that this Christmas would not only be nothing special, but quite likely the most miserable that she had ever experienced. She had been remembering how special it all seemed when she was younger, the anticipation growing all through the month of December at school and through the Sundays of Advent at church until Christmas Eve finally arrived, and the miracle of faith blossomed in the magic of the season. She had wanted to re-create that in her own home for her daughter, but the reality of the work routine had always made it difficult, until the strains of the marriage ruptured her dreams of one day fulfilling her expectations of what it would be like. But, she had been telling herself lately, it's only one day—remarkably like all the other days she had spent alone since the separation and divorce, and even before that. "Nothing special," she said, more to herself than to Les, as she turned from his window and took a step toward his office door. "And it's Carol," she said shyly.

Les nodded. "Well, Merry Christmas anyway," he said, reaching his hand out to touch her wrist. And then he added, "Carol."

She looked at him with the thought that she read warmth and sincerity in his voice. Had he read the disappointment and sorrow in hers? "Merry Christ—I mean, Happy Hanukkah!" she blushed with embarrassment.

"Whatever," he said with a forgiving grin. "I'll see you next week."

Carol sat down in her chair heavily. The momentary glimmer of a shared humanity had been eclipsed in her consciousness by her awkward attempt to reciprocate a greeting. She looked at the calendar on her desk and noticed that Hanukkah had ended more than a week earlier. The intercom buzzer on her telephone sounded, and she picked up the receiver.

"Carol, I tried to get you a few minutes ago. The boss wants the status of that commodities forecast. He had really wanted to be able to sign off on it today before leaving town for the holiday weekend."

"I'm pretty much done with the research," she said. "I'll come in the day after Christmas to write the report."

"Well, OK, but that doesn't give us much time to— "

"It will be on your desk first thing the next morning," she said. "Merry Christmas," she added.

"Yeah," said the voice on the other end of the phone, and he hung up. Carol went back to charting soybean futures.

The screen saver gave a blue glow to her office when Carol flipped off the light switch. She glanced at her wristwatch: 6:20. She heaved a sigh, a response to the monotony of her work and the loneliness of her life and the thought of walking through the cold to the subway station. It had been blustery that morning when she had walked from the Dundas Street station. Snow was forecast, but the thought of a Christmas Eve snow seemed more of a nuisance than a blessing. As she passed through the outer office, the little artificial Christmas tree by the receptionist's desk seemed a mockery of the season or a mockery of her. She walked out of the front door of the office suite as the cleaning crew was coming in—three expressionless faces, one black, one yellow, and one brown. She checked an impulse to wish them "Merry Christmas," excusing herself with the cliché that cleaning people did not speak English anyway, but thinking, during the elevator ride to the ground floor, that *her* sorrow was really *no* reason to be discourteous toward others. What did people like *that* do on Christmas Day? she found herself wondering. What were *their* memories of childhood Christmases, if they *had* any? What would their *children's* memories be? Did they know what Christmas *was*? And what it was *supposed* to be like?

The gold tinsel of the lobby seemed antiseptic compared with the pine garlands of Carol's childhood memories. The jazzed Muzak version of "Joy to the World" seemed an assault on her sense of the sacred. She shoved open the door of the office building and found the sidewalk not nearly as crowded as she expected; in fact, it was almost deserted. It was cold, but there was no longer any wind; the front that was bringing in snow had already pushed through the city. Carol was well bundled for the temperature. Maybe tonight, she would walk the extra distance to the St. Andrew subway station, as she sometimes did when she felt the need to relieve stress, rather than the shorter distance to Dundas or Queen Street. She looked up at the clock on the old city hall as she passed the portly stone building. 6:35, Christmas Eve. Her route took her past the big department store windows filled with Christmas displays and the corner of the store where, she knew, there was an entire room of Barbie dolls and paraphernalia. She could not help stopping and looking through the locked glass door at the shelves and shelves of dolls and doll clothes and doll houses, and then she could not help thinking about her daughter, and then she could not help crying.

Why must life be so unfair? Carol wondered. She felt robbed of everything that she had ever hoped for. In a city aglow with lights, she faced the darkest night of her life. The tinsel, the canned music, all left her soul empty and intensified her mood of despair. She turned the corner and walked west on King Street, wiping tears from her eyes with her gloved hand, wishing now that she had gone some other way than past the Barbie window. She did not begrudge her ex-husband a few days with her daughter—*his* daughter, *too*, after all. The failure of the marriage had been mutual. But, oh, the feeling of being alone in the universe!

Carol began running down the sidewalk, only occasionally passing other pedestrians now, heedless of the ice left here and there from last week's snowstorm, her vision blurred by tears. Two blocks brought her to University Avenue and the stairs down to the St. Andrew subway station. Across the broad boulevard, some people were emerging from the other entrance to the station, headed west toward the Presbyterian church after which the station was named or to restaurants in the theater district, perhaps before attending a play. She gripped the railing of the descending stairway and glanced down the block toward the church, slightly larger than the church of her childhood but similar in appearance, light filtering through the stained glass. Was it her imagination, or did she faintly hear a choir singing? She thought she could make out "Gloria in excelsis." Practicing, she thought, for a worship service. After all, it was Christmas Eve. The memories of childhood brought fresh tears to her eyes, so that she did not see clearly the ice on the step in front of her as she descended the stairway. She slipped, and fell on the stairs. She was not hurt, really, but it was the last straw. She sat there on the steps in a heap, crying uncontrollably, her right hand still gripping the railing.

It had been only two or three minutes. "Missy," she thought she heard a voice say timidly. "Missy, you all right?"

She tried to wipe the tears from her face.

"You all right, missy?"

She looked up into the wrinkled black face of a man dressed in a blue stocking cap with holes in it and a tattered raincoat. The accent in his voice identified him as an immigrant from somewhere in the Caribbean. "Are you hurt?"

"No, no, I'm . . . I'm not hurt. I fell, but I'm all right."

In truth, she was frightened; crime had increased so in the city lately, and much of it seemed to involve immigrants.

"Are you sure, missy? You're crying. Let Angel help you."

"No, really, I'm fine."

"Please let me help. Don't be afraid," he smiled, and Carol could see that the old man was missing several teeth. He put out a dry, weathered hand to help her stand up. "It's Christmas Eve."

She held out her hand partway toward his and imagined that she could feel his cold, rough skin right through her glove. "Can you stand up, missy?" he asked quietly.

"Yes," said Carol, and, feeling that she owed him some assurance on the subject, volunteered, in explanation of her tears, "it wasn't that."

The man cocked his head and the expression on his face became solemn. "What is it, missy? What's wrong?"

She had an overwhelming urge to tell someone. For hours, for days, for weeks, she had wanted to tell someone about how hopeless life seemed. Now, a total stranger, a homeless man living in the subway stations of a city of three million people, had asked her why she was crying! "Everything," she said. "Everything is wrong!" She buried her face, sobbing again, in the startled man's shoulder.

"Not everything," he said tenderly after a few seconds as he put his arm around her shoulder. "It's Christmas Eve!" He paused a few seconds and added, "Don't you know about the Savior?" After a few more seconds, he said, "Come along, missy. You need something warm. I was just going over to St. Andrew's to the soup kitchen, and then there's the church service at 7:30."

Carol looked at the man and smiled weakly. She let him lead her by the elbow across the street. Only then did she notice that it had started to snow. She looked up overhead and saw what looked like a million stars—snowflakes reflecting the lights of the city. They came to the street corner. Suddenly, the man stopped and motioned Carol to stop. "Listen!" he said. "You can hear the choir singing!"

Nativity of Jesus Christ/Christmas Day

Isaiah 57:7–10
Hebrews 1:1–4
John 1:1–14

"A Christmas Carol—Epilogue"

It was not many years, by earthly reckoning, after the remarkable visit to Ebenezer Scrooge by the Ghost of his deceased partner, Jacob Marley, and the successive appearances of the three Spirits on a single night, Christmas Eve, that the surviving member of the firm Scrooge and Marley passed from this worldly life to the next. By coincidence, or by irony, or by divine intention perfectly wrought, death came to Ebenezer Scrooge on a Christmas night.

It was now the third day since. Snow was falling lightly on the street outside the undertaker's establishment, and, within, the proprietor was making final preparations for the conveyance of the coffin bearing the mortal remains of the legendary, some might not long ago have said "infamous," businessman from the funeral parlor to the nearby church where Mr. Scrooge had become a regular presence on Sunday mornings and a liberal supporter of the parish's benevolences. The intervening holiday of Boxing Day had delayed newspaper announcement of Scrooge's death and arrangements, but there had been no interruption in the arrangements themselves, and today was the time appointed for the funeral. The undertaker had only the dimmest memory of the funeral of Scrooge's partner, Jacob Marley, some years past, perhaps because it had been such a modest affair of even more modest expense and with a yet more modest attendance of but one mourner, being Ebenezer Scrooge himself.

The undertaker assumed his habitual and practiced expression of somber dignity at the tinkling of the bell above the door. He emerged from the inner dominions of the funeral parlor to see a man, just stepped in from the now snow-covered street, dressed in topcoat and hat and scarf. "Is this where Mr. Ebenezer Scrooge is laid out?" the man inquired without either ceremony or sentiment.

"Mr. Scrooge is resting within," the undertaker responded, bowing slightly and indicating with his hand a passageway beyond velvet curtains tied back to a doorframe. "We will be transiting to the church shortly."

"I felt obliged to pay respects," the other man said. "I've just returned from several years abroad, and saw the announcement in the newspaper this morning."

"Would you come with me?" invited the undertaker, drawing aside further one of the curtains for the man's passage.

Upon entering a small candlelit room, the new arrival walked without hesitation directly to the coffin and peered at its inhabitant.

"No, no. I wanted to see Mr. Ebenezer Scrooge."

"This is the late Mr. Scrooge," the undertaker answered patiently.

"I think not," retorted the man. "Though I've been abroad in Canada these past several years, I know his face all too well, with a scowl so perpetual as to be chiseled in cold stone."

"This is indeed Mr. Scrooge, sir. I transported him here myself from the house of his nephew."

"See here. You're quite mistaken, I tell you. That smile and contented countenance are not those of the man I know, or, rather, knew. No mortician's artifice could so transform a disagreeable character long written so plainly on a face."

"I'm sorry, sir, but I really must now close the coffin. The hearse will be here any minute. Perhaps you would care to sign your name in the condolence register?"

"Surely no one will ever be interested to consult a record so thinly used," the man said with a sarcastic sneer. He glanced around the room and noticed a wooden stand with an open book. Walking over to the register and taking pen in hand and dipping it into the inkwell, he glanced at the page in front of him, and a look of amazement came over his face.

Ebenezer Scrooge's nephew Fred, the son of his sister Fanny of whom Scrooge had been so fond in their youth, now herself deceased many years, led the procession into the church behind the coffin accompanied by his wife and small children. His wife's sisters and their husbands were already in their places, as were the many score of other mourners who had defied the snow, still falling softly. Seated directly behind the family, in a location, as it were, of some special significance, was another family of husband, wife, and several children, one of whom was seated on the lap of his father. Just behind them were three women whose likeness of features hinted at their being sisters, perhaps slightly younger than Scrooge would have been, with their husbands, and then another older woman, seated by herself in mourning clothes, her face a study in deep introspection. At the front of the nave was an abundance of flowers in just a few rather elaborate displays but mostly in a large number of more modest arrangements. Quite a few of the mourners were weeping quietly, but despite their obvious sadness, they also bore, so far as an observer could interpret, gentle smiles suggesting warm memories.

It was more out of curiosity than any other motive, certainly not affection, that the man who had lately come to the funeral parlor was squeezed into one of the pews far to the rear of the sanctuary, somewhat uncomfortably crowded on this occasion. He could hardly credit the outpouring, which made him again question whether the man in the coffin was Ebenezer Scrooge and whether, indeed, he had come to the right church. "His poor heart just finally gave out, I understand," he had overheard a woman explain to her neighbor, a comment which further cast doubt on the identity of the deceased in his mind, for, like so many who had had business dealings with Scrooge and Marley, he had long since concluded as a certainty that the individual in question did not possess that bodily organ.

"'The Word was made flesh, and dwelt among us'" (John 1:14 KJV), the priest's voice awakened the man from his long muse on the crowd that had responded to the announcement in print and by word of mouth of Scrooge's death. "That testimony refers, of course, to our Lord, whose birth we celebrate this holy season. But it is no blasphemy to testify that our Lord's words themselves became flesh and dwelt among us in the person of Ebenezer Scrooge."

"Bless him," the man heard someone seated nearby murmur as others, in unison, as it were, nodded their heads in assent and confirmation at the words of the priest.

"No one among us was more generous toward those whom our Lord specially loves," the priest continued, "—the poor, the sick, the hungry, the imprisoned, the lonely. Ebenezer Scrooge visited them, carried food and medicine to them, gave without calculation his fortune for their care and support with the oft-stated goal that there need be not a single almshouse or prison in all of London."

The man's mouth fell agape. Had he not himself entered into arrangements with Scrooge to transfer notes whose payment was in severe arrears, and then watched from afar as Scrooge foreclosed without regard for circumstance, turning out widows and infants without delay? Had he not himself received only a blank look and sneer when he questioned Scrooge where the destitute were to turn for shelter and sustenance? He did not regard himself in the least bit sentimental, but he still harbored some feeling of humanity despite his belief in the sanctity of contract and the justness of return on investment.

"And, as if his daily liberality could be surpassed, this season of the year brought out from Ebenezer an especial sense of urgency to do good and to elevate the unfortunate to dignity and hope," said the priest. "Though it was certainly not his intention, his embrace of the Christmas spirit, shown brilliantly year 'round, many a time put my own humble efforts to shame." Here, the priest removed his monocle and dabbed his eyes with a handkerchief. "But, oh, what an example of Christlikeness with which he has blessed us!" he resumed after replacing his eyepiece. "It is said that he retained only such portion of his income, much more modest than many of us would claim by right, as was required to provide for his simple needs, and that he regarded any surplus as stealing from the poor."

The man sat as if in a daze. He noticed as for the first time the fact that many of his companions in the church were dressed rather more simply than he himself was, and, despite their efforts to primp and coif for the occasion, they could not conceal broken and missing teeth, many of them, and other evidence of hard lives.

"Abandoning the pleasures and privileges which others in his position of business and fortune might demand as their due," the priest went on, "Ebenezer Scrooge, as it were, eschewed the mansions of human ambition to make common cause with the wretched and the dispossessed. But never did he abandon his good cheer, on such full display this very season and up until just a few nights ago as he partook so joyfully and gratefully in the warmth of hearth and table at his nephew's house in celebration of our dear Lord's birth. Indeed, it could well be said, and truly, that he knew how to keep Christmas well, if any man alive possessed the knowledge. And indeed," the priest concluded, "may that be truly said of *us*, and all of us."

"God bless Us, Every One!" a child exclaimed from near the front of the nave, and the congregation turned toward the angelic voice, that of the boy seated on his father's lap, with nods and smiles and tears.

At the conclusion of the service, the mourners followed the coffin, borne by six pallbearers, into the churchyard and toward an open grave near the outer wall that enclosed the sacred precinct. The snow was no longer falling, but the sun was even beginning a rare peek through the wintry London overcast, scattering the customary grayness and awakening a flock of sparrows to song. The man followed in turn, and was beginning to wish that he had known the deceased man being carried to his final resting place in these his final few years. For the man in the coffin was one, from what he had heard that day, far different from the miserly curmudgeon whose memory he had come, out of a sense of hoary duty rather than tender affection, to honor in sterile custom, and mutter unfelt thanks to God for his brief sojourn on earth. He did not personally know these other mourners, so clearly and deeply affected by Scrooge's death, but recognized among them a few of the city's renowned philanthropists. Close by the grave, shoveling spades-full of earth upon the coffin following the priest's commendation, were those whom the man supposed were Scrooge's nephew and family, but also the man whose wife and children had sat close behind the nephew inside the church, seemingly most deeply moved of anyone by the ritual farewell. Curious, the man lingered behind the other mourners, none of them quick to leave the graveside after the gravediggers had completed their labors, to speak to the humble-looking fellow to learn more of the dead man's final years.

"Pardon me, sir, in your grief, but I was moved by your manifest esteem for Mr. Scrooge and wished to offer my condolences." He introduced himself as he reached out a hand from which he had removed his glove.

"Thank you kindly, sir," said the little man. "I was Mr. Scrooge's clerk these many years. My name is Bob Cratchit. And never was there a kinder, more considerate employer, and that's a fact."

"I knew Mr. Scrooge in former years, and, if I may say so without offense, few people I knew then would have described him in such words."

The little man turned and looked at his family, who were standing near the grave in consoling embrace. Turning back toward the businessman, Bob Cratchit explained simply, "He was a good and godly man, and no one can rightly say different. We're none of us perfect. We live by God's grace, bless the Lord. And Ebenezer Scrooge showed many a person the face of Christ and the love of him who created us and sustains us from cradle to grave. None knows that better than me, I should think."

"May I offer any assistance you might require in finding a new position?" the man asked, moved by Bob Cratchit's testimony and suddenly feeling no need of further attestation of the goodness of Ebenezer Scrooge.

"Thank you, most sincerely. Mr. Scrooge already saw to that, I am grateful to say."

"Well, then, goodbye. And I am most heartily sorry for your loss. I am grateful myself that Ebenezer Scrooge had such a loyal and faithful employee as yourself, and hope that I may someday come to inspire such esteem from those who work for me and with me. Indeed, you prompt me to start earning such respect this very day."

They shook hands, and the man departed from the churchyard.

By some mysterious gravitation, the man was moved to revisit the churchyard the next day and gaze upon the newly mounded grave. And when he did, he saw a curious thing: lying on top of the mound, nestled among a plethora of inexplicably fresh and unwithered wreaths and flowers, were a small child's leg brace and crutch.

First Sunday After Christmas

Isaiah 61:10—62:3
Galatians 4:4-7
Luke 2:22-40

"The Gift We Got"

Another Christmas Day is past. All the anticipation, all the preparations, all the expectations, have been folded into memories. Over time, some will be cherished, some will be forgotten, many having nothing at all to do with Gospel stories of unplanned pregnancy, humble birth, visit by shepherds, in one version, and wise men, in the other, but all of which have the potential of changing our lives, and most of which have the potential of bending the world toward God's hope, if we let them. The feasts have been complimented and digested, the leftovers have been reheated and nibbled, perhaps the ornaments and ribbons and decorations have already been put safely away and some of our living rooms look more bare than we remembered. And some of us have once again made resolutions to take more seriously the good news of a Savior come from heaven to bless and make holy not just one day of the year but all the other days, too, with God's gentle "Yes" on his creation, including all upon whom the world so often seems to pronounce its "No."

The full implications of that divine "Yes," portended in Simeon's warning to Mary—such an incongruous intrusion upon our holiday merrymaking—already paint Lent and Good Friday on the horizon of a dawning new year. The most genuine celebration of Christ's birth inevitably requires us to acknowledge his death, but, beyond that, his resurrection, too. Bethlehem, literally "the house of bread," is a reminder of the Last Supper, but also the

Lord's Supper at which Christ is still food for the hungry faithful. The holly in our wreath is a reminder of the crown of thorns pressed on Jesus' forehead. The myrrh brought by travelers from the East is a reminder of the spices brought by the grieving women to the tomb. The swaddling cloths in which the shepherds found the infant Savior wrapped are a reminder of the grave cloths in which Jesus' body was enshrouded when he was lowered from the cross. The angels who directed the shepherds to the manger to find the newborn Jesus are a reminder of the angel who informed the women at the tomb, "He has risen, he is not here" (Mark 16:6 RSV).

You and I have come to worship today, I think, out of profound gratitude that God's Christmas gift to us has surpassed all the others we received or could hope to receive, beyond all expectation, and fervently praying to be mindful of that daily until next Christmas, "[r]emembering," as the poet W. H. Auden put it,

> the stable where for once in our lives
> Everything became a You and nothing was an It.[1]

Billy Miller had been so hoping for the shiny toboggan he had seen in the store window. He had pictured in his mind dozens of times what fun it would be shooting down the hill above McLaughlin's Pond—if and when it snowed, of course. It hadn't snowed *that* much in a couple of years. To have tried to ride a toboggan on last year's deepest snow, it would have been splinters halfway down the slope. That didn't stop Billy from thinking about how much fun it would be to have a toboggan like the one in the store window. He would be the envy of his friends. They would line up at his door at the first snowfall, asking if he might be taking it out for a run that day, and he could tease them with, "I don't know whether I feel like it just yet," or "I seem to remember that you were mean to me on the playground last week," or "You can ride my toboggan if you'll let me ride on your horse Scotty." That's what he would say to Henry McCallum, who lived down the road from the Millers, and had the fastest horse in Dufferin County but would never let Billy ride him.

With a toboggan like that, the whole world would open up for Billy Miller. Every day, after school, he went to peer through the store window and admire the wondrous craftsmanship. Every evening, at dinnertime, he would drop the most transparent hints to his parents, so persistently that his sister Emily at dinner last night said "Here we go again" the second he

---

1. W. H. Auden, *For the Time Being,* edited by Alan Jacobs (Princeton, NJ: Princeton University Press, 2013), 64.

opened his mouth. *She* would have to *beg* and *grovel* to get a ride on the toboggan, he decided. Little Petey was a different story. As soon as Billy learned to steer and stop the toboggan, his baby brother would have the thrill of his life sitting right in front between Billy's legs.

But Billy had begun to worry as Christmas drew closer, and the toboggan was still in the window. His hints became even more obvious, but still the toboggan was there after school each day. What were his parents waiting for? he wondered. Suppose someone else should come along and see the fine toboggan in the window, and recognize it for the marvelous piece of equipment that it was, and snatch it up for *their* little boy? The longer it stayed there, the closer Christmas came, and the closer Christmas came, the better chance someone else would buy it first. People in this town weren't ignorant, after all—*anybody* would want to have that toboggan in their shed. And if someone *else* should get it, what a tragedy it would be. And if Joey Parker's parents bought it for *him*, Billy would just die! He could never ask Joey for a ride on it. Joey was the meanest kid in school, and he seemed to have a special loathing for Billy. Why, if Joey Parker were to get that toboggan, the Millers might just have to move away from Primrose, the pain and humiliation would be so great.

One afternoon, as Billy was looking through the window at the spectacular piece of merchandise, his threadbare coat slung over his shoulder in the warmth of the afternoon sun, Doc Pritchard happened to be walking along the sidewalk. "Hello, Billy," he said.

"Hi, Doc."

"What has you so occupied at that window?" asked the town physician.

"This swell toboggan. I keep telling my parents how it's exactly what I want for Christmas, but if they don't hurry, someone else might buy it!"

"Well," said the doctor from a lifetime of wisdom, "maybe they have something in mind for you that you need even more."

"I don't need anything else. I'd give just about everything I had to have a toboggan like this."

"Well," said the kindly old man, "I'm sure that, on Christmas morning, the very best Christmas present you can imagine is what you'll find under the tree."

"Well, I sure hope it's this toboggan."

The doctor continued walking down the street and, eventually, Billy made his way home.

Finally, it was the last day of school before Christmas. The teacher must have been relieved when 3:30 came and the excitement pent up in her classroom finally burst into the schoolyard. Riding the crest of the wave was Billy Miller, who ran toward the store window, just knowing that this was the day the toboggan would be gone. The question was, would it be *his* parents who had finally bought it, or someone *else's* parents? In fact, it was neither. The toboggan was still there, where it had been for over a month. Bitterly disappointed, Billy trudged home. As the sun kissed the horizon, Billy pulled his coat on. It had holes at the elbows this season. It did little to keep out the growing cold, and nothing to keep out the growing despair.

Billy's mother had a list of chores for him to perform that kept him from going into town the next few days, plus the family outing into the woods to cut down a Christmas tree. Billy shivered all the way back from the forest as the wind changed from a westerly breeze to a northerly blast. When they got back home, his mother's hot chocolate and donuts made him forget about the cold. Petey's eyes were aglow with excitement, and he clapped his hands when Billy's father set the tree up in the corner a few feet away from the fireplace. They popped corn that night and strung it, and hung the paper and glass ornaments that were a treasured part of the Miller family Christmas.

The next day was Christmas Eve, and the family went as usual to the church service that night. Once again, the Millers and all the people of Primrose heard the story of a child who came to fulfill an age-old promise in a most unexpected way. Once again, the Millers and all the people of Primrose sang of angels and shepherds and a young mother and a tiny baby. Once again, the Millers and all the people of Primrose were reminded to be thankful for the loving care of a God who gave us such a perfect gift. When the Millers came out of the church, they bundled in blankets for the wagon ride back home. That felt especially good to Billy. On their way home, Billy's father drove the wagon along the main street of the town, past the store which had been Billy's destination after school each day, but there was frost on the window—the night was clear and very cold—and Billy couldn't tell whether the toboggan was there or not. He wanted to ask his father to stop the wagon and let him jump out to go over and see, but that seemed too bold a demonstration of his desires.

Billy woke the next morning before the sun came up, even earlier than on school days, and roused Emily and Petey. Their parents had expected that, and were coming out of their bedroom in robes to meet the children around the tree. Billy hoped as he jumped out of bed and hoped as he ran through the bedroom door and hoped as he bounded down the stairs and hoped as he rounded the corner into the living room, but his hopes faded quickly when he saw nothing that looked at all like a toboggan under the tree, and they were dashed entirely when his mother handed him a flat, oblong box wrapped in green and red paper with a red bow on it. Bravely, Billy slipped the ribbon and paper off and opened the cardboard box and looked at a heavy plaid winter coat. "Thank you, Mom and Dad," he said as, without any perceptible enthusiasm, he tried it on for size. There were some smaller presents, too, including oranges and nuts in his stocking over the fireplace, but no toboggan.

It never did snow much to speak of that winter in Dufferin County. It was cold, though—one of the coldest winters that anyone could remember.

In the charming glow of the manger scene, it is easy for us to forget that the Christ child was not exactly the gift that most people were expecting or even hoping for from God. When, in the course of time, he grew to adulthood, and asked embarrassing questions about where people put their treasure, and asked embarrassing questions about what sinlessness entitled anyone to judge another person, and asked embarrassing questions about why the self-righteous abused the poor, a lot of people decided that they would do away with the source of the embarrassment. Who did he think he was, anyway? The Son of God? The Messiah? Where were his armies? Where was his crown? Where was his throne? And, standing bewildered at the base of the cross, his mother's memory probably flashed back to the time that an old man praying in the temple had come up to her and said, "Behold, this child is set for the fall and rising of many in Israel, and for a sign that is spoken against (and a sword will pierce through your own soul also), that thoughts out of many hearts may be revealed" (Luke 2:34b–35 RSV).

But, whether those who were hoping for and expecting some other Messiah realized it or not, the man Jesus was just what they needed. And, whether *we* realize it or not, even if we were hoping for and expecting and still search for some *other* Messiah, the man Jesus is just who *we* need. He is the gift we got for Christmas from the one who knows beyond all human desires the truest yearnings of our heart, the truest needs of our soul. The infant Jesus grew to be manifest as the Son of God and servant of all, put to death for his obedience, raised from the dead for his faithfulness. That is the reality that makes this gift so right for every person of every time and every place.

> Remembering the stable where for once in our lives
> Everything became a You and nothing was an It.[2]

That is the gift we got. How appropriate.

---

2. W. H. Auden, *For the Time Being*, edited by Alan Jacobs (Princeton, NJ: Princeton University Press, 2013), 64.

The Day of Epiphany

Epiphany of the Lord

Isaiah 60:1–6
Ephesians 3:1–12
Matthew 2:1–12

"Epiphany"

Peter Jorgenson cast an exasperated glance at his wife sitting beside him in the front seat of their car. "I certainly thought that we were supposed to take a right back at that intersection," she said apologetically as she looked at the hand-drawn map in the faint circle of yellowish light from her flashlight.

"Hardly qualifies as an 'intersection,'" he muttered. "We should never have tried to do this at night."

The two women sitting in the backseat wisely chose to stay out of the discussion.

"Betty," Anna Jorgenson said, turning her head halfway around to address the woman sitting behind her. "Do you remember?"

"I'm not sure that was actually the intersection," Betty Chung answered rather timidly, hoping not to fuel Peter Jorgenson's growing disgust. He had clearly not wished to come on this errand anyway, and had been muttering little complaints the entire way down from Albuquerque to Belen and out onto the dirt road that was leading them farther and farther from the inhabited part of town. "It could be that we hadn't reached the correct turn-off. I think Mr. Garcia said that it was about a mile and three quarters after the end of the pavement."

"That's what I heard him say," offered Safira Daoud, the fourth occupant of the car. "Have we come that far?"

"Well, nearly," Peter Jorgenson informed the three women, all volunteers for the Albuquerque Interfaith Refugee Committee.

"What's that light off to the right of the road?" Betty Chung asked, looking out of her side window. "I see a light over there. There must be a building. Maybe that's the place."

It was the day before that Anna Jorgenson, Betty Chung, and Safira Daoud had received the directions from Eduardo Garcia, the director of the Refugee Committee, to a tiny house south of Belen, and Anna had drawn her map based on his instructions, which seemed clear enough at the time, but had become rather doubtful on this moonless midwinter New Mexico night.

"OK," said Peter Jorgenson with only a slight improvement in his mood. "I can see what looks like a road branching off to the right up ahead."

"See if it doesn't lead us toward that light," his wife advised unnecessarily. Peter Jorgenson looked at her with an expression that it was just as well could not be distinguished in the darkness of the automobile interior.

"This whole thing is foolish," he grumbled as he pulled onto a rutted dirt track that sent them all four bouncing in their car seats.

"But they need these things," his wife countered, her voice rising and falling with the lurches of the car as its suspension system received a severe test. "They came here with next to nothing."

"Why should they be encouraged to come here at all?" he responded brusquely, his eyes focused on anticipating the ruts. "Aliens." Peter Jorgenson had been unhappy ever since his wife became a volunteer for the Refugee Committee, and he had on more than one occasion spoken against their church's involvement in the refugee resettlement effort—in fact, every time it came up in worship or church meetings. "They don't belong here," he would say. "What do we even have borders for?" he would ask anyone within earshot. "You're just encouraging them to breed," he hissed when his wife announced that the Refugee Committee had accepted the task of providing supplies for the recently arrived baby of José and Maria Reyes. Anna Jorgenson wondered whether her husband had agreed to drive the three committee volunteers, after insisting that she not attempt the journey on her own, simply to take advantage of another opportunity to complain about immigrants. Several times, she had tried to explain that they were fleeing death threats and joblessness and hunger in their Central American homeland. All they wanted was a place where they could find jobs and raise their child in safety and dignity, she kept repeating.

It was a couple of weeks earlier that the Albuquerque Interfaith Refugee Committee had gotten their names from Juan Bautista, the coordinator of the refugee clearing agency, and now the three women were taking a case of infant formula, a supply of cloth diapers, and baby powder to the little adobe shack that the committee had rented on behalf of the families who moved in and out as they arrived in the greater Albuquerque area while waiting for more appropriate accommodations as they earned their first paychecks. The house they were seeking that night was a one-room building with electricity and a well and an outhouse—an old migrant workers' dwelling in the middle of a dry patch of what had once been farmland but which, when the level of the Rio Grande became too low to supply water to the neighboring irrigation ditch, had been abandoned. The landowner rented it to the Refugee Committee for a few dollars a week. Now, the outline of the little structure started to be visible below a lone light bulb hung from a tall post at the side of the building that served as a utility pole for the incoming electrical service. The headlights of the car illuminated the shack's front door.

"See the way these people live," Peter Jorgenson snorted.

"Yes, see how they are forced to live," his wife responded, sympathizing not with her husband's sentiment but the plight of the refugees. "But," she said in an explanatory tone to the women in the backseat, "as Mr. Garcia says, it is at least something. Now we need to work to get them into a place that's more suitable. And try to find a job for Mr. Reyes. I understand that he was a farmer, used to hard work."

Peter Jorgenson looked at his wife in mock disbelief. He was about to make a response when the door of the tiny house swung partway open, and a man stepped through it, his hand up to shield his eyes from the car's headlights.

"Turn off the lights," Anna Jorgenson instructed her husband, who did so after a few seconds' delay, but left his parking lights illuminated.

The man lowered his hand and took another tentative step toward the car. "Amigos?" he asked quietly, and then again more loudly.

"Señor Reyes?" Anna asked as she stepped from the passenger seat.

"Si," he responded.

By now, Safira Daoud had stepped from the car and was coming around the rear to converse with the man. She was the best Spanish speaker among the three volunteers, and it had been decided earlier that she would take the lead in communications. They already knew from Mr. Garcia that Mr. and Mrs. Reyes did not speak English. So, in Spanish, she continued the conversation.

"We are from the Albuquerque Interfaith Refugee Committee, and we brought you some things. I think someone from the agency told you that we would be coming?"

"Yes," José Reyes replied in Spanish. "What is 'Interfaith?'"

"Well, we are a group of people from different faith groups in Albuquerque who have banded together to assist newly arrived people fleeing bad conditions in their homeland," Safira Daoud explained. "Like you and your wife, we understand."

"Why don't you ask him why he doesn't go back where he belongs?" huffed Peter Jorgenson. "He's not welcome here."

"Peter!" Anna Jorgenson spoke sharply. "Please. That's terrible."

"I'm just saying what's true."

Though her voice betrayed that she had been rattled, Safira Daoud continued. "I am from the Albuquerque Islamic Brotherhood." If it had been daylight, her companions might have seen her face redden slightly with the mention of this last word. "My name is Safira Daoud. And this is Betty Chung," she said turning to the woman of Asian descent who had emerged from the passenger-side backseat and who now bowed to the new father.

"I'm from St. Matthew's Catholic Parish," Betty Chung said, briefly forgetting that the man standing in front of the house could not understand her English. Safira Daoud quickly translated, and the man bowed toward her with a smile in recognition of his fellow Catholic.

"We are Lutherans," Anna Jorgenson said, nodding toward her husband and nearly exhausting the limits of her Spanish language ability. "Anna Jorgenson and Peter." Peter Jorgenson, standing just outside the driver's door, made a show of his disinterest.

"So," continued Safira Daoud in Spanish, "you have a new little baby. That is very exciting."

"Yes," answered José Reyes. "He is our first. I suggested delaying our trip to the United States, but we had to escape the cartel." He paused, then continued. "They threatened me, threatened to harm Maria if I didn't agree to go to work for them. There isn't any other work in our village, or any of the villages nearby. I had been trying to find work ever since our crops failed in the drought."

Safira Daoud held up her hand. "Please, just a moment while I tell the others," she said, then translated into English what she had just heard.

"I would never work for them," José Reyes added before Safira Daoud could begin her translation. "But they killed our neighbor, and some others in the village nearby. Our neighbor's wife—they took her and . . . well, I could not let that happen to Maria."

The faces of the other two women registered immediate empathy when they heard the story, but Peter Jorgenson seemed unmoved and remained on the far side of the automobile.

"Please, come in," José Reyes said, turning slightly toward the door of the house and gesturing with his hand.

"Just a moment while we get the things," Safira Daoud said, nodding toward the trunk of the car.

Peter Jorgenson roused himself from leaning against the sedan to walk around to the rear of the car and open the trunk. Each of the women reached into the trunk in turn, picking up a box and then walking toward the door which José Reyes held open, Peter Jorgenson trailing behind.

"Maria," her husband said as the visitors entered the doorway. The woman was reclining on a dilapidated double bed and shifted her legs making ready to stand.

"No, no," said Betty Chung.

"You just stay lying down," Safira Daoud said to the young mother. "You don't need to get up for us."

Maria Reyes smiled weakly in gratitude and shifted her gaze toward the far corner of the room, out of the direct glow of the one light bulb dangling from the center of the ceiling. In the dimness, the visitors could make out a wooden box elevated on a couple of sawhorses, padded with blankets and containing a sleeping infant. "Oh, may we?" asked Anna Jorgenson, Safira Daoud eventually translating the question as she remembered her role as interpreter.

"Of course," said José as he and his wife both registered pride in their tired faces.

"First, where would you like us to put these?" Safira Daoud asked, nodding slightly toward her and the other women's boxes. "Baby formula, diapers, and baby powder," she explained.

"Thank you very much," said Maria. "We need those things. It is very kind of you, and to bring them all the way out here."

"We were grateful to see the light outside your house," Safira Daoud said. "It helped."

"Just here by the stove," José suggested, drawing attention to the antique-looking appliance with two heating elements. Each of the women from the committee crossed to it and set down her box on the dirt floor. There was no refrigerator, just a small open cabinet with vegetables and sacks of flour and ground corn and a few spices, along with a bowl of eggs and, beside the cabinet, a small cooler.

"This is all they're doing for you?" Peter Jorgenson asked as his eyes surveyed the interior of the house. "How can you live like this?"

Safira Daoud did not bother to translate as she and the other women from the committee crossed the small room to the makeshift bassinet. "Beautiful," Anna Jorgenson cooed as all three looked at the baby with adoring eyes. Their admiration required no translation.

Peter was still looking around, his expression one somewhere between disbelief and disgust. "This is how you people have to live," he said under his breath. "How can anyone want something this badly?" Only then did he really notice the bassinet in the corner, except it wasn't a bassinet—just a wooden box propped up on sawhorses.

"Where did you give birth?" Safira Daoud asked Maria. "Where was he born?"

"Here," the young mother answered. "Right here. Just a few days after we arrived. There was a doctor," she explained. "And a nurse came out every day for about a week."

"The baby came early. We were thankful it did not happen on the road. They bring ice and milk each day," José added. "And some food. They will take me in to Belen to look for work next Tuesday. But I needed to be here to . . ." He did not finish the sentence, as no further comment was necessary.

"We had our own field in Guatemala," Maria said, sitting up now on the edge of the bed. "It was beautiful, so green. Home," she said wistfully. "But when the crops failed because of the drought, we had to sell it. That, plus our savings, is how we managed to come north. I did some sewing, but that wasn't enough for us to live on."

"We couldn't stay anyway," José reiterated, looking at Maria, his face showing that he was reflecting on a painful memory.

As Anna Jorgenson and Betty Chung and Safira Daoud had turned their attention to Maria, they hadn't noticed that Peter Jorgenson's facial expression had changed while listening to the conversation. He had drifted toward the bassinet and was now gazing down at the sleeping child. Peter and Anna had been following the progress of their daughter's own pregnancy back east, excited at the prospect of being grandparents, concerned, as parents must be, for their daughter's health. They had talked about what it would be like, to be grandparents, wishing that their daughter and her husband did not live so far away, hoping that they had everything they needed, the best obstetrician, adequate health insurance, proper advice about nutrition, and so many other details. If all went as it should, the arrival date would be in about a month. Then, they would fly to Virginia to meet the first member of their family's next generation. It would be so special.

"What's his name?" Peter asked quietly, his back turned toward the others so that they barely heard his voice. "Como se llama?" he asked of the little bundle in the box sitting on the sawhorses.

Anna Jorgenson was totally surprised to hear her husband ask the question in Spanish. She had never heard him speak Spanish before; indeed, he usually complained when anyone around him spoke in any language other than English.

"Epiphany"

Not needing to wait for a translation, José Reyes said to Peter from the opposite side of the little room, his voice lowered in volume to match the inquisitor's, "We haven't given him a name yet. We are still trying to decide," José explained. His wife had risen from the bed and now stood beside him, her hand on his arm. "Maria was so certain he was going to be a girl." Safira Daoud translated this for the benefit of the other two visiting women, who laughed quietly, remembering that the baby was sleeping. Peter Jorgenson, too, smiled, not needing the translation and still looking at the baby, his mind completely in the room but completely elsewhere at the same time. "Do you have a suggestion?" José asked, coming up alongside Peter, who responded in Spanish.

"No, that's the privilege of the parents. He needs a name that has special meaning for you."

Anna Jorgenson did not know enough Spanish to understand her husband's words, but just prayed that he was not being rude or insulting. But she saw that he had reverted to the manner of the kind man she had married years ago and still recognized as his truer self. José Reyes was smiling as he nodded in reply to her husband's comment. She also saw her husband now reach his hand into his pocket and pull out a billfold. He extracted several bills and handed them to José. Continuing in Spanish, he said, "Here's a start on his education fund," words which Safira Daoud translated quietly for Anna's benefit.

Flabbergasted, José said, "Oh, no, we can't accept so much money."

"Por favor," Peter urged.

"Thank you, thank you, thank you, Mr. . . ."

"Peter," Peter responded. "Just Peter. Pedro."

"That would be a good name," Maria said.

Ordinary Time after Epiphany

Second Sunday After Epiphany

Isaiah 62:1–5
1 Corinthians 12:1–11
John 2:1–11

"From Water to Wine"

Shelley sat in the middle of the living room, opening boxes that had been sealed only a week earlier, but half a continent away. It had been difficult leaving the old neighborhood—well, not that old; she and Frank and the boys had only lived in Brampton for three years, but that was a fairly long stay for them. And they had made friends there. Frank's job had kept them moving ever since they were married a dozen years before. So far, Shelley had always managed to find a job in her field wherever Frank's job had taken them, but she had grown weary of the repeated uprooting and the feeling that *her* career was somehow subordinate to *his*. "Resentment" was probably too strong a word, but "weary," yes. And then there were the boys—it always seemed to fall to *her* to get them established in school. Soccer and hockey and softball had become her strategy for getting them to feel like they *belonged* in a new place. And boating or camping—that was how they managed to spend time together as a family whenever Frank had the weekend off and the boys were not involved in sports.

Shelley pulled a photograph album out of the box and opened the cover and began turning the pages—pictures from the days of romance before their wedding. How naïve to have ever thought that they could spend every weekend on Frank's boat, just the two of them, away from work and free from any responsibilities. The dreams had seemed so wonderful back then—just the two of them, and *forget* the *world*. The arrival of their first son had come so quickly that they had never really been a romantic married twosome. They came to realize that the boat was in the driveway far more than it was in use—the boys' sports activities were impinging more and more on the weekends now, anyway, and Frank often was out of town or too tired for family outings. So, they had sold it as they prepared to move to their new landlocked community, many miles from any body of water larger than a pond.

Shelley gazed at the page in front of her, and hardly recognized now the face of the young woman who smiled back at her from the deck of the "We've Got Ours"—the name they had given the boat. She closed the book and set it on the coffee table and pulled out the next volume—their wedding pictures. She almost set it on the coffee table without opening it, but something nudged her to leaf through a few of the pages. The first page featured a storybook portrait, she and Frank in the front of the church that she and her parents had attended from time to time, usually around Christmas and sometimes at Easter. It was a pretty sanctuary with elegant stone and carved wood; the pink and white flower arrangements framed the bride and the groom perfectly. She skipped over a few pages to where she and Frank and the minister were standing together. She couldn't remember the minister's name offhand, but she did remember that she felt rather uncomfortable in the premarital counseling that he insisted she and Frank go through. She had felt compelled to be careful not to make reference to their living arrangements. She didn't know how to answer some of the questions the minister had asked about how they expected their faith to play a role in their marriage—that was hardly the sort of thing she and Frank had ever talked about. She had been unhappy that their favorite song was relegated to the reception, rather than being considered appropriate for the wedding. She flipped past the picture of the minister to the pictures of cutting the cake at her parents' club. How did the little wrapped-up piece of wedding cake survive *this* move? she wondered.

It was not a bad marriage. She and Frank had had their differences, of course, even some genuine arguments. But Shelley had already reconciled her romantic dreams with the realization that it wasn't destined to be the world's most fantastic marriage. The physical passion had subsided, as her female relatives had told her that it would, and there was little excitement now when Frank came home to her or she came home to him. So this was what parenthood and mortgages and orthodontists and paychecks did to couples? It seemed all so *ordinary, commonplace*—just what she had promised herself she would never let happen to *her* marriage.

Shelley suspected that this was the great truth about life. She had decided after her second child was born that she must come to terms with it, scaling down her expectations and reining in her imagination. And now, even the boat was gone. She would contribute to the family income by finding a new company that would want her as a staff accountant, immersing herself in raising her boys, doing her part to get them to soccer and hockey and softball, showing her support like all good parents should, filling up their lives with activities and thus keeping them out of trouble, and at the end of the day indulging in a good book in the bathtub while Frank watched TV with his sons. Maybe, after all, that's what everyone ultimately decided to do.

The doorbell rang. As Shelley laid the album on the coffee table, the pages flipped back to the picture with the minister. She got up from the floor and walked to the front door, pushing some stray hairs away from her face as she went. "Hello," said the woman on her porch when she opened the door. She was about the same age as Shelley. "I'm Margaret McDonald. I live a couple of houses down on the other side of the street. I noticed that you moved in last weekend, and I wanted to come over and welcome you to St. Albert and to the neighborhood."

"Thank you," Shelley said awkwardly, thinking that her living room was a mess. "I'm afraid the house is sort of cluttered."

"Oh, well, that's the way it is when you're moving in, isn't it?" the neighbor said, standing her ground at the door.

"Well, if you don't mind..." Shelley's sentence drifted off as she looked around over her shoulder and then motioned the woman inside. "I was about to fix myself some tea," she said, recovering her sense of hospitality. "That is, I think I know where the kettle is. Would you like some?"

"Thank you, yes," Margaret said.

"Why don't we just go into the kitchen?" Shelley suggested, trying to remember just where the kitchen was and where the teakettle might be, and also the tea. "I'm Shelley Harris," she said, leading the way through the maze of boxes and furniture. Margaret glanced at the picture album on the coffee table as she passed by.

"I know it must be a busy time for you," said Margaret, taking her coat and hat off and putting them on the back of a kitchen chair, "but I thought that it might be a help to know the names of some of the neighbors and maybe a doctor and a dentist and so forth. I noticed children playing in the snow in your yard the other day."

"Thank you," Shelley said, fumbling through the cabinet and finding the teakettle but no tea. Above the stove, she thought to herself. "Yes, we have two boys—Greg and Jeremy. I started them in school on Monday— grades six and four. My husband, Frank, works for the government, and

I'll be looking for an accounting job." As the kettle warmed, they briefly exchanged family histories (the McDonalds had a girl Greg's age and a boy about Jeremy's age), compared the climates of the Great Lakes and the northern prairies, and talked about the schools. As they sat down at the kitchen table and Shelley poured out the tea and set out some biscuits, Margaret gave her the names and addresses of the McDonalds' family physician, dentist, and insurance agent. Then she said something that caught Shelley off guard. "And, though I don't know your faith tradition, I would like to invite you come with John and our children and me to Knox Presbyterian Church on Sunday, if you don't have other church plans."

"Church? Sunday?" Shelley stammered.

"I saw the wedding picture on the table in the living room. You haven't changed much at all."

"Oh, well, that was twelve years . . ." Shelley stopped before finishing the sentence. She hadn't been in a church in ages, except to attend some weddings. In fact, she wasn't sure that she and Frank had *ever* been to church together, except for their *own* wedding, and perhaps her sister's; other than that, she thought, she had gone to half a dozen weddings by herself. "Well, I don't know. I'd have to ask Frank, and we're hoping to get the boys involved in—"

"Knox would be a wonderful place for that. They have a children's after-school activity group once a week, and a youth choir and Sunday school, of course. Amy and Philip would be happy to introduce them to the other children, and John and I would be pleased to have you come with us to the adult class."

"You agreed to do *what*?" Frank asked, looking at Shelley in amazement when he got home from work that evening.

"Well, I didn't know how to turn her down. She just got going, and nothing came to mind. I mean, I couldn't tell her that the boys had a soccer game in the middle of *January*."

Frank sighed deeply and sat down heavily in the one chair in the living room whose seat wasn't piled with boxes.

"Besides, she's the first person I've really met in the neighborhood, and I *didn't* want to *offend* her."

"Why didn't you just tell her we were Buddhists or something?"

"Frank!"

"OK, OK, OK." He sighed again.

"How bad could it be?" Shelley asked. "I mean, just this once."

"But how do you know it will be 'just this once?'"

"Look, I'll simply tell her if she asks again that it just didn't feel quite right for us."

"What did the boys say to the news? Or did you tell them yet?"

"It was kind of cute," Shelley responded. "They said, 'What's Sunday school?'"

The words sounded sort of familiar when class members read the various verses, but it had been somewhat embarrassing for Shelley and Frank to be fumbling through a Bible in search of 1 Corinthians. "Frank," Shelley said, turning on her side toward him in bed Sunday night. "Those were the words that the minister read at our wedding."

"Hmm?" he grunted from his side of the bed.

"About love—what we read in the class this morning."

"I was uncomfortable," Frank said.

Shelley was silent for a while. "I was uncomfortable at first, too, but I'm glad that we went. The McDonalds are a nice family, and the kids got along."

Nothing from Frank.

"And the service was nice." She paused, and then ventured, "And I thought the sermon was good—about living for others, like Jesus said to do."

"We have each other," Frank finally said. "We have the boys."

"But I've been thinking. Maybe we should try doing something for others more, and now that we're in a new place, it would be a good time to find something that we could do together that would make a difference for someone else."

"Like what?" Frank asked. "You've always said that our family should come first—the boys, so that they don't get into drugs and stuff."

"I don't know. It's just a feeling that I've been having. And then the minister this morning kind of put her finger on it for me—that Jesus opened people up to the joy of living for *more* than just themselves, told them not always to be worrying about their own comfort, that *God* will take care of their needs, and to do something for others, even if it's risky."

"You mean like going to that place in the city that guy talked about this morning in church, I suppose? That night-shelter place, with all the derelicts and bums? That's a great place for decent people to be!" Frank said this in a tone that signaled he hoped the discussion would end. But Shelley persisted.

"Maybe, maybe not, I don't know. It's not something I would want to do alone." She was quiet for a couple of minutes. Then she asked, "Would you go with me, Frank?"

"*What?*"

"Would you go with me if I called the church and volunteered to go down there some night next week?"

"Shelley, you're crazy. Aside from the dangers of going down to that neighborhood and everything else about it, we've got a household to unpack and things to do to get situated. We don't owe those people anything."

"We owe *some*body *some*thing!" she said, rather more boldly than she usually spoke to her husband or anyone else. "A single evening won't make that much difference in unpacking. I think it's time for us to do something out of the ordinary. Even something that's not exactly comfortable and not exactly safe. The story that man told this morning about the teenage boy who was trying to turn his life around . . . Frank, that could be somebody's son. That could be the child of a couple like us. That could be Greg or Jeremy a few years from now."

"Not if we keep them busy with sports and stuff," Frank objected.

"It could be, Frank. Hockey's no guarantee, or soccer, or softball." She was quiet again, and then almost whispered, "But Sunday school couldn't hurt."

Frank answered with a soft sigh.

"Frank?"

"What?"

"I was thinking this morning while they were reading from the Bible in that class we were in. Those words about love being patient and kind reminded me of something the minister said before we were married."

"And what's that?"

"He said that *our* love wasn't just for our *marriage*. He said that it wasn't to be kept just to *ourselves*. He said that if we grew in love for *each other*, that would be a sign of success in our marriage, but that our marriage would only be a *real* success if our love grew and spilled over to *others*. That's what marriage is really all about. He said that we could settle for an ordinary, everyday kind of marriage, or we could have an extraordinary marriage, if Jesus was a part of it and *our* love became more and more like *his*. Do you remember that?"

"Sort of," Frank said, and then there was silence. Finally, he asked, "So what would we do with the boys if we went down to the city at night? We can't leave them home alone in a strange neighborhood."

"Maybe they could play at the McDonalds' that night," Shelley suggested. "Or maybe they could come with us and help."

It was almost ten o'clock when Shelley and Frank and Greg, who had gone with them to the night shelter, and Jeremy, who had spent the evening at the McDonalds', entered their new house. By the time the boys were in bed and Frank turned on the television, the newscast was ending with the evening's hockey scores; the hometown Oilers had beaten the Stars with a tie-breaking goal in the last ten seconds of the game. "That would have been something to see," Shelley commented when she overheard the report while she was putting on her flannel nightgown.

"Yeah," Frank responded as he turned off the TV and got in bed. "But I'll bet those hockey players couldn't have been any more excited than that kid was tonight when he finally beat me at checkers—it took him five games, but then he did it. I wouldn't have thought that a teenager covered with tattoos . . . well, you know."

"Charlie? I know," Shelley said with a laugh. "It just about knocked me over when he said the prayer before dinner."

Frank reached over to the nightstand and turned off the light.

"Frank," Shelley said, snuggling up to him and putting her arms around him.

"What?" he asked.

"Have I told you lately how very much I love you?"

Fourth Sunday in Ordinary Time

Micah 6:1–8
1 Corinthians 1:18–31
Matthew 5:1–12

"Beatitude"

Mr. Groves looked impatiently at the gold-cased clock on his desk. He had planned to leave the office early to avoid some of the traffic on his way to the dinner, but now he felt doomed to be late. At this time of the day, his big European luxury car would be nothing more than an expensive easy chair hemmed in by all the other steel tortoises inching along the 401 freeway. He, the guest of honor, would be late. His donation to the Hospital for Sick Children was one of the largest that the institution had ever received, and had attracted media coverage from across the country. His name, and the name of his company, were being broadcast into every home from coast to coast. Tonight would be a triumph, if he ever got to the suburban hotel where the banquet was being held.

"Look," he barked into the telephone, "I don't care *what* your problems are. We both knew that this wouldn't be easy. I want results. I pay you for results. You just find a way to get the information. I want the complete design of Digitech's new model in time for *us* to beat *them* to the market."

He swiveled his leather chair around to look out on the lights of the city and the lake beyond illumined by the rising moon, listening to the person on the other end of the line. The view from his office was superb, but if anyone else had been in the room, they could have seen that it was not *appreciation* on his face, but a growing sense of *agitation*. "I *know* it's confidential. *Of course* it's confidential. That's just the *point, isn't it*? Why do you think we're *playing* this game? We're going to *beat* Digitech to the market this time, and that's going to put us on top once and for all." He listened again. "Well, just do whatever's necessary, and make sure that your tracks are covered. Call me by Friday, and I mean with the full schematic." He slammed the receiver down. "Incompetent," he muttered as he stood up and opened his briefcase, picking up a file folder from his large mahogany desk.

The intercom buzzed. "Yes," he said, absently setting the file folder down again. His secretary announced that he had another call waiting. "I'll have to call him back tomorrow," he said, and then he added, "Call down and have my car brought around."

No time, he thought. *At the top of the heap, a seven-digit salary, and never time to enjoy it.*

He had risen far and fast in the industry, and was in fact one of the most powerful and admired of the new generation of business leaders. Market analysts had almost universally acclaimed him as a wizard, and had declared that the sky was the limit for his company.

Mr. Groves reached in his pants pocket and pulled out a money clip. He quickly flipped through the bills, counting mentally, and frowned. "The ATM in the lobby," he mumbled to himself as he fastened the clasps on the briefcase and crossed his large corner office to the door. "I'm late," he said as he paused at his secretary's desk. "Call Jack Conrad in Chicago and tell him that I want his report overnight—*fax* it. And call Robert Higgins and tell him that I'll be a few minutes late for the testimonial dinner. He may still be at the hospital, or he may be en route to the hotel. Tell him I'll make it up to him by cutting the length of my speech and making an additional contribution." The secretary did not know if this was meant to be a humorous statement or not, but before she could decide whether she should laugh, Mr. Groves had disappeared into the hallway walking briskly toward the elevator.

The high-ceilinged lobby of the office tower was adorned with considerable greenery, including several potted ficus trees, that constituted an exotic contradiction to the winter drabness outside. While Mr. Groves had been on the telephone in his office high above the ground level, a team of deliverymen from an office furniture company had arrived in the lobby with their merchandise destined for a suite on the forty-third floor. One of the deliverymen had slipped on the water that had melted off of his shoe, and had fallen backwards, bumping into one of the potted trees that stood near the automatic teller machine not far from the bank of elevators. He had knocked the tree and its planter over, spilling a pile of dirt onto the polished marble floor. As the elevator doors opened and Mr. Groves stepped out, he emerged into a scene of considerable confusion—a chaos of deliverymen, office desk and chairs and credenza, and Homer, one of the office building custodians, just arriving with a broom and a dry mop.

"What's going on?" demanded Mr. Groves of the custodian as he tried to find a path through the chaos to the automatic teller.

"Just a little accident, sir," explained Homer in a genial voice as he set down his cleaning instruments.

"Well, I'm in a hurry," said Mr. Groves as he pushed past the deliverymen, who were still flustered by the disarray they had created.

As Homer and one of the deliverymen were setting the planter and its tree upright, Mr. Groves placed his briefcase on the little ledge alongside the automatic teller machine and opened it, extracting a plastic card which he inserted in the appropriate slot, entered a code number and the amount of cash he wished to withdraw, and waited for the machine to discharge the bills. In the brief time it took for the machine to deliver the money, the furniture deliverymen had resumed their work, blocking access to the elevators in the process. Mr. Groves counted the money and lifted the lid of his briefcase to return his ATM card to the place where he always kept it when he noticed that something was missing from his leather case. He flipped through the various documents that he was taking out of the office with him, but did not find what he was looking for. "My speech. Where's my speech?" he said to himself softly but loud enough for Homer and the others nearby to hear. He replaced his papers as he searched his memory. "My desk. Must've left it on the desk when Sheila buzzed me."

Just then, Mr. Groves looked toward the elevator and saw the continuing chaos caused by the delivery of the office furniture, then quickly glanced at his watch. "Great!" he muttered. He quickly pushed his way past the deliverymen again toward the elevator panel. "Get out of the way!" he said at one point, shoving against a uniformed deliveryman whose colleague had stopped one of the elevators. Mr. Groves leaned on the button which had an arrow pointing "up." Under the circumstances, the twenty seconds it took for a pair of elevator doors to open for him seemed like twenty *minutes*, and when they *did* open, a crowd of people emerged, taking up more precious time.

"Back so soo—," his secretary began, rising up from her chair as he brushed past her desk.

"Forgot something," he said brusquely, opening the paneled door of his office.

"I made your calls," she said as her boss emerged again, drawing a perfunctory "Thanks" as he disappeared again into the hallway. She sat down with a sigh, looking at the pile of work that would keep her once again past quitting time into the early hours of the evening, long after her children's dinnertime.

The elevator became crowded as it descended from the uppermost floors of the office tower. The office furniture deliverymen were squeezing their chairs into another elevator car when Mr. Groves passed them, locked in the middle of the crowd that had spilled out toward the lobby. Two other elevators had arrived on the ground floor at the same time, so that there was now a tide of humanity surging toward the glass doors and out into the darkness of a late winter afternoon.

Mr. Groves reached in his pocket to tip the attendant who had driven his car to the front door from its heated parking space, and realized that the money from the ATM was not there. Instantly, he realized that he had left the money—several hundred dollars' worth—and his briefcase, sitting alongside the automatic teller machine. A sense of disaster came over him, not because he couldn't afford to *lose* the money—in fact, he was worth many millions of dollars—but because it was an indication of an unaccustomed stupidity. He cursed softly under his breath as he closed the driver's door of his car and hustled back into the lobby of the office building. It would take a *miracle* for the money still to be there, and *another* miracle for the briefcase to be where he left it, and he did not believe in miracles.

His fears were quickly confirmed—or one of them was. His briefcase was still in its place, now with the lid closed, but the money was gone. A few feet away, Homer was dry-mopping the floor. Mr. Groves grasped the handle of the briefcase, and then noticed that the clasps were still unfastened. He cast a suspicious glance at Homer.

"Oh, there you are," said the custodian as he turned and saw the business tycoon.

"Yes, here I am," the businessman said, with deliberate slowness. He knew that Homer was only one of a hundred people who could have taken the money in the time that it took him to go back up to his office to retrieve the file folder containing his speech for the testimonial dinner.

"I noticed that you forgot your briefcase," the custodian said, matter-of-factly.

"Clumsy of me," the businessman said. "I was distracted."

"That happens to all of us, I guess. I hope you don't mind, but I closed it for you," the custodian continued.

"Thank you," said Mr. Groves. He paused, then added, "Did you notice anything else?"

"Yes, I did. I put it inside. I thought that it shouldn't be left out in full view. And then I've been kind of watching it while I've been cleaning up here. Quite a little mess. But accidents happen. That's what I'm here for."

"I'm much obliged," said Mr. Groves, but there was no warmth in his voice. He needed to be on his way to the dinner, but he was intrigued by the little drama that had just taken place. "How much do you earn each week?" he finally asked.

"Oh, well, now, Mr. Groves, I don't like to boast."

Was he serious? Mr. Groves wondered. He stifled the impulse to laugh. "Well, then, just an approximate figure. I'd really like to know."

"It's quite enough to provide a roof and place food on the table," said Homer. "The Lord knows what I need. And the Lord provides," he added, patting his stomach and grinning good-naturedly. In fact, Homer was of slender build, a man in middle age, a quiet worker who possessed a certain native dignity. "I'm even able to help my sister and her children a little bit after giving to the Lord."

"Five hundred, six hundred a week?" Mr. Groves persisted, rather rudely, actually.

"Oh, not quite so much as that," said Homer, blushing slightly. "I don't know what I'd do with all that." He tried to resume mopping the floor.

"Do you know what *I* make a year?" Mr. Groves asked.

"No, sir," replied Homer, looking at the perfectly clean floor that he was still mopping in embarrassment. "No, sir, I never really thought about it."

"My salary this year is $1,200,000. And I receive an annual bonus half again that much. And stock options—"

"My goodness," Homer said, still refusing to lift his eyes from the floor. "You must work awfully hard, Mr. Groves. But then, I know you do. And I know that you do some real good with your money, too. I've seen in the newspaper about your gift to Sick Children's." He finally looked up. "God bless you, Mr. Groves. That's a wonderful thing. Anytime I think of a child being real sick, it breaks my heart. My niece and nephew were both born with a serious condition. They've been in and out of Sick Children's."

Mr. Groves opened his briefcase and looked at the stack of bills placed neatly in one corner. He made a sound somewhere between a snort and a chuckle. "Did you count the money that you put in here?"

"Oh, no sir, it's not my business."

"Let's count it together," said Mr. Groves, taking the bills in his hand. "I'll set them down and you count them aloud."

Homer was clearly uneasy. "Yes, sir," he said slowly, "if I can be of help."

Mr. Groves began laying them down on top of his briefcase one by one. Homer stammered his words. "One hundred, two hundred, three hundred, four, five, six, seven, eight, nine, ten, eleven, twelve, thirteen, fourteen, fifteen. That would be one thousand five hundred dollars."

"That's right," said Mr. Groves. "You had fifteen hundred dollars in your hands. Have you ever had that much money in your hands before, Homer?"

"No, sir, I don't suppose that I have."

"How many people do you think passed by this pile of money before you saw it and put it in my briefcase?"

"Oh, I wouldn't know," said Homer, who could only guess at the point that the businessman was making with his excruciating questions. "This time of day, several dozen, I suppose."

"And any one of them—any person in this lobby—could have taken this money without my ever knowing it. And if I questioned any of them about it, including the person who took it, they could say that someone else must have taken it. Don't you think that's so?"

"That's why I thought I should put it in your briefcase. So nobody *would* take it. I hope I didn't do anything wrong."

"As much as you could make in a month."

Homer stared at Mr. Groves blankly, totally oblivious to the implications of what the businessperson was saying. Then suddenly, he understood what Mr. Groves had been hinting at.

"Why, I'd never—my Lord would be awfully disappointed in me."

"Homer," said Mr. Groves, fastening the clasps on his briefcase, "you're a fool." He turned toward the entrance and went out to his car.

An hour later, Homer was walking through the dark cold from the subway station to his rooming house. The snow along the sidewalk left over from the big blizzard a couple of weeks earlier looked tired and hard and dirty under the feeble light from the street lamps. When he arrived at his little apartment, he made himself a supper of some canned meat, vegetables, and bread, asking God's blessing at the beginning of his meal and reading a psalm of thanksgiving at the end. Then he called his sister as he did every night to see how her day at work had been, how the children were, and whether she needed anything. He opened the mail—a bill and an advertisement—and then read from the Gospels for a while, and then a chapter from Sir Walter Scott—he loved Luke and he loved Sir Walter Scott. Tomorrow night would be choir, but tonight was a night for reading. Finally, he changed into his night clothes and turned on the little black-and-white television that sometimes worked and sometimes didn't work. Tonight, it was working. And as the news came on, the first report was about the lavish dinner that had been held earlier that evening to honor Mr. Groves the famous business wizard for his large donation to the Hospital for Sick Children.

Transfiguration of the Lord

Transfiguration of the Lord

Exodus 24:12–18
2 Peter 1:16–21
Matthew 17:1–9

"Eyewitness to Glory"

We had been with Jesus for several months by then—the other eleven and I who traveled with the Master throughout the hills and villages of Galilee. I remember that it happened just after Simon had startled us all by saying that Jesus was the Christ, the Son of the living God. Not that Simon really understood what that meant, certainly not that he understood Jesus must go to Jerusalem and suffer many things from the elders and chief priests and scribes, and finally be crucified. As a matter of fact, Simon had tried to talk Jesus out of going to Jerusalem if he was going to be killed there, but Jesus had rebuked him for saying that. Simon really didn't understand. Well, none of us did. We had seen with our own eyes that Jesus had the power to calm the wind and the waves, that he even had power over demons. We had heard him preach and teach in words that rang with truth like no other preacher or teacher. We had watched how he lived, how he treated even the most lowly peasant with dignity and even the most wretched sinner with respect, how he often went off by himself, praying to the Father. All that, and we never realized. Now, of course, we do understand. Or at least we understand more than we did, since he has been raised from the dead.

Well, as I was saying, it was just a few days after Simon had declared Jesus to be the Son of the living God and after Jesus had said that his followers must deny themselves and take up their own crosses and follow him, that he summoned the three of us, and said that we were to go with him up to a high mountain near where we were staying. Frankly, we had been puzzling over Jesus' words about taking up our crosses, and we were starting to be rather nervous about what might be in store for *us*. It was still a new thought to us, and an uncomfortable one, that we might be endangering our own lives by following Jesus. Why would anyone want to kill Jesus? He hadn't hurt anyone. Oh, some rich people and a few scribes and Pharisees might have been offended by some of the things that he said, but we had never really thought that anyone might try to harm him, or us. And it had always seemed that Jesus could cheer us when we were discouraged and could calm our little fears and anxieties. But the fact that he was now obviously thinking about the possibility of his own death was upsetting to us in itself, and then the thought that we, too, might have to face death simply because we were his followers . . .

Anyway, we went up the mountain together, and I think that all three of us were glad to have the opportunity of being alone with Jesus. So often, lately, we had been surrounded by such crowds that we all longed for some quiet moments with him. He had not told us what was going to happen, but we were happy simply to be in his company. We started out in a lighthearted mood, joking with each other, feeling the relief of the tension of the last few days. But we eventually realized that Jesus was not entering into our banter, that something was still weighing very heavily on his mind and his heart, and our jocularity faded as an awareness of his own solemn mood spread over us. We remembered again his words about suffering and dying, and began to sense that something momentous was going to occur on the mountain, that he had something very serious to say to us or to show us. But we could never have anticipated what happened.

We reached a level place, and there, in our presence, a strange and marvelous transformation came over Jesus' appearance. We had seen Jesus on the fishing docks; we had seen him dining with tax collectors and harlots; we had seen him embracing lepers and kneeling down over the lame. He walked where we walked; he ate where we ate; he slept where we slept. But there, on the mountain, his face became bright, shining as the sun itself. And his tunic and his robe became dazzling white, so that we had to shield our eyes from the bright glare. And suddenly, there appeared two other men with him, and the three of them were talking. I don't know how it happened, but it occurred to us that these men were great men out of our history—Moses, who led our people up out of Egypt and delivered the blessed Law, and Elijah, the mighty prophet of old. We all three saw this wonderful thing.

We were bewildered and amazed and not a little embarrassed to be there in the presence of the fathers of our people. I suppose that we each thought that we should do something, but we didn't know what. Finally—it seemed like a long time passed, but I suppose that it was just a few moments, really—Simon, who could never keep silent for long in amazing situations, asked Jesus if he might build three booths, one each for Jesus and Moses and Elijah, to commemorate this great miracle. But before Simon had finished his question, a bright cloud appeared over Jesus, and we heard a voice speaking out of the cloud, saying, "This is my beloved Son, with whom I am well pleased; listen to him" (Matt 17:5b RSV). Well, when we heard the voice, we were of course amazed even more, and, realizing that we were in the very presence of God, we fell with our faces to the ground.

I don't think that it had ever really sunk into our minds, what the voice had said—"This is my beloved Son." In the years since then, and since his being raised from the tomb and appearing to many of the disciples, reports have come to us that when Jesus was baptized by John, people heard the same words spoken by a voice as if it were from heaven. And of course, when the three of us eventually talked about this among ourselves, we recalled that Simon had announced the same thing just a few days before, that Jesus was the Son of the living God.

Soon, while we were still hiding our faces to the ground, we felt the Master's hand touching us. Ever alert to our fears and our doubts, he told us calmly to rise and not be afraid. And to our surprise, when we lifted our heads up and looked about, the two men—Moses and Elijah—had vanished. Responding to our Master's calm voice, we raised our eyes and saw only Jesus.

He said nothing else, but started back down the mountain, and we scrambled up from the ground and followed him. We were still very much agitated, as you can imagine, but Jesus said nothing more until we were well down the mountain. Yet it was clear to us that Jesus' mood had changed, that some of his anxiety had passed, that he was at peace, like a person who has long wrestled with a proper course of action. And finally, perhaps sensing our amazement, Jesus turned abruptly to us and told us not to tell anyone what we had seen, not until, as he said, "the Son of man is raised from the dead" (17:9c RSV). Of course, we obeyed, in spite of the astonishment that we all felt, and not knowing exactly what he meant by "the Son of man being raised." Probably, no one would have believed us anyway. And I'm not sure that we understood well enough ourselves what had happened on the mountain even to try to tell the others about it. Then, sooner than we were ready, we were back down among the throngs of people who had come to ask Jesus to heal them and their friends. And he did.

To this day, I am not sure that I really comprehend what it all meant. But I have thought about Moses, how he went up on Mount Sinai with

Aaron and Nadab and Abihu and they saw God, and how Moses later went up alone and for six days a cloud covered the mountain, a sign of God's own presence, and on the seventh day the Lord called to Moses. And Moses was given the Law. The scriptures say that Moses' face shone like the sun after he had spoken with God. I think about *Jesus* on the mountain—how *his* face shone like the sun that day and how his clothing turned a dazzling white, and then how the bright cloud appeared and the voice spoke those words, "This is my beloved Son." And then I think about the cloud that darkened the land on the day that Jesus was crucified, and how the women who were there at the cross heard from the lips of a Roman centurion what he said about Jesus—"Truly, this was the Son of God" (27:54c RSV)!

But then Jesus was raised from the dead. And I think that I begin to understand. It's as if we had never before truly seen Jesus up until then, but for a brief moment, we were blessed to have a glimpse of Jesus as he really was and we were witnesses to a promise that he would be glorified and that he will come again, in glory, just like he said. It's as if a veil was lifted for just a few moments, there on the mountain.

One thing I do know—all that Jesus said, all that Jesus did, has taken on new meaning for me. For I have become convinced—slowly, I confess, but convinced—that I have beheld the very glory of God in Jesus, as Moses once long ago beheld it on another mountain. And everything that came before—including Moses and the Law, Elijah and the other prophets—found its full meaning in Jesus' life and death and resurrection.

We who knew Jesus can never again be the same as we were. And the *world* can never the same, either, because God—yes, *God!*—has been among us. The words that Jesus spoke, the things that Jesus did; the way that Jesus blessed others with healing and forgiveness and hope—God was in them every one. And those are the things that *we* should be doing, *too*, just as Jesus said, whatever the cost may be, glorifying God in what *we* do, even if it means rejection or ridicule or poverty or pain, even if it means the *cross*. For we know that Jesus was the Christ, the Christ who will come again, and the unveiled brightness of his radiance will be like the dawn of a new day, like sunlight breaking through the darkness of a vanishing night, as all people acknowledge his Lordship and conduct themselves according to God's will.

We, too, can be transformed into that same glory; we, too, can become sons and daughters of God, living like Jesus did. Now we can face our own suffering, now we can face even our own cross, because God himself was in all that Jesus did, and blessed Jesus' suffering with the glory of the resurrection. We were eyewitnesses to Jesus' majesty, with him on the holy mountain, when he received honor and glory from God the Father and the voice spoke from heaven. And we are eyewitnesses of his glory *today*, beholding and proclaiming what he is doing in the hearts of believers and in the life of the world even now. His face shines bright as the sun in every obedient act, his garments become dazzling white with every word of hope. And he is lifted to the *mountaintop* every time that he is proclaimed to be the Christ, the Son of the living God.

Lent

Ash Wednesday

Isaiah 58:1–12
2 Corinthians 5:20b—6:10
Matthew 6:1–6, 16–21

"The Committee"

"It's past seven o'clock," Sally Milton observed, signaling an end to the pre-meeting visiting among the committee members who had gathered in the church parlor. "Let's begin the meeting. Cliff, would you open us with prayer?"

Clifford Nelson, the pastor, was used to being called on, spur-of-the-moment, to offer a prayer at the beginning of meetings of various kinds. He did so again, thinking to himself that he really needed to do something to cultivate the *lay* people's ability to pray publicly in impromptu situations. "Amen," the committee members all answered at the conclusion of the prayer.

"Now then," said Sally, who was the moderator of the committee, "the Session has approved our proceeding with fundraising for the homeless family facility." As a bank executive, Sally had been the unanimous choice to chair the homeless shelter fundraising committee. "Of course, it's a blessing in these economic times that we don't have to build a building from scratch. But, as we all heard at the congregational meeting, the conversion of the ground floor of the education wing is going to cost about $365,000."

"$366,950," contributed Harry Hamilton, who could always be counted on to expand or refine someone else's comment.

Sally looked at Harry with an expression that was something short of appreciation. "Yes," she continued. "And, at present, we have about $75,000 in the building fund, which the congregation has agreed to put toward the project."

"$73,989.24," Harry added as he looked at the treasurer's report, "according to last month's bank statement."

"Yes," Sally said again, this time followed by a quiet snort.

"The time deposit has been making about $600 each quarter," Betty McGregor, the church treasurer, added, less in an attempt to be helpful than to dilute the effect of Harry's interruption.

"Thank you," Sally said with a glance and a nod which made it clear that her approval was directed toward the treasurer rather than toward Harry Hamilton.

"This is going to be a fine step toward caring for the homeless in our community," Rose Allison interjected. She was generally known in the congregation as a person who had an encouraging word to say about almost everything.

"Yes," Sally said in a tone that did not particularly amplify Rose's judgment of approval. "So it's up to us to determine how we will finance the balance of the project."

"$292,960.76," Harry said, looking up from his hastily scratched figures.

"Of course, it will be less than that if we get some more interest on the time deposit," Betty McGregor added.

Sally Milton looked slightly pained.

"I think we should have a bake sale," Rose Allison said. "And perhaps the youth group could sponsor a car wash."

"Cookies and soap suds aren't going to raise that kind of money," Jim Farmer said. "We ought to see whether the Rotary Club would contribute. And maybe some of the other churches."

At this suggestion, Reverend Nelson decided to enter the discussion. "I believe, when the suggestion for a homeless facility was first proposed to the congregation, that the intention and understanding was that it was something *our* congregation should do as a ministry to the *community*, including the full expense of renovating the space that wasn't being used for church purposes. The expectation of the Session has certainly been that the funding would come from the congregation itself. And while bake sales and car washes can be motivational and foster a spirit of camaraderie in the project, there is going to have to be some kind of pledge campaign. I would encourage you to set a goal of, say, $280,000, which would still leave plenty of room for things like bake sales and car washes. And, although times are tough, I think that a congregation of our size ought to be able to pay off a loan for that amount in ten years' time. We shouldn't go much beyond that, because there are going to be other major repairs that will be required on a building like ours in ten or fifteen years."

"I don't know, Pastor," Winnie Lewis said. "That's an awful lot of money. Most of our families are giving as much to the church as they can already."

"I think they will give, once they understand the need," Sally Milton said.

"Usually, you begin a pledge campaign like this by going to some of the wealthier church members, asking them to make a major gift that will sort of point the direction for smaller givers," Reverend Nelson explained. "You might be surprised that you can probably trim the total amount down to maybe $200,000 just by making three or four or five personal calls. I could help you identify some likely major givers."

"Wow," Jim Farmer said. "I don't know about that, not here."

"I wouldn't think that our congregation is so different from others that fit that pattern," the minister responded.

"I think we should have a plaque of some kind that will identify the donors," Mike Shelton said, making his first contribution to the discussion.

"Well, we can discuss that further into the project," Sally said.

"No," Mike insisted, "it needs to be a part of the deal up-front. People need to know that they're going to be recognized for their donations. It's the right thing to do. Besides, how else are you going to get anybody to donate? They've got to see their names up somewhere. And it ought to be right in the entrance, where anybody who comes in off the street knows exactly who it is who's been generous enough to put a roof over their head."

"Is everyone who buys a plate of cookies going to get their names up on the wall, too?" asked Winnie Lewis with an obvious note of sarcasm in her question.

"Folks, it seems to me that we're getting ahead of ourselves," Sally said, trying to exert some control over the meeting. "We haven't even decided what the target for a pledge campaign will be, or whether we're going to have just a single pledge drive or plan to have multiple drives over a period of years."

"I agree with Mike," said Harry Hamilton, ignoring Sally's attempt to redirect the discussion. "People don't just give out of the goodness of their heart. They're going to expect some recognition, especially anybody who's giving tens of thousands of dollars, like the parson here seems to be proposing."

"Well, I certainly *hope* they're going to give out of the goodness of their heart," Rose Allison said, then added, "whether they're going to get a *plaque* or *not*."

"Could I just say—" Reverend Nelson began.

"We have to be realistic," Harry persisted. "People want other people to *know* that they've been generous. Every time I walk into the hospital, I pass this great big wall of brass nameplates. Of course, the *amount* of money the people gave isn't listed. But their names are all there. And some of the nameplates are bigger than other ones. You *know* that means *they* gave *more* money. Some of the leading citizens of this community are listed there, including some of our members, and even some corporations. And you know *they* wouldn't have given a *dime* if they couldn't get some publicity out of it. As for the regular people—it's just human nature."

"Folks, we really need to back up here," Sally tried again.

"And if anyone for some reason doesn't want to have their name in lights, we can get some nameplates that say 'Anomalous,'" Harry concluded.

"Anonymous," Mike corrected him.

"What?" Harry asked. Mike sort of shook his head.

"Wait a minute," Rose Allison interjected. "Wait a minute. The hospital can do whatever it wants to. And it may be that some of those people wouldn't have contributed to building the hospital if they didn't get recognition for it. But that's not what *our* motivation should be in the *church*. We don't expect to have our names in lights when we give to the church on *Sundays*. And we certainly don't grade people's Christianity by how much they *give*."

"Oh, I wouldn't say that," Jim Farmer said. "I've heard that it's only the bigger givers who get to be on the Session."

"Jim, that's not at all true," said Betty McGregor, the treasurer.

"I'm not saying there's anything *wrong* with that," Jim added. "Those who pay the piper get to call the tune, and that's maybe as it should be."

Several people now tried to talk at once, including Sally Milton, who recognized Reverend Nelson by raising her voice above the others. "Cliff. Everybody else, please be quiet."

"Thank you. First of all, let me assure you that nomination to the Session is not based on being a big pledger." He looked at Jim Farmer, then moved his gaze around the circle. "That is not how the church of Jesus Christ operates. The disciples were not wealthy people. If any of you has been in a church that operated that way, I regret that it was so off base. The day that that becomes the standard *here*, I'll be looking for another church."

Harry began to speak, but Sally cut him off. "Cliff still has the floor," she said curtly, and nodded back toward the minister.

"If we're going to lead the people to be good Christian stewards," Reverend Nelson said, "we're going to have to educate them a bit on the Christian basis for giving. And if we're going to encourage them to give toward a project that will minister to the poor, it will be especially important for them to base their gifts on *proper* motives. And it seems to me . . ." He paused a few seconds, taking in his breath as if preparing to say something that he knew would not be popular, then he continued. "It seems to me that we are creating a homeless family facility because Jesus expects his followers to care for the homeless poor simply out of love, not for hope of any gain, not even public acknowledgment."

"That's kind of high-and-mighty," Jim murmured to no one in particular but with the intention that everyone would hear.

"Our goal here, I hope," Betty McGregor, the treasurer, spoke now, quietly, "is not only to create a homeless shelter, but to help our own people grow in their Christian faithfulness. Of course we are doing this for families in our community that have fallen on hard times. But, in the process, we are also doing it because our own *congregation* needs to *give* at least as much as those *families* need to *receive*." She looked at the minister. "Am I wrong about that, Reverend Nelson?"

"No, Betty," he answered. "I think you are exactly right. If, at the end of this process, you want to put up a simple plaque acknowledging those who gave toward the project, that's fine. But I strongly encourage you not to suggest in any way that public recognition is a motive for doing what we *ought* to be doing *anyway*." The parlor was suddenly quiet, though there was some fidgeting. Jim Farmer was looking at his hands folded in his lap and Harry Hamilton was pretending to study the figures he had written on a piece of paper when he was calculating the exact amount of money that would need to be raised. "Madam moderator," Reverend Nelson looked at Sally, "I think we need to get on with the business of planning a pledge campaign."

Ten months later, on the dedication Sunday for the church's new homeless family facility, Terry Marshall, moderator of the homeless shelter planning committee, stood behind the pulpit at the front of the sanctuary. As Reverend Nelson had predicted, four families had agreed to contribute a total of $85,000 toward the project, and one man and one woman from two of those families had even joined the fundraising committee. The gentleman had been the chef at the fundraising pancake supper that had been held on Shrove Tuesday, the night before the start of Lent. Very few people in the congregation knew how much he and his wife had contributed toward the project, though some were surprised when they saw the CEO of a major local corporation with his sleeves rolled up and wearing a chef's hat. The pledge campaign had not raised the entire amount required, but the pledges were to be paid over a period of three years, and it was understood that there would be a second pledge drive after that, with the expectation that the building loan could be paid off at the end of the second three-year pledge period. "Now comes the important part," Terry Marshall said in conclusion of his dedication speech, "—our *personal* involvement with the guests who will be sheltered here. *Some* communities, even some *churches*, might contribute to the building of a shelter so that the homeless would be out of sight and out of mind. Well, *this* homeless family shelter was built in *this* church so that this congregation would become more aware daily of Christ's call to reach out to people in need and serve them with generous love—the love that God has for each and every person." Reverend Nelson nodded approvingly from his chair off to the side of the chancel.

The mayor had already spoken, congratulating the congregation on helping to solve what he called "the homeless problem." The president of the local ministers' association had also thanked the congregation for its generosity. Now, it was Sally Milton's turn. "As moderator of the fundraising committee," she began, "I want to say how very grateful and proud I am of your faithful response to our request—invitation, really—to give what was needed. Our hope is that, one day, this facility will need to be remodeled again, and turned back into church school classrooms, not simply because our congregation has grown in size, but because homelessness will have disappeared, not only in our community, but in our country, and in our world, not just because it embarrasses us, but because it violates God's will, and because it insults the image of God in each individual. In the meantime, it will be a reminder to us of the need to work daily for a world in which everyone is treated fairly, and everyone is safely sheltered. All of us who served on the committee have grown in the process." Here, she looked at the committee members, who were seated together in the front pew. Jim Farmer and Mike Shelton both nodded introspectively. "When we go downstairs in a few minutes to see the finished product and welcome our first two families . . ." At this point, she nodded toward two family groups, each with at least two young children, seated in a pew at the side of the sanctuary. ". . . you will notice that there is no roll of honor on the wall as you might see in some places, listing all of the contributors. The fact is, we *all*, this entire *congregation*, contributed, even those who might not have been able to give money. We *all* contributed our hopes, offered our encouragement, and prayed for a good result. And all of us who were able to give did so because Christ first gave himself for us, and called us to follow him by giving ourselves for others. *God* knows," she concluded her remarks, "and that's all the recognition that *any* believer needs."

Terry Marshall then invited the congregation to follow him down the stairs to the new homeless family facility to see what, together, and with God's help, they had created.

Fifth Sunday in Lent

Ezekiel 37:1–14
Romans 8:6–11
John 11:1–45

"To Live Again"

Evelyn heaved a sigh as she folded the last of Buzz's shirts. She sat back in the chair and looked at the plaid flannel, frayed at the points of the collar. It had been one of his favorite work shirts. Had she purchased it for him as a gift? She tried to remember. He had had it for a long time—so long, in fact, that she could not recall its ever not having hung in their closet. When was the last time she had seen him wear it? It was hard to say, it was such a familiar sight. Probably not since he had been ill—really ill, too ill to do any odd jobs around the house. His arms had grown too weak in his last few months even to nail up a picture hook—so unlike the vigorous man that he had been as recently as his sixty-fifth birthday. How cruel it seemed. How unfair. They had so looked forward to retirement—doing things together, traveling, enjoying the grandchildren. And then that wicked, relentless disease . . . Her mind recalled the last Christmas they had put up a real Christmas tree; surely Buzz was wearing that old flannel shirt then, when they brought the tree into the house and set it up in the stand. Yes, yes, she was quite sure of it. And Mike and Connie were home that Christmas, and what joy filled the house.

Tears came to Evelyn's eyes, but she fought them back. No, no, she would not cry again. She must close the chapter, just as she would close the lid on the cardboard box that held Buzz's clothes. Mike had taken a few things after the funeral. These rest would go to the Salvation Army. She would close the lid; she *must* close the lid, just as the lid had been closed on the casket before the funeral, and remained closed. She knew the teachings of the Bible—she had known them all her life—and she truly believed that she and Buzz would one day be reunited in the presence of the Lord. But, in the meantime, the hurt was fresh and the wound in her heart seemed that it would never heal. With a strong dose of will, she folded over the cardboard flaps of the box and slipped them under each other. There, it was done.

She sat back in the chair and looked out through the window at the bare trees and brown grass of late winter, and the lumps of snow here and there that marked the places large drifts had been a few weeks earlier. Buzz loved spring—he always looked forward to yard work, to the earth coming to life again after months of short days and cold nights. That tree by the driveway—Evelyn remembered the spring day many years ago that she and Buzz had planted it, together, had watered it, had pruned it, and how it was now mature enough to shelter birds' nests and provide welcome shade in the heat of the summer. Another occasion on which Buzz had worn that flannel shirt, surely, perhaps with the sleeves rolled up as a sign that winter was over.

But it had been a long winter, this one—a winter of sickness and hopelessness. There could only be one outcome, Evelyn remembered the doctor saying. There might be a temporary arrest of the deterioration, but there could only be one outcome. But then, there is really only one ultimate outcome for *any* of us, she had told herself—it is the same whether you are healthy or sick; if you're not sick now, one day you *will* be. Evelyn remembered thinking that when the minister had first come to see Buzz in the hospital. Cynicism had crept into her soul these past several months. She never before would have considered each day of living just a delay in the inevitable. But now, the "inevitable" had come to pass for Buzz, and she was alone. There were decisions to be made, which she had no interest in making. There were documents to be signed, which she had no energy for signing. There were thank-you notes to be written, which she had no eagerness to write. She no longer felt at home in the world, or even in her own house; her discipline of routine had withered with the waning strength of Buzz's body.

Evelyn had become numb to the expressions of sympathy that acquaintances offered. She knew that people were trying to be helpful. Nice words, she thought, not one of which will bring Buzz back. Why hadn't people been as vocal to *Buzz* about how much he meant to them during his *illness* as they had been to *her* after his *death*? And now he was gone, and she felt utterly empty. She was not a bitter woman by nature, but perhaps her very lack of experience with bitter feelings was making it more difficult for her to rally out of her bitterness now. Never before had she had such difficulty sleeping as the last several nights, nor such trouble getting out of bed in the morning. A friend had said something about depression being a stage of grief, and about bitterness, too, but it had not seemed worth looking into. Of *course* she was depressed, and she had every *right* to be, didn't she? The truth was, she felt as dead as her husband. Nothing seemed pleasurable to her anymore. No effort she might make seemed worthwhile.

She missed him terribly—after forty-two years of marriage, that was natural. They were not all perfect, of course—forty-two years of washing his dishes and washing his clothes were hardly romantic. Yet, now that there was no one whose dishes and clothes needed washing... It had been a good marriage. They had grown close in a thousand ways that young starry-eyed lovers never consider. If only she could have had another year with him, another day with him. If only there had been a cure. Why were we put on this earth to live and love and die? She had always believed in the goodness of God and in the resurrection—had taught this to her children and to her Sunday school children—but her belief had never been so tested. She could still say the words, but her prayers for understanding seemed to go unanswered.

The telephone rang. Evelyn got up and walked across the bedroom to the nightstand and picked up the receiver. "Hello," she said weakly.

"Evelyn?"

"Yes."

"This is Judy Hudson. I'm sorry to bother you at a time like this."

"No, that's all right. Thank you for coming to the funeral."

"Well, I wanted to be there. You know, Buzz was such a wonderful person, always so cheerful and pleasant and kind. We will certainly miss him at the church."

"Yes, he was all those things," Evelyn agreed.

"Well, if this is something that you don't feel up to doing just now, please feel free to say so."

"What is it?" Evelyn asked apprehensively.

"Well, you know that we both ended up on the funeral dinner committee of the women's association this year."

"Yes."

"I'm afraid that we've had another death in the congregation. The family has asked if we could provide a meal at the church. Again, if you don't feel up to it now—"

"Well, I'm not sure that I do, really."

"I certainly understand, Evelyn. I know that it has been a difficult time for you. It is so hard to lose someone who has been so close to us. We are certainly praying for you, and for Mike and Connie, too. Please let me know if there's anything that I can be doing for you."

"Thank you," said Evelyn.

"Bye now," said Judy.

Evelyn hung up the receiver. She and Buzz had always been moderately active in the church. They had done their share, up until the time that Buzz became ill. She just wasn't up to this now. They ought to know that at the church. She hoped that they understood. There were others who could and should be doing the work now, anyway. Evelyn was feeling old today. Judy was a nice person, a woman in early middle age who seemed sincere in her sympathy at the funeral and afterward, when she had brought a casserole by the house and had put her arm around Evelyn's shoulder and offered a brief prayer. She should have told her again that she appreciated her kindness, Evelyn thought. Perhaps a little note to her—yes, she ought to write a note to her while she was thinking about it.

Evelyn went to the kitchen and reached up above the desk for some stationery and the church directory to look up Judy's address. As she did, a copy of Buzz's funeral worship order fell from the shelf down onto the desk. On the cover was a picture of the sun breaking out from behind a cloud, and a Bible verse was printed in script in the bottom part of the picture. Evelyn picked it up and looked at it. Had she noticed the words earlier? Surely, she must have read them at the funeral, perhaps over and over. But just now, she could not remember ever having seen the words before. "Blessed be the God and Father of our Lord Jesus Christ," the scripture read, "the Father of mercies and God of all comfort, who comforts us in all our affliction, so that we may be able to comfort those who are in any affliction, with the comfort with which we ourselves are comforted by God" (2 Cor 1:3–4 RSV).

"'So that *we* may be able to comfort,'" Evelyn said the words slowly to herself. "'Who comforts us in all our affliction, so that we may be able to comfort'" (1:4a RSV).

Suddenly, it dawned on Evelyn that she had not even asked whose family the meal was for. She felt a flash of embarrassment, but it gave way to a genuine desire to know who in the congregation had died, and who, like herself, was now grieving the loss of someone whom they had loved. She opened the church directory and found Judy Hudson's telephone number. "Judy," she said when a woman answered at the other end of the line. "This is Evelyn. I'm sorry, I didn't think to thank you just now for being so kind to me these past couple of weeks."

"Oh, it's not necessary to thank me. That's what it means to be a church family."

"And I didn't even think to ask who it was that died."

"Philip Martinez. Did you know him? They are fairly new in the church—a young couple with a baby girl. His wife's name is Clarissa."

"No, I don't think that—wait a minute. You mean that young couple who have been sitting up near the front? And that adorable little baby?"

"Yes, they're the ones. They started coming back about Christmastime, and joined in January. Their baby was baptized last Sunday—I guess you weren't in church, it being so soon after Buzz's death."

"Oh no, oh no," said Evelyn, suddenly forgetting everything but the picture of the young family in her mind. "Oh no. What happened?"

"It was an industrial accident at the place where he worked. Yesterday afternoon."

"No, no, no. They couldn't have been married but a few years. They had so much to look forward to."

"I know," Judy agreed.

Compassion flooded Evelyn's soul, extinguishing every concern except for the grieving young widow. Perhaps Evelyn's own recent loss made her more sensitive to the pain that this young mother must be experiencing, but it was a real concern for Mrs. Martinez and not any projection of her own grief that now prompted Evelyn to ask, "Judy, do you have their address?"

"Yes, I think that I wrote it down when I saw it in the last newsletter. Just a minute." There was a rustling of papers at the other end of the telephone. "Here it is—2716 Birchmount Avenue, Apartment 308."

"Thank you, Judy," Evelyn said as she scribbled the address on the back of Buzz's funeral order. "Oh, and, please, I *do* want to help with the meal."

"I'll put you down and I'll be back in touch," said Judy.

"Goodbye," said Evelyn.

She had not been out of the house in days. She glanced quickly in the hall mirror now as she opened the closet door to get her coat and scarf. Her dress was not exactly what she would have chosen if she had *planned* to go out, but she felt an urgency about her task that would not permit her time to change. On her way out the door to the garage, she picked up her purse. She opened the garage door, got into the car, turned on the ignition, and backed out of the driveway. "2716 Birchmount," she said aloud to herself, committing the address to memory. So intent was Evelyn on thinking of the fastest route to Birchmount Avenue that she did not notice the buds on the tree alongside the driveway, and how one of them had sprouted a new green leaf.

Palm/Passion Sunday

Isaiah 50:4–9a
Philippians 2:5–11
Luke 19:28–40

"Conversation in a Workshop"

Hand me that tool over there, will you, my friend? No, the other one. Thank you.... My son Elias? He's gone down to the market to help out my cousin for a few days—you know, with the Passover crowd in the city, there's so much more business at the market. So, here I am to do the work around the shop myself, and at my age!... All right, all right, so I'm younger than Uncle Mordecai who still works by himself, but he doesn't have this many mouths to feed, does he, eh? Please to hold that crosspiece steady for me for a moment.... Yes, it's a little job for the governor.... Listen, I will work for *Satan* even, if he pays me fairly. Times are hard. This soldier comes this morning banging on my door, says it's a rush job and I've got the sturdiest timber in Jerusalem. So, he shows me the money, so I get to work. Everybody's mind is on celebrating the Passover, not carpentry, so I welcome the work, even with Elias gone.

    So, what's new with you? Your brother's wife had another child, did she? Boy or girl?... Ah, I thank you, God, that you made me a man.... A parade? No, I know nothing about a parade. When?... No. What was it about? Have the Romans blessed us with another garrison?... A Jew?... From Galilee? And what might a Galilean have done to deserve a parade?... Oh, another miracle worker, is he? We've had enough of them lately—curing the same cripple in every town, restoring sight to the same blind man every day, not a one of them able to work a real miracle and make the tax collectors disappear! . . . You say he has tax collectors among his *followers*? *I* want no part of him, then. What could he possibly do miraculous enough to turn a tax collector from his rolls, anyway? . . . Well, that's a new one, I must say! In Bethany, was it? And not just sick, but really dead? . . . Four days in the tomb? . . . Bless me, this one must be bold indeed. I suppose that *would* draw something of a crowd. . . . They did *what*? Laid their clothes down on the road in front of him? . . . That's a fine way to treat a good garment, letting a donkey walk on it!

. . . "Blessed is the King who comes in the name of the Lord! Peace in heaven and glory in the highest!" Quotes the Psalms, does he? He'll soon find himself an enemy of Herod *and* the Romans if he's calling himself a king. . . . All right, then, even if he allows his *followers* to call him "king"— they'll see it as a threat just the same, and even more so, if the crowd shows any sign of disorder. If Pilate can kill a bunch of Galileans quietly making their sacrifices in the temple, he can easily enough kill a single Galilean inciting a riot! . . . Yes, well, your Galilean may well *talk* peace, but it takes Pilate very little threat of disobedience to react with an iron fist. If you ask me, he likes nothing more than an excuse to crack down on the Jews. And Herod—Herod will brook no rivals to his pomp and his wealth. . . . You say this one seeks no riches? Since when did a king not covet money and jewels? Even David had his palace! If this man would be a king, surely he has no aversion to power and prestige and an army to guarantee it all. . . . Not that kind of king? Then *what* kind? . . . A kingdom in heaven? . . . Give all you have to the poor? Forgive your enemies? Bless those who curse you? This sounds like no king I have heard of! More like a fool, or a dreamer. Well, it sounds like he's harmless after all. Few enough people will really be willing to follow a revolutionary who promises his supporters poverty and tells them to be humble.

So what sort of people were there at this parade for a king with no kingdom—the city rabble and ne'er-do-wells? . . . All the way up from Jericho, eh? Well, I suppose if they were *responsible* folk, they'd have plenty of work of their own to do instead of hanging around the latest celebrity. Hold that still, now. . . . You think they were sincere, then, do you? And did you see this man of miracles yourself? What did you make of him? . . . I think you get carried away too much with the emotion of the crowd, my friend! Be careful—the next thing you know, *you* will be a follower of this Galilean, praying for poverty and learning to be humble!

So what has become of him since he came to the city? . . . At the *temple*, was he? . . . No, I have heard nothing—I mind my own business and my customers mind theirs, what few customers I have had this week. I am a carpenter, not a gossip. Mind you, I could tell you all sorts of things about my neighbors and my customers, but I say nothing! I knew about the scandal of your sister for days before I heard it from the butcher, did I not? And even then I did not tell anyone but my family and my closest friends whom I could trust to keep quiet, as you know. So, tell me about this Galilean at the temple.... He did *what*? By what authority did he drive them out?... Ha! He has a strange way of impressing the officials, this Galilean whom people call "king." True enough, those thieves in the temple should have been thrown out long ago. But no, no, this Galilean of yours goes too far! There must be order, especially in the house of God.

... What? He dared to go back to the temple and teach after all that?... You heard him, then? And a large crowd?... And what did he say, this Galilean teacher and man of miracles?... You seem quite moved by him, my friend.... What? You are considering becoming a follower of his? Are you serious? Leave Jerusalem, leave your family and your job to follow a vagabond teacher from Galilee? Think of your responsibilities, man! Consider your reputation! I admit that, from what you tell me, his words sound very fine, but if the priests do not endorse him and if, as you say, the scribes are unhappy with him, how can what he says be right? And even if he does speak the truth, they are not likely to let him go on *this* way very long. They are powerful men, and learned in the scriptures. They are respected, and they respect the mood of Pilate too well for you to suppose that they will let your Galilean give him any excuse for doing away with their privileges. Mark my words, if this teacher is as popular as you say, and if he is attracting crowds like you say, they will find some way to have him silenced, even if he *is* a Jew, even if he says his kingdom is not an earthly one!

... What? You say there is more? ... The Messiah? Who says this?... But if he is the Messiah, surely the priests and the scribes would be the first to hail him! And even the Pharisees!... Well, I am sure that even God himself works through the established channels. The priests and scribes speak for God, do they not? They are intelligent men, are they not? They know his ways, do they not? Surely, God would have the courtesy of informing them if the Messiah were coming. Besides, from what you say, this Galilean is hardly what we have been told to expect!... A God of love and mercy? What then becomes of righteousness under the law? I spend my whole life doing what the priests and the scribes say to do, I try to live as carefully as the Pharisees, and what is to prevent a sinner from saying, "God, forgive me," and suddenly he is as righteous as I am, who have obeyed the law? Preposterous! This is a far cry, I think, from the Messiah. Now, hold this up while I lash it in place, then I will drive these nails in to keep it rigid.

"Conversation in a Workshop"

Say, what's all the commotion in the street? You! Boys! What is going on? . . . A crowd at the governor's palace? For what? . . . Pilate might release Barabbas? There's a bad one, if you ask me. That madman Barabbas will bring the death of us all, him and the Zealots. . . . Well, you are a good friend and if you do decide to follow this dreamer and king and teacher and miracle worker, then God go with you, but if it doesn't work out, don't say I didn't warn you. True enough, your Galilean must be a remarkable man, in his own way. But it seems to me there's danger in it. And even if Pilate and Herod and the priests and the scribes leave him alone, many of his followers will find a life of poverty and humility and forgiveness to be less romantic and filled with more hardship than they may think. But I know you must follow your heart. I suppose that is why I love you as my own brother—and why I am so worried by what you have told me.

Well, that job is done. That soldier should be back for it soon with some of his comrades. Help me to get it out onto the street—I really don't want Romans under my roof, especially at Passover. . . . Yes, I know it's heavy—I told you that I have the sturdiest timbers in town. . . . Thank you for your help, my friend. . . . No, I don't like making this kind of thing. It's certainly not why I learned to be a carpenter. But, as I told you, orders have been slow, and I don't relish the thought of what might happen to me if I defied the request of the governor. . . . I just wonder what poor soul they're going to crucify today.

Good Friday

Isaiah 52:13—53:12
Hebrews 4:14-16; 5:7-9
John 18:1—19:42

After Jesus had spoken these words, he went out with his disciples across the Kidron Valley to a place where there was a garden, which he and his disciples entered. Now Judas, who betrayed him, also knew the place, because Jesus often met there with his disciples. So Judas brought a detachment of soldiers together with police from the chief priests and the Pharisees, and they came there with lanterns and torches and weapons. Then Jesus, knowing all that was about to happen to him, came forward and asked them, "Whom are you looking for?" They answered, "Jesus of Nazareth." Jesus replied, "I am he." Judas, who betrayed him, was standing with them. When Jesus said to them, "I am he," they stepped back and fell to the ground. Again he asked them, "Whom are you looking for?" And they said, "Jesus of Nazareth." Jesus answered, "I told you that I am he. So if you are looking for me, let these men go." This was to fulfill the word that he had spoken, "I did not lose a single one of those whom you gave me" (John 18:1-9 NRSV).

> Judas, that *rat*. Curse him! His name sticks in my throat. I never liked him. I never trusted him. From the very beginning, you could tell that he was scheming. I didn't understand why Jesus wanted him to come with us. We should have known he was plotting something like this—when he got up and left the dinner. It was obvious that Jesus had something important on his

> mind, things that he wanted to tell us. But before he had gotten very far into it, Judas up and left. Just like that! And after Jesus had washed his feet, and the rest of us, too! At the time, I just thought he was being rude. Little did I know that he had an appointment with the police, those Roman dogs. We should never have come up to Jerusalem. It was too dangerous. And we should have warned Jesus about Judas. I suppose he got *paid* for his treason. I swear, if I ever see him again alive . . .

Then Simon Peter, who had a sword, drew it, struck the high priest's slave, and cut off his right ear. The slave's name was Malchus. Jesus said to Peter, "Put your sword back into its sheath. Am I not to drink the cup that the Father has given me?" (John 18:10–11 NRSV)

> Only Peter had any guts last night. Why didn't the *rest* of us put up a fight? Why didn't the *rest* of us try to defend Jesus? Yeah, we were scared. We were surprised. We were confused. But that didn't stop *Peter*. And Jesus told *him* to put his sword *away*. At least Peter *tried*. *So what* if we couldn't *win* a fight against the police and the soldiers? At least now I wouldn't feel like such a contemptible coward. Why Jesus didn't *want* Peter to defend him, I don't know. Something he said made me think that he didn't want any of us to get hurt. It was almost like Jesus was resigned to what was happening—thought that it had to be. He used to talk sometimes about dying . . .

So the soldiers, their officer, and the Jewish police arrested Jesus and bound him. First they took him to Annas, who was the father-in-law of Caiaphas, the high priest that year. Caiaphas was the one who had advised the Jews that it was better to have one person die for the people.

Simon Peter and another disciple followed Jesus. Since that disciple was known to the high priest, he went with Jesus into the courtyard of the high priest, but Peter was standing outside the gate. So the other disciple, who was known to the high priest, went out, spoke to the woman who guarded the gate, and brought Peter in. The woman said to Peter, "You are not also one of this man's disciples, are you?" He said, "I am not." Now the slaves and the police had made a charcoal fire because it was cold, and they were standing around it and warming themselves. Peter also was standing with them and warming himself (John 18:12–18 NRSV).

> You'd think people would have some rights. They didn't even say *why* they were arresting Jesus. But they dragged him off to Annas' house. Peter and another of our number followed along, at a distance, staying in the shadows. We *all* should have gone

> to complain about what had happened, to demand justice. But we were stunned. It had happened so *quickly*. And we were *scared*. If they'd arrested *Jesus*, wouldn't they arrest *us, too*? And we didn't know *why* he had been taken, so we couldn't know that they wouldn't accuse *us* of the *same thing*, whatever it was. But we *should* have gone. *I* should have gone. But maybe we would have buckled when we got there. Peter did, I gather from rumors. Some of the others have criticized him severely. But I can't. Peter, at least, had the courage to *go* there, to be *close* to Jesus and see what they were *doing* to him. The *rest* of us were just looking out for *ourselves*.

Then the high priest questioned Jesus about his disciples and about his teaching. Jesus answered, "I have spoken openly to the world; I have always taught in the synagogues and in the temple, where all the Jews come together. I have said nothing in secret. Why do you ask me? Ask those who heard what I said to them; they know what I said." When he had said this, one of the police standing nearby struck Jesus on the face, saying, "Is that how you answer the high priest?" Jesus answered, "If I have spoken wrongly, testify to the wrong. But if I have spoken rightly, why do you strike me?" Then Annas sent him bound to Caiaphas the high priest (John 18:19–24 NRSV).

> I think they don't even know *themselves* why they arrested Jesus—I mean, what his real crime was. They just didn't *like* him. They didn't want people to *listen* to him, to hear what he had to *say*. They were *jealous*. They love their power, the priests do, and *Jesus* was becoming more popular than *they* are. I mean, think of the crowd when we came into the city! His reputation had preceded him all the way up from Galilee! *They* were the ones who should have been *afraid*. And I guess they were.

Now Simon Peter was standing and warming himself. They asked him, "You are not also one of his disciples, are you?" He denied it and said, "I am not." One of the slaves of the high priest, a relative of the man whose ear Peter had cut off, asked, "Did I not see you in the garden with him?" Again Peter denied it, and at that moment the cock crowed.

Then they took Jesus from Caiaphas to Pilate's headquarters. It was early in the morning. They themselves did not enter the headquarters, so as to avoid ritual defilement and to be able to eat the Passover. So Pilate went out to them and said, "What accusation do you bring against this man?" They answered, "If this man were not a criminal, we would not have handed him over to you." Pilate said to them, "Take him yourselves and judge him according to your law." The Jews replied, "We are not permitted to put anyone to death." (This was to fulfill what Jesus had said when he indicated the kind of death he was to die.) (John 18:25–32 NRSV)

> So scrupulous they are to avoid breaking any of the laws! Why, if a person were lying bleeding in a ditch alongside the road, they'd probably walk on the other side to avoid being contaminated by the blood; they'd rather see a person *die* than think that *they* might be *defiled*! So unlike *Jesus*, who taught us that the sabbath is a gift from God, not an excuse for avoiding helping your neighbor. I hear they wouldn't even enter Pilate's *house* last night because then they would have to go purify themselves for the sabbath. All careful to avoid the ritual dirtiness of being under the roof of a Roman, but quick enough to call on a Roman to do their dirty work!

Then Pilate entered the headquarters again, summoned Jesus, and asked him, "Are *you* the King of the Jews?" Jesus answered, "Do you ask this on your own, or did others tell you about me?" Pilate replied, "I am not a Jew, am I? Your own nation and the chief priests handed you over to me. What have you done?" Jesus answered, "My kingdom is not from this world. If my kingdom were from this world, my followers would be fighting to keep me from being handed over to the Jews. But as it is, my kingdom is not from here." Pilate asked him, "So you are a king?" Jesus answered, "You say that I am a king. For this I was born, and for this I came into the world, to testify to the truth. Everyone who belongs to the truth listens to my voice." Pilate asked him, "What is truth?"

After he had said this, he went out to the Jews again and told them, "I find no case against him. But you have a custom that I release someone for you at the Passover. Do you want me to release for you the King of the Jews?" They shouted in reply, "Not this man, but Barabbas!" Now Barabbas was a bandit (John 18:33–40 NRSV).

> Pilate! Roman scum! He's never had the backbone to stand up for *anything*! And he refused to stand up to the *priests*, though he suspected they hadn't any right to have Jesus *arrested*. Keep the order! Keep the peace! But what kind of peace is *this*? One based on lies. What kind of order is *this*? Simply how people act when they're afraid. Pilate tried to worm his way out of responsibility, tried to turn the decision over to the crowd. But they just wanted to be entertained, just wanted the spectacle of another crucifixion. Didn't they know the things that Jesus had *done* for people? The things that Jesus could *continue* to do for people?

> *They* didn't care any more about the truth than *Pilate* did! "Give us Barabbas!" they shouted. A thief, a liar, an anarchist! So *he's* loose on society again by their own fickle desire. And the kindest, most caring, most wonderful person that I've ever known is . . .

Then Pilate took Jesus and had him flogged. And the soldiers wove a crown of thorns and put it on his head, and they dressed him in a purple robe. They kept coming up to him, saying, "Hail, King of the Jews!" and striking him on the face. Pilate went out again and said to them, "Look, I am bringing him out to you to let you know that I find no case against him." So Jesus came out, wearing a crown of thorns and the purple robe. Pilate said to them, "Here is the man!" When the chief priests and the police saw him, they shouted, "Crucify him! Crucify him!" Pilate said to them, "Take him yourselves and crucify him; I find no case against him." The Jews answered him, "We have a law, and according to that law he ought to die because he has claimed to be the Son of God" (John 19:1–7 NRSV).

> The Son of God? I don't know. He was certainly human enough to get hungry and to feel pain. But if Jesus *wasn't* the Son of God, then how did he bring Lazarus back to life? Oh, I don't know. These questions are too big for me. Look, the point is, he never hurt anybody, only helped people, did wonderful things. Certainly more than *King Herod* ever did, that pompous Roman puppet. *Herod* cares for no one but *Herod*. There isn't *anyone* that *Jesus* didn't care about. There isn't *anyone* that Jesus didn't . . . *love*. Is there some law against *love*?

Now when Pilate heard this, he was more afraid than ever. He entered his headquarters again and asked Jesus, "Where are you from?" But Jesus gave him no answer. Pilate therefore said to him, "Do you refuse to speak to me? Do you not know that I have power to release you, and power to crucify you?" Jesus answered him, "You would have no power over me unless it had been given you from above; therefore the one who handed me over to you is guilty of a greater sin." From then on Pilate tried to release him, but the Jews cried out, "If you release this man, you are no friend of the emperor. Everyone who claims to be a king sets himself against the emperor."

When Pilate heard these words, he brought Jesus outside and sat on the judge's bench at a place called The Stone Pavement, or in Hebrew Gabbatha. Now it was the day of Preparation for the Passover; and it was about noon. He said to the Jews, "Here is your King!" They cried out, "Away with him! Away with him! Crucify him!" Pilate asked them, "Shall I crucify your

King?" The chief priests answered, "We have no king but the emperor." Then he handed him over to them to be crucified (John 19:8–16a NRSV).

> No king but the *emperor*? A fine lot of Jews are *these* children of Abraham! They complain that Jesus blasphemed by calling himself the Son of God, committed treason by calling himself the king of the Jews, and then they pledge all *their* allegiance to a Roman emperor who calls *himself* a god! *They* should have been on trial, not *Jesus*. *They* should be facing the ultimate punishment, not *Jesus*. And if Pilate really thought the charges were baseless, or petty, the Roman swine, he could have let Jesus go—or at least let Jesus *live*. But *no*. He handed Jesus over to the *rabble*. And he washed his hands of the whole affair. The world has gone insane.

So they took Jesus; and carrying the cross by himself, he went out to what is called The Place of the Skull, which in Hebrew is called Golgotha. There they crucified him, and with him two others, one on either side, with Jesus between them. Pilate also had an inscription written and put on the cross. It read, "Jesus of Nazareth, the King of the Jews." Many of the Jews read this inscription, because the place where Jesus was crucified was near the city; and it was written in Hebrew, in Latin, and in Greek. Then the chief priests of the Jews said to Pilate, "Do not write, 'The King of the Jews,' but, 'This man said, I am King of the Jews.'" Pilate answered, "What I have written I have written." When the soldiers had crucified Jesus, they took his clothes and divided them into four parts, one for each soldier. They also took his tunic; now the tunic was seamless, woven in one piece from the top. So they said to one another, "Let us not tear it, but cast lots for it to see who will get it." This was to fulfill what the scripture says, "They divided my clothes among themselves, and for my clothing they cast lots." And that is what the soldiers did (John 19:16b–25a NRSV).

> I wasn't there. But those who were say that they tried to strip every bit of Jesus' dignity away from him, humiliated him in every way possible. They mocked the notion that he was the king of the Jews, with that sign, with that robe, with that crown of thorns. Then they left him naked on the cross for hours while they gambled for his clothes. I can't image the pain, the blood, the flies, the insults. How could God have allowed this to *happen* to such a good man? Why didn't he *do* something? Why didn't *Jesus* do something? He'd done wondrous things for *others*.

Meanwhile, standing near the cross of Jesus were his mother, and his mother's sister, Mary the wife of Clopas, and Mary Magdalene. When Jesus saw his mother and the disciple whom he loved standing beside her, he said to his mother, "Woman, here is your son." Then he said to the disciple, "Here is your mother." And from that hour the disciple took her into his own home.

After this, when Jesus knew that all was now finished, he said (in order to fulfill the scripture), "I am thirsty." A jar full of sour wine was standing there. So they put a sponge full of the wine on a branch of hyssop and held it to his mouth. When Jesus had received the wine, he said, "It is finished." Then he bowed his head and gave up his spirit (John 19:25b–30 NRSV).

> It's not possible to believe that he's dead. He can't be! But he is. I've heard that they didn't even bother to break his legs, like they do so cruelly to make victims die more quickly. He was already dead. And then they stabbed him in the side on top of that. But before he died, I understand, Jesus did one last kind deed—he made sure that his mother would be taken care of. Maybe he would have asked *me* to do that if I had been there. Of course, he knew that I *wasn't* there. So he knew that I, too, had abandoned him. What must his last thoughts of me have been? I *should* have been there. I'm glad I *wasn't* there to see him in such pain and agony. But I *should* have been.

Since it was the day of Preparation, the Jews did not want the bodies left on the cross during the sabbath, especially because that sabbath was a day of great solemnity. So they asked Pilate to have the legs of the crucified men broken and the bodies removed. Then the soldiers came and broke the legs of the first and of the other who had been crucified with him. But when they came to Jesus and saw that he was already dead, they did not break his legs. Instead one of the soldiers pierced his side with a spear, and at once blood and water came out. (He who saw this has testified so that you also may believe. His testimony is true, and he knows that he tells the truth.) These things occurred so that the scripture might be fulfilled, "None of his bones shall be broken." And again another passage of scripture says, "They will look on the one whom they have pierced."

After these things, Joseph of Arimathea who was a disciple of Jesus, though a secret one because of his fear of the Jews, asked Pilate to let him take away the body of Jesus. Pilate gave him permission; so he came and removed his body. Nicodemus, who had at first come to Jesus by night, also came, bringing a mixture of myrrh and aloes, weighing about a hundred pounds. They took the body of Jesus and wrapped it with spices in linen cloths, according to the burial custom of the Jews. Now there was a garden in the place where he was crucified, and in the garden there was a new tomb in which no one had ever been laid. And so, because it was the Jewish day of Preparation, and the tomb was nearby, they laid Jesus there (John 19:31–42 NRSV).

> Joseph—he is a good man. He did what all of *us* should have done, at least—to take care of Jesus' body, to give him in death the dignity that the soldiers took away from him in his last hours of life. And now, it's over. Our hopes, our expectations, our friendship, our purpose for living. And we *still* don't know but that they might come hunting for *us*. Yes, I'm still scared, and still feeling a coward. I guess I'll have to live the rest of my life with the knowledge that I let him down—the best person who ever lived. How I yearn to hear him say he had forgiven me for that! But now he's dead. And my spirit—it feels dead, too. I hear that Mary, the one from Magdala, is eager to go to the tomb as soon as the sabbath is over. I don't see what good that will do anyone. What could she possibly hope to find but a place full of death?

Eastertide

Third Sunday of Easter

Acts 2:14a, 36–41
1 Peter 1:17–23
Luke 24:13–35

"Word and Sacrament"

Will McFarland drew in the reins, bringing Jenny to a halt in front of the icehouse, thinking to himself that *this* horse would never be as smart as Bonnie had been. The two of them had worked together for almost twenty-five years, and he missed her. She had learned every stop on his route after not more than a few weeks, and would obediently come to a halt at just the right spot in front of each house or behind in the alleyway to give Will the shortest route to the door. It was as if she knew that the blocks of ice were heavy and was trying to help as much as she could—something that Will had appreciated more and more as he grew older and rheumatism had set into his shoulders and arthritis into his knees. There was a time when he had been burly enough not to *feel* the length of the day when it finally came to its end, but that had been many years ago. Now, the workday was shorter, but it wore him down much more than it had in his twenties and thirties. Not that he was all that old—he was barely into his fifties. But rainy days were more miserable now. And *ice-cutting* days were more *lonely*. And he sensed that his whole way of life was vanishing—he had lost nearly two dozen customers this year alone to Frigidaires, and he was one of the last deliverymen in Summerside *not* to have a motor truck. Maybe he should have taken Bonnie's death as a sign, the morning he had come out to the stable and found her massive body lying cold and silent in the straw.

It was the wrong customers that were buying Frigidaires, of course, or *not* buying them. Reverend McGill, for instance—the parsonage, naturally, would be one of the *last* places in town to have electrical appliances. But every time he climbed up the stairs to the back porch of the parsonage, he shuddered from a dread more chilling than the block of ice on his back. "You ought to be attending to the word of the Lord, Will McFarland," Mrs. McGill said every time he made a delivery. "You're not so much made of ice that the fires of hell won't burn ye."

"Same amount next week?" he would ask.

"Of course," she would answer, and, feeling already the flames of perdition licking his heels, he would trudge back to the ice wagon looking forward to the coolness emanating from behind the front panel.

It was his sabbath-breaking that officially kept him from earning a communion token, but he noticed that the *church members* on his route were as anxious to get *their* ice as the *non*-church members. But only Mrs. McGill regularly lectured him about his sins of *commission*—cutting ice on Sundays—and his sins of *omission*—not, therefore, being in church. It wasn't that he hadn't tried to confine his ice-cutting to Sunday *afternoons*, leaving his mornings free for accompanying his family to worship. Now that he had less ice to *cut*, thanks to the Frigidaire salesman, he actually had time to get to church, and had even done so a few times when his business first started to drop off, but he had been so self-conscious about returning to church after so many years' absence that he imagined everyone was looking at him and whispering about his sins of sabbath-*breaking* which, on balance, so far outweighed his modest successes of sabbath-*keeping*, that the whole exercise of churchgoing seemed like a walk *into* the valley of death rather than *out* of it. He didn't remember much about the last worship service he attended, but it did strike him as strange that the Bible passage that day had to do with Jesus' disciples walking through a grain field and picking some of the grain, and Jesus getting into trouble because it had been on the sabbath, and Jesus somehow saying that it was really all right. The sermon, as best he could remember, was a harangue about how the Jews should have known who Jesus *was*, scarcely *mentioning* the fact that Jesus condoned plucking grain on the *sabbath*. His wife had been pleased that he had been in church, as was his daughter, who was grown now and married to a bank teller. The minister had announced at the end of the worship service that communion would be offered the next Sunday, and that, in preparation, each family would be receiving a visit from the elders that week. Will had found some excuse not to be home when they came.

Will unhitched Jenny and led her into her stall, where he gave her a quick brushing and let her nibble some oats from his hand and then rubbed her nose and thought about Bonnie. He grieved for her still, but for other things, too, that he had lost. The world was changing, and the ripples of change were lapping up on the shores even of this little island, far remote from kings and presidents and prime ministers. The strange magic of electricity was part of the change. But Will McFarland didn't know how to change his way of *life*. He could only mourn its *passing*.

"Supper's on," his wife greeted him at the backdoor.

"It's early, then," he said. "I just got back."

"It's the elders coming," she replied. "I need to have things cleaned up before they arrive."

He responded with a look of not quite understanding what she had said.

"It's communion on Sunday."

"Oh," he said simply, not having any other reply to the unanticipated news.

"I was hoping," she said, and paused, considered, then started over again. "I was hoping you could be here this evening when they come."

"Well," he said, looking down at the plate she set before him, "the iron's worn thin on the rear wheels." Actually, it was a task he'd been putting off for more than a month, but this evening it suddenly seemed like the job had acquired a special urgency. "I was going to pull them after supper."

His wife looked at him with a mixture of skepticism and disappointment. She screwed up her courage. "It gets, well, embarrassing—I mean, every quarter, when the elders come, you're gone."

"Maybe they'd like to come to the stable and help me, then?" he said, managing only a half smile, indicating that he was not serious, but neither was what he said meant to be amusing. After they had started their supper, he said, "The Thompsons bought a Frigidaire." They ate the remainder of the meal in silence.

He had only just managed to prop the rear axle up on a block when Will McFarland heard a knock on the door of the stable.

"Mr. McFarland?" a voice came from outside. "Will? May I come in?"

Will was not accustomed to visitors in the stable, and he could not quite place the voice—it sounded sort of familiar, but he couldn't think exactly where he had known it.

"Yes, come in," he shouted back, with a touch of anxiety.

The door creaked open about two feet, and Rev. Thomas McGill slipped into the light of the kerosene lanterns that Will had lit to illumine his workplace.

"Reverend," he said, surprised, reaching for a rag to wipe his grimy hands, and then extending his right one out in response to the minister's gesture. "I'm afraid it's kind of dirty out here," he apologized, looking at the minister in his clerical suit.

"Our Lord was a carpenter," the minister said, shrugging his shoulders slightly. "Dirt comes off."

"I didn't know you were coming," Will said. Then, he added, "I've got to replace the iron on these wheels."

"May I help in some way?" the minister asked.

Will surveyed the suited clergyman who, aside from his clothing, did not appear to have the musculature required for the task at hand. "No, no, thank you," Will said. "I can manage. It's something I've done a lot of times before."

The minister smiled in response, though Will did not know whether it was a sign of *relief* or an expression of *pity*. After a few seconds of silence, Will asked, "Is there something I can do for you?"

"No, I just wanted to visit with you for a while," the minister said.

Will felt his jaw tighten.

"I've been thinking that I ought to get out to see my parishioners in their workplaces more." He paused, then added, "I missed seeing you on Easter. You used to come to church with Emily on Easter."

"Oh, well . . .," Will said, without any plan for finishing his sentence.

"I've been wondering how you're faring these days," Reverend McGill continued.

"Well enough," Will replied, "though none of us are getting any younger."

Both men chuckled in a socially obligatory way. The minister continued, after a few seconds of awkward silence, "I've noticed, as I've accompanied the elders now and then on their communion visits, that more and more people are replacing their iceboxes. In fact, some of our parishioners take me right into their kitchens to show off their new Frigidaires."

"They seem to be much in fashion," Will responded, forcing a smile through his understatement.

"In fact, the trustees have offered to purchase one for the parsonage," the minister said.

So this was the purpose of his visit, Will thought—to inform him that he was canceling the church's account. Well, of course—the minister didn't owe it to the McFarlands not to buy an electric icebox, especially since Will was not exactly a model church member. Why shouldn't the trustees get in tune with the times, even if it *did* cost money?

"But," the minister said, "I've talked it over with *Mrs.* McGill, and I've told the trustees that I think we could put the money to better use repairing the roof at the orphanage."

Will, of course, had been expecting different news. The minister continued, "That gale last January did a lot of damage, I understand, and the orphanage's trustees just don't have the money to put things back right. If the church could help them purchase the shingles, maybe some of our menfolk could donate a Sunday afternoon to do the labor."

"Labor on the sabbath?" Will blurted out before he could stop himself.

The minister's face reddened slightly, and he cleared his throat. "Our Lord labored on the sabbath, when it was a matter of helping somebody." Reverend McGill looked down at his shoes, which were now uncharacteristically coated with a fine layer of dust. "I was reading an article just the other day on the subject. That made me think about how folks who earn a living the *other* days of the week might help the orphanage. Perhaps you could *help* us next Sunday afternoon, if you're not too busy with your business?"

"I suppose," Will said, inconclusively.

"Actually, I don't want you to think I just came out to ask you to donate your time," the minister said. Will looked at him, again bracing for a lecture. "I've been wondering, with so many people buying electric iceboxes, how you were getting along? I can imagine that it's had an impact on your business."

Will did not respond immediately.

"So much in our world seems to be changing. 'Modern conveniences,' they call them. 'Progress.' But it's not an easy adjustment, not for any of us. Please don't think me presumptuous, but I imagine this might be posing a hardship for you and Emily."

Now, it was Will's turn to clear his throat. "Well, I do have fewer customers, of course," he said. "That has some advantages, naturally. And, thank the Lord, Andy's a good provider for our Lydia."

This time, when the minister smiled, Will was sure it was a smile of pity.

"You're a hard worker," he said. "Our Lord's afflictions hallow the hardships of us all, certainly working people. And when God raised him from the dead, that was a promise to glorify *all* of those whom life has ground down." Then Reverend McGill added, "Is there any way that I can be of help to you?"

This was totally unexpected.

"I don't know what it could be, Reverend. Neither of us can stop progress."

Just then, Jenny whinnied from her stall. "But some of the new ways seem not to offer the simple satisfactions of the old ways, do they?" the minister observed, glancing toward Jenny, who was now standing looking at the two men. "Take motor cars, for instance—it's hard to feel a partnership with a gasoline engine." He turned his face back toward Will. "I was mentioning to Mrs. McGill just the other day—when I think of the many years that you and your horses have faithfully served the people of Summerside, cutting ice and carting it, storing it and then delivering it dependably, regardless the weather."

"Well," Will said, now somewhat embarrassed by the praise. "The ponds will be melting now. So I can probably help you next Sunday afternoon."

"I wish you would also come to worship Sunday morning, if possible."

Will looked hard at the eyes of the man whose wife constantly envisioned him roasting in hell, and who had himself condemned him on occasion, at least so Will thought, for working on the sabbath.

"Oh, I almost forgot," the minister said, and thrust his hand into his coat pocket. He pulled out a little metal disc, and held it out to Will. "This is communion Sunday."

Will took the token and stared at it. It had been many years since his calloused fingers had held a communion token. It had been many years since the Session had found him worthy to sit at the holy table, to taste the holy meal. The minister looked at him sheepishly. "Christ died for all of us. God raised him for all of us, too. That's the miracle of Easter."

Emily McFarland was surprised to see her husband take his suit out of the wardrobe on Sunday morning, but she did not say anything about it. She and the elders who had come to the house on Thursday evening had discussed the importance of salvation. She was unaware that the *minister* was on the premises—he had left the others as they came up the front walk, and disappeared around the side of the house, and then rejoined them after they had come out following their visit with her. But when her husband appeared at the breakfast table looking uncomfortably stiff in the only white shirt and the only suit and tie that he owned, she could not help smiling at him, and she bent over and kissed him on the forehead. "Fixing the roof on the orphanage," he said, which did not really explain his Sunday haberdashery.

The sermon was about how Jesus had appeared to some of the disciples after the resurrection, but they hadn't known that it was him, and how just talking about Jesus and knowing about the Bible doesn't mean that we really love Jesus or *experience* God's love in our lives. It usually requires an encounter with Jesus, often in a form in which we don't at first recognize him. Will McFarland understood what was said, but his mind was somewhat preoccupied with the greeting that the minister's wife had given him when she passed his pew on her way to the front pew, where she customarily sat. "It's so nice to see you this morning," Mrs. McGill had said, and had stretched out her hand to shake his. Perhaps there really *was* something to this talk about the miracle of Easter.

Then came the moment that Will McFarland had been denying for many years. But as Reverend McGill began to ask people to come forward by pews to sit at the table for communion, he broke off his instructions in mid-sentence. "Sometimes," he said, "the holiness of this meal makes it seem almost unapproachable for those of us who live in the world, whose lives are buffeted by the world's realities of hardship and happenstance. But it is at just such times that we learn, perhaps for the first time, the blessing of Christ offering himself to us in this sacrament. It was in the midst of their painful grief, unfounded as it was, that the two disciples had the joyful privilege of dining with their risen Master, and it was in the sharing of bread and wine that they recognized Christ with them, alive at their table." Will McFarland's hand was trembling as he gave his communion token to the elder when he entered the chancel of the church of which he had been a member ever since his childhood, but from whose table he had been absent for so long. "Take, eat; this is my body which is broken for you." The minister was looking directly at him as Will McFarland took the little piece of bread and placed it in his mouth. He returned the gaze, and then looked around at the faces of his neighbors and customers, people he had known all his life. "This cup is the new testament in my blood." As Will McFarland drank from the cup, tears came to his eyes, and not just a few, but a stream, and then sobs. Emily McFarland put her arms around her husband as the congregation looked on in hushed amazement, or maybe it was embarrassment at the scene of a grown man crying; for some, at least, it was embarrassment at the thought of Will McFarland's long absence from communion.

"I've seen Jesus today," Will finally managed to say, looking at his wife through his tears, and smiling.

"So have I," whispered Reverend McGill to himself.

Fifth Sunday of Easter

Acts 11:1–18
Revelation 21:1–6
John 13:31–35

"Revelation"

Deborah had always known that there was something different about her son. She was no expert on child behavior, but from an early age, Michael's interaction with girls and boys had not been what she would have expected of a boy of his age. Her husband, Jake, had also noticed, and had increasingly blamed her for turning him into a "mama's boy," though she had always encouraged Michael to do things with his father, and to play with other children in the neighborhood and school. And eventually, when the differences took on a more recognizable nature, Jake's criticism of her became more emotionally abusive and he increasingly ignored his son, seldom speaking to him after he once called him a "sissy," leaving the room when the boy would enter it.

Deborah had sometimes considered seeking help—going to a psychologist or a counselor—but always ended up feeling too embarrassed to do so, and, in truth, afraid of what she might learn. Instead, as Michael grew older, she would ask whether he wouldn't like to invite a girl over to the house, or go to a movie, perhaps. Sometimes, in the beginning, Michael would just turn away. As he progressed through his teens, such conversations sometimes ended up in shouting matches, Deborah arguing that his lack of interest in girls wasn't normal, Michael responding that he should be allowed to live his own life. Then, one day, their confrontation had led to tears, a slammed door, and the sound of the boy's uncontrollable groaning and sobbing from behind it. Once, Deborah had considered talking with the minister about Michael, but then he had preached a sermon on the abominable sinfulness of people like Michael, and how they were destroying the country's moral fiber, and she had abandoned the plan. It was shortly after that that Jake had left her and Michael, saying that her coddling of the boy had deprived him of the son he had wanted and expected and deserved.

As Deborah turned from closing the front door behind the two men who had been in her living room for the past twenty minutes, with despair and shame and anger competing for supremacy within her, she saw Michael standing at the head of the stairs above the entryway. His face showed profound sorrow. She wiped her eyes and sniffed, and then said in his direction, "Two of the elders."

Michael responded, "I know." Then he added, "I heard."

Anger was now in the ascendancy within Deborah's heart, and her face was turning red. She looked toward the living room and away from the child she had carried within her for nine months, whose diapers she had changed, whose fevers she had worried over, whose behavior she had agonized about, and for whom she had prayed daily since even before the doctor had confirmed that she was pregnant.

"I can't help it, Mama," Michael said in a voice twisted with pain over the pain that his *mother* was feeling. "I'm sorry."

Tears now flowed freely down Deborah's cheeks. She shook her head, though neither of them knew exactly whether it was in anger at the visitors or in dismay at the situation or in rejection of the apology or in denial that any apology was necessary.

Michael walked down to the landing. "I'll leave and go somewhere else to live if you want," he said limply. "I don't want to cause you any more trouble."

Deborah turned to look at her son, and her tears became a convulsion of grief—grief, mainly, at the thought of losing her boy.

"I love you, Mama," Michael said, tears now trickling down *his* cheeks, too. Deborah climbed the stairs and put her arms around her son as he put one arm around her waist—the first time in many months that they had touched—and they stood there on the landing for several minutes, both continuing to cry, neither knowing what more to say. The grandfather clock below them at the foot of the stairs chimed seven-thirty.

"Hadn't you better get to class?" the mother said to her son, more telling than asking. They both knew that he didn't feel like driving to the college campus for his night class in English literature.

"Yes, I guess so," he answered weakly.

"Are you coming home afterward?" Deborah asked. "Or . . . ?"

Michael pursed his lips. He considered for a few seconds, but then said, "I'll be home about ten."

The telephone rang a few minutes after Deborah heard Michael driving off down the street. "Mrs. Simms," the voice on the other end of the phone began. Deborah recognized it as belonging to Margaret Durkin, the woman who chaired the ladies' guild at the church and who once had been Michael's Sunday school teacher and had advised that she didn't think he was yet ready for baptism. "I know you signed up to bring a casserole to our lunch next week. But I really think it would be best if you chose not to come. I know that you had a visit from George Haines and Cleve Barker tonight, so I'm sure that you understand." Deborah replaced the receiver without responding. For the time being, there were no more tears left in her. She simply sat in her chair at the kitchen table, hardly thinking, little aware of the accustomed surroundings. In front of her was a short stack of mail, mostly junk solicitations, addressed to Jake, that had been accumulating until, as usual, she would bundle it into a large manila envelope at the end of the week and send it to his apartment address.

She was still there at the table when, two hours later, Michael said, "I'm back." Although she had not been conscious that he had come into the house, she was not startled. Her back was turned to him, and he could hear only a quiet reply to his greeting. After a few seconds of waiting to see whether she had anything else to say, he went upstairs to his room. Deborah continued to sit at the table long into the night.

Deborah had never warmed to her coworkers. In part, she feared what the office gossipers would do if they knew about her family and home life, so she had seldom spoken at work about Michael and, in the last couple of years, less and less about her husband. Today, she was grateful that much of her work was routine and rather mechanical; she was not in the mood to do anything that required much concentration. It was unusual for her to take a break from her work, although that morning she had brought a section of the newspaper with her from home to read over again a notice that she had seen under the listing of church events. She could not easily set aside her lifelong habit of attending worship and being moderately involved in other congregational activities. The latter practice had waned as tensions had increased at home and nearly stopped altogether when Jake left. But she had recently started to participate in the ladies' guild—a group to which, it now seemed, she was no longer welcome.

Rather than turning against God, she had decided to investigate other churches, sad as that was for someone as sentimental as herself, and so had looked over the newspaper that morning before leaving for work. Under the listed events for one church—a congregation belonging to a denomination that she had frequently heard denounced by people in her own church as "liberal"—she had noticed the mention of a support group for parents and grandparents of gays and lesbians. A few years earlier—even a few *weeks*—she might have considered the notion of a church hosting such a group as strange or even shameful. But her experience over the past several months, culminating in the visit from the elders and the telephone call from Margaret Durkin, had produced a change in her outlook—those things, and the fear that she might lose contact with her son, whom she had always loved even though she could not always understand. Indeed, one of the things she had thought about long into the night, sitting at the kitchen table, was Michael's words, "I love you," and how, for too many months now—or was it years?—she had been unable or unwilling to say the same thing to him.

She found again the church listing and noted the time and day of the meeting—Tuesday at eight p.m. It was now Friday morning. She resolved to go to the meeting. No one would know her. After all, she was quite certain that she didn't know anyone who had a homosexual child or grandchild. But could she really bring herself to attend that other church on Sunday? For years, she had lived in dread that someone would make a comment, that someone would ask a question, that someone would make a doctrinaire statement about homosexuals burning in hell and she would break down uncontrollably and then the secret would be out. And then, after all of her self-conscious caution, Jake had said something to somebody about having moved out and why, and it had gotten back to the church and to the elders and, obviously, to Margaret Durkin. And George Haines and Cleve Barker had been sent to make sure that she was aware that the Bible said homosexuality is a sin. They would be praying for her, they had said, that she would be a good parent and get Michael "straightened out," and that he would recognize and acknowledge and repent of the grave error of his choice. In the meantime, he would not be welcome at the church, and the tone of their visit indicated that everyone would be more comfortable if *she* were not around, either, until the family again followed the ways of scripture.

In the eyes of her own congregation, attending such a church as the one that offered the support group was almost as objectionable as homosexuality itself. But, she told herself as she folded up the newspaper section and put it back in her purse, she was a *Christian*, and Christians needed to worship *God*. If her *own* church would not allow her to fulfill a Christian duty, she reasoned, she would fulfill that duty *elsewhere*. And if there was a church that was willing to help her deal with the circumstances in which she found herself, then she would take the risk of worshiping *there*. She refused to punish *God* for her sorrows. She would even put money in the offering plate, if they had one.

Deborah Simms found a seat near the rear of the sanctuary on Sunday morning—a section of the room that seemed to be particularly popular. Much about the service was unfamiliar, with music and responses that she had never heard or spoken. There was also rather more scripture read than she was used to, and there seemed to be special attention given to the words and deeds of Jesus. The minister talked a lot about mercy and grace and not so much about judgment and damnation. She herself was focusing on being inconspicuous, and prayed that no one would try to engage her in conversation at the end of the service. Except for the persistent anxiety about the events that had caused her to attend the church in the first place, she was not uncomfortable in the worship service despite the differences from what she considered normal. But toward the end of the service, she noticed a man and woman seated on the other side of the sanctuary and somewhat closer to the chancel than herself. From her angle, they appeared familiar, and when, following the benediction, they turned to greet someone who had been sitting behind them, she recognized Miles and Stacy Harbison, who had disappeared rather suddenly from her own church about two years previously. She slipped out of the sanctuary and into the parking lot without speaking to anyone, although several people tried to offer a word of greeting.

On Tuesday evening, Deborah returned to the church and followed the signs to the room where the support group would be meeting. She was normally early for appointments and events, but, on this occasion, she chose to sit in her car in the parking lot until just a few minutes before eight o'clock. When she arrived at Room 114, there were already about a dozen people present, both men and women, ranging in age from their mid-thirties to their seventies. One woman gestured to Deborah to sit down in the empty chair alongside her. Just as she did, another couple entered the room. Deborah looked at them, and was shocked to recognize the faces of Miles and Stacy Harbison. Before she could feel embarrassed, and before she could formulate a plan to slip out of the room without their noticing, Stacy's eyes met hers. The other woman crossed the room and embraced her. "Deborah! How good to see you. I've missed you since we started coming here."

"Hello, Stacy," was all Deborah could bring herself to say.

"We've been here about two years now," Stacy explained, "and we've found it so warm and accepting. About a year and a half ago," she continued, "we became a part of this group, and now we're leading it, since the original leaders moved away."

By now, Miles Harbison had noticed his wife talking with a new participant, and then, recognizing Deborah, came across the room to greet her.

"A few years ago, we finally acknowledged the truth about our Rachel," Stacy explained.

"I remember Rachel," Deborah said. "She was so beautiful and charm . . ." Deborah stopped in disbelief. The question escaped from her lips unintended. "You mean that Rachel . . . ?"

"Pastor Blaine said we should disassociate ourselves from her," Stacy said.

"We were always being told to ask what Jesus would do in different situations," Miles took over. "Well, we didn't think that's what Jesus would *do*."

"And, as we've talked with other people in the same situation, we've become convinced of it," Stacy added. "We had some very difficult times. But today, our family is stronger than it has ever been. And Rachel is so happy and doing so well, now that she, now that we . . ." Stacy's sentence trailed off. Eventually, she added, "There's so much love back in our lives."

Miles spoke again. "We'd better get started," he said. He and his wife sat down together. "Hello, everybody. Let's begin the evening with prayer." Before the meeting was over, Deborah Simms had shed many tears. But, by the end of the meeting, the tears she was shedding were tears of joy and thanksgiving.

When Deborah got home that night, she climbed the stairs and knocked on the door of her son's room. She hadn't told him at dinner where she was going, only that she had a meeting to attend, and he hadn't questioned her about it. "Come in," she heard him say from within.

She opened the door to find Michael rising from his desk and closing a textbook. "Michael, would you come to church with me on Sunday?" she asked. It had been many months since he had attended a worship service. "At the place I went last week," she added.

"Well—" he started.

"Honey, it's different there."

"Yes, I guess so," he shrugged.

Deborah crossed to where Michael was standing and put her arms around him. "Michael, I love you so much," she said to her son. And there were no tears in her eyes.

Ascension of the Lord

Acts 1:1–11
Ephesians 1:15–23
Luke 24:44–53

"Witness to the Power"

Even after all these years, I can remember it vividly. And, of course, it was the sort of thing that stays etched in your memory—something so very extraordinary. What is that? Well, yes, it was *all* extraordinary, though we didn't realize it at the time it was happening. All the days in the hill-towns of Galilee, and out on the lake, even in Jerusalem, one wonderful word after another, miracles of sick people being made well, of blind people being made to see, of lame people being made to walk, of people possessed by demons even being restored to their senses, of people deep in sin being assured that God loved them nevertheless, and the *difference* that piece of news made in their *lives*. And all people were called to repent. They were bewildered, so many of them, bewildered but joyful at the change that came over them—like they had been born anew from heaven. No doubt it *was* a new birth from above—the Spirit of God coming upon them.

What did you say? Yes, of course, we *should* have known, we *should* have been aware that such things can only come from God. Somehow, we just got *used* to things like that happening when we were with *Jesus*. Every day was so wonderful that we lost track of just how special it all was; perhaps we came to *expect* miracles when we were with Jesus. I'm ashamed to say that we all rather came to take it for granted. No matter how perceptive his teaching, no matter how extraordinary his deeds, we all just sort of remained oblivious to the implications. We still thought only about today and tomorrow—where we would sleep, how we would eat, what the difficulty of the day's travel would be, *when* Jesus was going to start the *revolution* and restore the kingdom of Israel. That came more and more to occupy the minds of some of us. We would have carried him to the throne of David, we loved him so much. And his way with people—well, with most people—if anyone could have led a revolt against the Romans and purged the temple of the hypocrites, it would have been Jesus. But we didn't understand. That wasn't what he was all about, although his teaching certainly *is a judgment* upon society and politics and living conditions. But what he tried to teach us was so much *more* than that. He kept *trying* to tell us, but we just didn't understand. How blind we were! How self-centered and petty and blind!

What? Oh, yes, yes, after the empty tomb. Well, the empty tomb itself was so extraordinary, wasn't it? And such a shock! Who had taken him away? we wondered. Where had they laid him? What was it all about? You must remember our fear in those days—how we imagined that the authorities might be coming after *us* next. What Jesus had done that was considered so very bad, we didn't know—he had helped people, he had been kind, he had showed the love and mercy of God to everyone, even those who would destroy him. He even forgave them, yes, right from the cross, he asked God to forgive them. But you have heard about that, I am sure. That was extraordinary, too—I mean, forgiveness is hard enough for any of us, but to forgive your accusers and your torturers and your executioners, and to forgive us who turned away. But then, when, later the same day that the women discovered the empty tomb he appeared to two of our number as they were walking along the road to Emmaus, and went into their house and ate with them—well, they didn't realize at first that it *was* Jesus, but then, as he talked with them about the scriptures, and was at table with them and took bread and blessed it and broke it and gave it to them, then they knew that it was Jesus. It was so characteristic of him. But then, just like that, he vanished. And they came and told the rest of us about it, and just then, Jesus himself appeared to us *all—in the flesh*! "Look at my hands and my feet," he said; "see that it is I myself. Touch me and see; for a ghost does not have flesh and bones as you see that I have" (Luke 24:39 NRSV). And right there, he asked us for some food, and we gave him a piece of broiled fish and he ate it with us. It had to be Jesus himself—ghosts don't eat, do they? And he told us all about the meaning of the scriptures—how they all speak about him, and what happened to him, and what it all means. So, you see, it was *all* extraordinary. Astounding. What more could happen that would demonstrate that he was none other than God's own Son, raised by God from the grave to show the truth of all that he said, to guarantee God's blessing on all that he had done, to indicate God's pleasure in him and approval of him in every way?

Now here is the thing that you asked me about—after a time, when Jesus was with us in bodily form, raised from the dead, teaching us, promising the baptism of the Holy Spirit upon us, we were gathered with him out by Bethany, up on the Mount of Olives, and suddenly, after he had told us that we would be his witnesses to every corner of the earth, he was lifted up from our sight.... Yes, yes, lifted up in the air as he was blessing us, and then vanished in the clouds.... No, I have no way of explaining it. I can't begin to. We all stood with mouths wide open, amazed—not fearful, for it was Jesus, after all, and we never had to fear when he was near. But I have come to realize that the important thing is not *how*, extraordinary as it all was. There was something more extraordinary still. Let me tell you, something came over us—not yet the tongues like fire—that was later—but a definite power. Peter was so emboldened—he really began to speak out, to exercise leadership, to grasp the import of it all. But not just Peter. We *all* came to understand that Jesus' power was still *with us*—his influence upon us, but more than influence, the very power of God that had been at work in all of his teaching and healing and forgiving, the very same great power that raised him from the tomb, now seemed to be enlivening his *followers*. *He* went away, but his power to continue doing the things he had done stayed *among us*. That's the *really* extraordinary thing.

I can't begin even now to speculate about how he rose into heaven. But, you see, that's not the really fantastic thing. It was necessary, that we know now. He *had* to depart from us, or we would never have come to experience the power of the Holy Spirit for *ourselves*. He *had* to depart from us, or the teaching and the healing and the forgiving would have been possible only where *he* was. And the power *had* to come, or we would still be standing there now, I suppose, looking wistfully up to the sky, instead of obeying Jesus by doing the things he told us to do. He gave his church work to do, and the power to do it. Now, you see, the gospel has been carried to every corner of the world—even as far as our own land. It is not just for the Jews, it is not just for the people of Israel. It is so much more than restoring the throne of David and driving out the Romans. God, we know now, is not just for the Jews, but for *all* people. Salvation is for the gentiles, too; no one has a monopoly on salvation, just as no one has a monopoly on sin. Jesus is where God is, and he knows no limit of time or space.... No, we can't prove it, and that means that some refuse to accept the truth of it. What we *can* do is to give witness by pointing to what has happened *since* then, among *ourselves*, and among the people who believe what we testify. His influence is stronger now even than when he was walking among us. We can sense his presence with us more surely even than when we saw him with our own eyes. Just look at it—the church, made up of people of every nationality and race, women sitting at table with men and Jew sitting at table with gentile and slave sitting at table with master; old arguments settled and enmities overcome as pride and jealousy and fear are cast aside in a spirit of love and forbearance. These things are not of *human* doing. These things are of God, and they are the very sorts of things that Jesus taught about and showed us. Jesus is Lord!—that is the only explanation—sitting right alongside God in heaven. From Jerusalem to Judea to Samaria to the ends of the earth! It has happened just as he said.

You say your church isn't quite like that? That you yourself sometimes have trouble loving and forgiving and sharing and hoping? Then think more of Jesus—keep your focus on him and the power of God to overcome all that is negative and unworthy of Christ. Think of our own experiences—setbacks and persecutions and discouragements of every kind, but always above and beyond the frustrations of the moment, *Jesus* reigning in power at the right hand of God. I remember Paul—what a time we had, not just with the authorities, but with other believers! Corinth—now there was a case! But the power of God in Christ is greater than any obstacle to sharing and living out our faith.

What is that? Yes, that was a wonderful time. What? No, no, you mustn't think that. Belief is not tied to having walked around Palestine with him. Listen, many have experienced the Lord with them, and the power of the Holy Spirit, who never even knew of him during those three years. That is what this is all about, this ascending into heaven. Look at Paul, who never knew Christ until many months later, and yet, could anyone doubt that he encountered the risen Christ? See how infused he was with Christ, so long after Christ was crucified and raised from the dead! That was not just a *memory* that seized Paul—not just a *story*. It was the power of the living Christ. And Christ is powerful and present right now! Never wish to live in the past, never desire to find refuge in the old days. God put you here in these times for God's own purpose—to transform the present, by the power of the Spirit, so that it bears the marks of the kingdom.

What did you say? That these are difficult times for the church? That people do not seem to have the same zeal that they once had? Yes, I grant you that the flame seems to have blown out in many places—there are some places that were once ablaze and now are merely embers. But the power is spreading still, is bringing about miracles still, where people have not given up trust in that power. We forget after a time, it seems—we begin to imagine that the church depends on *us*, that it is *ours*. We grow lazy in our prayers. We grow contented in our ease. We grow comfortable in our supposing that *we* are in charge. We forget the power of Christ, and lose the commitment it takes to teach, lose the boldness it takes to proclaim, lose the humility it takes to forgive. We succumb to the temptation to measure progress by worldly standards. But that is not the failure of *Christ's power*, only *our* failure to *use* it. He said that we must be witnesses—we must tell about him and show his power to bring about the wholeness that God intends, not only healing, but generosity and mercy and kindness and trust. And we *have* been—it is so extraordinary, all that has happened, such a miracle, that the Church should have spread throughout the world, proclaiming the gospel, showing his love, that it should even exist at *all* among a race that speaks much about religion but is still hostile to the gospel.

No, do not be discouraged. Never give up. Christ is *still* at God's right hand. Yes, I know your efforts sometimes seem futile. Read the letters, read the story of the apostles, read the memoirs of the evangelists. You will see that nothing was ever gained without effort. Nothing ever occurred without risk. But neither did any miracle ever happen without faith. See how the world had judged Christ as a failure! See how we ourselves thought that Calvary was an *end* of it all. See how death was in truth only the beginning of real *life*. That's how it was in those first days of the gospel—that's how it was for all of us called "apostles." And so it is for *you*—to die to your fears of failure, to die to your anxiety about the future, to die to your need for security in the way of things you can see and touch, to die to your presuppositions about the way things must be, to die to your dependence upon yourself, and to live in trust in Christ. Isn't that faith? And it is no different now than it was then, only perhaps even *more* wonderful. There is a whole new generation that has never heard the gospel, I mean, never *really* heard it, among all the commercialism around holidays, amid all the noise about making money, in spite of all the politicizing of the Bible. There is a whole new generation that needs to know that God has given Christ rule over all creation, that his being raised to heaven didn't *remove* him from earth's joys and woes or mean that he is *unconcerned* about our successes and disappointments, but that it was for the purpose of empowering his followers to be his hands and feet today in every land, witnessing to him in words and deeds.

What is that? Yes, yes, I am so glad to have had the opportunity to tell the story again. Sometimes, when we think about how far we have yet to go, we forget how far we have already come. Let God do the measuring; sometimes, the best thing we can do is wait upon him. But never let that be an excuse for spiritual sloth, or for failing to discern the work that Jesus has put before us and given us power to accomplish. Yes, it was all so extraordinary, so wonderfully extraordinary. And it is extraordinary still.

Pentecost

The Day of Pentecost

Acts 2:1–21
Romans 8:14–17
John 14:8–17, 25–27

"When the Spirit Moves You"

The needle danced back and forth across the face of the VU meter, occasionally venturing into the red zone. Terry Peters instinctively pulled the slide back three-eighths of an inch on the large mixer in the control room—"the board"—that he captained every afternoon from three to seven. It occurred to Terry that he had forgotten what song he was playing. He turned up the volume on his headphones, but did not recognize the tune. Actually, he very seldom listened to the music that he played anymore. It was the *music* that had *prompted* Terry to get *into* the radio business, but fifteen years and half a dozen stations later, he had come to realize that the *music* was *irrelevant*. At bottom, it was all about *sales*, and *sales* depended upon *ratings*, and *ratings* depended upon *programming*, but *programming* no longer had anything to do with what was, in *his* opinion, good music. So much of it was just loud and foul. Terry hardly ever bought CDs for himself anymore, even, he had become so numb to his youthful passion, and he seldom listened to the radio in his car as he traveled around town, except occasionally tuning in to listen to the jokes of his coworker, evening disc jockey Leonard Emmett Hamilton III, known to his listeners as Johnny B. Bopp.

Leonard was the only real friend that Terry could claim from fifteen years in a business known for transiency and competition, and even *that* friendship was not what you would call "strong." There *was* that guy in . . . what town was it? Des Moines? Wait a minute—had he ever even *worked* in Des Moines? Yeah, Des Moines was in there somewhere. What town was *this*? Terry had to think. The control room looked remarkably like all the others. He looked at the call letters above the microphone. They meant nothing to him—not like the days of his youth, when radio stations were legendary and helped to *define* a place. KFRC *was* San Francisco. KIMN *owned* Denver. KOMA *meant* Oklahoma City. WLS *dominated* Chicago. CKLW was *synonymous* with Detroit, even though it was actually in Windsor. He knew that he couldn't be in *Des Moines* anymore. Fort Wayne. It must be Fort Wayne. The truth was, through six radio stations in six towns, Terry Peters could not say that he had ever moved *up*. He had just moved *around*.

Terry noticed that the needle was resting against the left peg. How long had the song been over? He didn't know. And he still had no idea what it was. He had no comment to make about it, or about anything else, for that matter. He was surprised to realize that he didn't care. An urgent tapping on the plate glass window beyond the board broke into his consciousness. The receptionist was standing there, looking disgusted and pointing to her ear. She had noticed that the speaker in the lobby had gone silent. Terry nodded and looked quickly at his log to see what commercial or promo he was supposed to be playing. A mouthwash commercial, to be followed by an Italian restaurant. "Wrong order," he thought to himself as he pushed the button to play the mouthwash spot. Within a short thirty seconds, offensive herbs, dangerous bacteria, and dreaded gingivitis had all been addressed, and he hit the next button. "Tight," he said to himself, glancing out the window into the lobby, where the receptionist had gone back to whatever it was that she did all day. Wasn't her name Lopez? Yeah—Julie Lopez. Or was that the one in Evansville?

Terry vaguely remembered having loaded all of the players with CDs and tape cartridges, and he mechanically hit a "play" button when his restaurant spot was over. He should have *said* something. He should have said something *witty*. But what *could* he say about a song he didn't *know* and didn't *care* about? Actually, it had gotten worse lately—his apathy about popular music. He had been righteously upset when he lost his first radio job because the station had gone country—it was not merely the fact that all of the jocks had been dumped. It was an offense against rock and roll. That was Sioux Falls. Then came Peoria. *That* was Julie Lopez. How was Julie doing? he wondered. They had gone out a couple of times. She took him to a church picnic, up at Starved Rock. He remembered that. Nice people, genuine, down-to-earth. Seemed really to care about each other. That had been his first experience with a church since he had left home. His church attendance had been sporadic since Julie and Peoria, but he had started reading the Bible lately, and was currently in Acts, with its record of the persecutions of the apostles. That got him to thinking about his own church youth group, and Ed and Frances Williams, the associate pastor couple who led the youth group. Some people within the congregation had asked Ed and Frances to leave the church after they picketed the defense contractor that was his hometown's biggest employer because it had been polluting the creek that ran beside its plant, killing the fish and endangering the public supply of drinking water. Ed and Frances had thought that it was unconscionable for the company to continue to pollute while fighting a court-ordered injunction.

This time, Terry actually *saw* the needle fall off to the side. He immediately hit the station's jingle, only it *wasn't* the station's jingle. It was the news intro, twenty-two minutes early. He fumbled a "Sorry about that" into the microphone and followed it with, "Your Fort Wayne forecast next," and hit the button for the next commercial. This was for a fast-food chain and its latest toy craze with the children's meals. "Junk," he muttered. Not three seconds later, the receptionist was pounding on the window again, running her flattened hand back and forth in front of her neck. "Huh?" he said, failing to comprehend her message. Suddenly, it occurred to him that he had not cut off the microphone before his editorial comment about the toy promotion at the fast-food chain. "Fort Wayne weather: Breezy, cloudy, with a high of 48 today, possibility of rain, down to 30 tonight with periods of light snow, 52 tomorrow and clearing, with warmer for the weekend. Right now, it's 46 degrees in Fort Wayne." He hit the button for the station jingle, and then the next song.

"What are you *doin'*, man?" asked Leonard Emmett Hamilton III as he poked his head in the door of the control room. "I was listening on my way in. You'd better wake up!" He ducked back out the door. Never before had Terry Peters lost concentration like this on the air. The receptionist was glaring at him from behind the counter in the lobby.

Terry took a sip of a soft drink to perk himself up. The station manager did not like the disc jockeys to have soda pop in the control room, fearing that it might get knocked over and short out the board or, even worse, might cause them to belch on the air. But the station manager was at a meeting in Indianapolis or somewhere, and the station engineer had brought Terry a soft drink to celebrate. Terry took a gulp, and then, knowing that Leonard, alias Johnny B. Bopp, was right, he decided to listen to the song he was playing to see whether he recognized it. He did. It was a highly successful singer who had made a reputation for her wholesale embrace of the consumerist culture, singing about sexual exploits. Terry sighed. He looked at his log and saw that a public service spot was next on the list. He popped it in as the song was coming to an end. "Donna Morris, from her album 'Gimme It,'" he said without enthusiasm, and then hit the button for the public service spot.

"Holy Week," it began, "is a special time of worship and reflection, of remembering God who sent Jesus for our salvation, of gathering together with people of faith to give thanks for the resurrection, and of looking forward to the promised coming of the Holy Spirit. Let the Spirit move you to worship in the church of your choice this week at the table, at the cross, at the empty tomb, and to become Christ's own forever. This message is from the Fort Wayne Area Council of Churches."

Terry leaned back on his stool, feeling a wave of shame and embarrassment for playing the Donna Morris song during Holy Week. He had always been a bit uneasy about playing her songs, but something came over him now that he could not repress. "I'm sorry, folks. I'm sorry for playing that song, especially in the week before Easter." Terry Peters looked up and saw the receptionist, sitting behind the counter, her mouth open with disbelief. But he continued, feeling helpless against the urge to say what he believed. "That isn't the sort of stuff to be listening to. Really. Don't buy that trash." He checked the receptionist again. She was still sitting behind the counter aghast. "And speaking of not buying trash, this tactic of coaxing kids into getting their parents to spend, spend, spend is wrong. Take this fast-food promotion, for instance . . ." The receptionist was now running past the window and down the hall.

Terry was rolling. He went on to declaim against consumerism in general, and the exploitation of children and youth by Madison Avenue and the media in particular, and about corporations that had been charged with violating child labor standards in their offshore factories and had been shown to have encouraged children to smoke and drink. He attributed it all to selfishness and greed and insensitivity to the welfare of others. Terry had already graduated to environmental pollution and was starting in on the error of replacing faith in God with faith in worldly wealth when Leonard Emmett Hamilton III burst through the door and lunged at the board, cutting off the microphone and pushing Terry off of his stool at the same instant. "Johnny B. Bopp with you a little early today. Now back to music. News is coming up on the mighty 97.3."

The sound of the front door banging open was loud enough to rattle the plate glass window of the control room. Within the space of a heartbeat, the station manager was in the studio. "What *is* this? Are you *drunk*? Or just *crazy*? Get out of here. You're *fired*. Get out of here this minute. And if I ever hear that you're trying to get another job in radio, I'm going to be on the horn to those saps about you so fast that your head will spin." The station manager had returned early from Indianapolis or wherever he had been and had grabbed Terry by the arm and was shoving him out of the control room. Spying the illicit pop can, he picked it up and hurled it at Terry as the door to the control room was closing behind him, with the effect that the contents splattered on the wall all the way up to the ceiling.

The telephone in Terry's apartment rang a little before eight o'clock—news time, Terry thought as he set down his Bible—he was just finishing Acts—and reached to pick up the receiver.

"Terry?" said the voice on the other end of the phone. "This is Johnny B."

"Oh, hi, Leonard. How's it going tonight?"

"Never mind that," Leonard replied. "Are *you* OK?"

"I think so."

"I thought maybe the manager would settle down, but I guess he was ranting and raving the rest of the afternoon. I think your job's gone for good. What in the world got into you?"

"I don't know," Terry answered quietly. "But I *wasn't* drunk. And I'm *not* crazy. Something just came over me."

"Well, we'd better get you exorcised of that devil, or you're going to be hungry. I've got a friend at a station up in Grand Rapids I could talk to about giving you a shot . . ."

"Thanks, Leonard, but I'm not sure. Let me think about things for a few days, OK?"

"Sure," Leonard said.

"Better get back to the show, hadn't you?"

"Yeah. Look, I'll call you in a day or two. Oh, I've got a call on another line. I'll talk to you later."

"Thanks," Terry said, and hung up the phone.

The telephone rang again a few minutes later. "Hello," Terry answered.

"Is this the residence of Terry Peters?"

"Yes, it is."

"The disc jockey?"

"Yes."

"Terry, I don't know if you'll remember me, but we used to work at the same station in Peoria. I'm Julie Lopez. Actually, Julie Phelps, now. I was married . . .'"

"It's nice to hear from you, Julie," Terry said, genuinely meaning it but totally surprised. "But, how . . . why?"

"I heard you this afternoon. I've been listening *every* afternoon. My little girl and I live here now. After my husband died, I moved to Fort Wayne. My sister and her husband live here."

"I didn't know you had married. I'm sorry to hear about your husband. When . . . ?"

"We were married about eight years ago, and he died in an accident last year. He was a truck driver, and he had volunteered to drive a load of food and medicine from a local mission organization up to North Dakota after the flood. A car pulled right in front of him on the interstate and he swerved to avoid hitting it and . . ." Julie's voice trailed off into silence.

"That's a terrible thing," Terry volunteered. "At least he died trying to do something worthwhile. That will mean something to your daughter someday."

"The food and medicine got transferred to another truck and still got up there," Julie said. "Maybe it did some people some good."

"I'm sure it did," said Terry. Then, he added, "How did you get my number?"

"The office was closed. I just called the studio line. When I explained who I was, the disc jockey said that it was against company policy to give out home numbers, but he thought you might like to talk to me."

"I'm awfully glad he did," said Terry. "That would be Leonard . . . I mean, Johnny B. Bopp."

"I'd been meaning to get in touch with you anyway, to let you know that I was here and that I'd been listening, but when you said what you said today, I just had to call and thank you for taking a stand. And you were right, you know. Why do we spend money on this stuff? And what is it doing to our souls? It's all so far from what God had in mind."

"My 'stand' got me fired."

"I figured it would. But there are other stations. And if there aren't other stations, there are other lines of work."

"Funny thing is," said Terry, "I don't know what came over me. I've never done anything like that before. I was just sitting there thinking, and, like, *whoosh*, all of a sudden, these words were coming out of my mouth. I didn't even think about it—they just came. Kind of like . . ." Terry glanced at the open Bible on the coffee table.

"The church I'm going to here has a support group for people who are out of work—to keep up their self-esteem, help them think about their careers, prepare resumés, and so forth. Would that be a help to you?"

"Maybe. Yes, I think it might."

"Where do you live?" Julie asked. "I'd like to come over and see you. I thought you could use the company. Maybe go out for a soft drink, talk about things . . ."

"A soft drink," Terry echoed with a chuckle, thinking of the scene in the control room.

"Would that be OK?" Julie asked, more tentatively.

"That would be fine," Terry said. "I might even go to church with you Sunday. It's Easter, isn't it?"

"Yes," Julie answered.

"Grab a pencil and paper, and I'll give you directions to where I live."

Ordinary Time after Pentecost

Trinity Sunday

Isaiah 6:1–8
Romans 8:12–17
John 3:1–17

"Nicodemus' Diary"

Attended a meeting of the elders today. Much was simply trivial routine, as the Roman procurator does not permit us to deal with anything that he deems to be political or would infringe on his administration of Roman law and justice. We did have appear before us a rabbi from Jericho, whose teachings on some points of the Torah seemed to require correction. On the whole, he submitted unquestioningly to our authority in matters of interpretation of the law, though some of the elders warned him that they would be alert to any deviations from the tradition. And there was also some talk about a Nazarene—a rabbi, some of us suppose, although that is rather unclear, especially since the rumors are that he has violated the sabbath on multiple occasions, which scarcely seems possible for a rabbi. So the council of elders spends its time these days—hardly the way things were in Moses' day when the seventy were appointed to help him govern the people. Not that anyone wants to return to the wilderness, but God's presence with the people seemed more direct in those days.

Attended another meeting of the council of elders. No new information about the situation in Jericho—the rabbi whom we dealt with last time—but more about this Nazarene fellow. Talk of a miracle he performed at a wedding in Cana. Rather sketchy and unreliable, in my opinion. Who can trust reports from a drunken wedding party? A few of my colleagues very agitated at the news of water being turned into wine. At most weddings I've attended, it goes the other way—the longer the party goes on, the more like *water* the *wine* becomes. The wise host knows that some people will *eventually* drink *anything*.

Emergency meeting of the council today, called to address the matter of this rabbi or teacher or whatever from Nazareth. The news is, he came to Jerusalem yesterday and immediately caused a scene at the temple, turning out the money changers and letting the sheep and cattle out of their pens—the ones that are on hand to be purchased for making sacrifices. The money changers and vendors are rapscallions, of course—and resented by the common people, deservedly so, profiting as they do on the good intentions of the pious. But it was apparently a most unseemly performance by the man, who came to town with a number of his followers and now has won to himself several others. Of course, preparations for Passover are consuming the time of most of us, and the coming to Jerusalem of the Passover crowds is what makes that man's behavior such a sensitive issue just now. I have no idea why the temple guards didn't step in. It seems that the man just walked out of the temple after having his say and having his way with the profiteers. One of the elders wanted to charge him with desecrating the temple, although, of course, cleansing the temple of the money changers was hardly a desecration—in fact, in my book, just the opposite! Good riddance!—though, of course, it would make it inconvenient to pay the temple tax. Furthermore, he seems to have upset some people who confronted him about his authority for doing such things—he answered them by saying something about destroying the temple and raising it back up in three days. I rather distrust the accuracy of that report. Who could say something so absurd? I pointed this out in the council. Others said that it wasn't right for anyone to be so disorderly and disruptive in the temple. No matter what we might think of the money changers and sellers of the sacrificial animals, they were there legally and performing a necessary function and ought to be able to do so without some crazy Galilean coming in and causing them trouble. Seems to me that there might be more behind this man's behavior than insanity, though. Some of our number volunteered to try to be present at some of the man's gatherings to collect evidence about just what it is he is saying and doing, whether he is twisting the scriptures that he quotes. I personally have more important things to be doing as the Passover approaches.

Another emergency meeting of the council of elders today. There are reports that the Nazarene is performing feats of magic around town as well as teaching about the scriptures in a new way. People are saying that he preaches with confidence and certainly speaks words that ring true. Not sure that what he is doing should be called "magic"—doesn't sound like he's just doing things to *impress* people, but to *help* them, including several reports of healing and exorcism and the like, especially among the lower classes. Poor souls, can't afford doctors, quite likely. They're probably delighted to have someone pay them some attention and take their complaints seriously enough to try to do something about them. Still, he's dabbling where someone who's not a *physician*—or a *priest*—shouldn't. I'm starting to sense trouble ahead.

One of my colleagues today persuaded me to go with him to hear the Nazarene. His name is Jesus, and he seems to have come to the city from Capernaum. Of course, there are a lot of Galileans and all sorts of other people coming to town for the Passover. I must say, I was very impressed with him, though it was a little disconcerting that he did not invoke the authority of the *rabbis* for what he had to say. No, he just taught as if on his *own* authority. What he said certainly moved many of the people who were listening—plain language, speaking straight to the heart, as it were, telling people to repent of their sins but also that God is merciful. Then, when a man in the crowd shouted out asking for healing for his deformed foot, Jesus went to him and told him to take a few steps. The man objected that it was too difficult, but Jesus told him to do it anyway, and the man did so, and said that he had been healed. I couldn't get very close, but the people around the man were turning to the crowd and shouting that the man's foot had been straightened! And then Jesus put his hand on some people's heads and blessed them, and then he left, followed by some of the crowd as others dispersed to go on their way. I admit, there is a personal magnetism about him. But if he's going about performing healings without the approval of some higher authority, well, that's irregular. Still, the man can walk upright now, without limping.

I went out to hear Jesus again today, this time on my own. The same sort of thing happened as yesterday—teaching the same sorts of things that the prophets wrote, but somehow fresh and pertinent for our own day, and some more healings of people with various ailments. But there was something more—he forgave a woman who confessed to being a sinner. Now, that seemed to be going too far. Only *God* can do that. The woman whom he forgave—who knows what sort of things she had done? I suppose I may have to report that. And yet, she was so grateful (as well she might be!). It was as if a tremendous stone had been lifted from her shoulders. In my own seeing, she almost appeared to be a new person altogether, the creases in her forehead gone, color in her cheeks, whereas she had been pale and haggard-looking. I know that forgiving another person of their sin is wrong. It's a lie—no one has that power, only God. And yet, to bestow such peace upon another person with just a word! Can he be permitted to make people think that they won't be judged for their sins, that they don't have to make sacrifice for atonement, that violating the law doesn't doom them on the day of judgment? Isn't he putting their souls in jeopardy by giving them false hope? Or is he restoring people to God? I am feeling confused.

Another emergency meeting of the council today. Many spoke about what they had seen and heard of Jesus, the Nazarene. Some were very angry—jealous, almost, it sounded, that some upstart from the countryside was attracting attention. I remained silent. What I could tell them would have added nothing. Except about forgiving the woman, of course. But I'm not ready to tell about that in the council. I think it would be best if I went to speak to Jesus privately, to ask him to explain, to find out what is in his mind and on his heart. He seems approachable. Maybe tonight. After people have gone to their homes, and the streets are quiet. In the dark.

Maybe I should not have gone. My mind is so confused. I began by telling him that I was impressed with what he has been saying and doing. I even told him that I was sure that God was with him—I didn't mean to say that, it just came out. But I guess that's what I've been thinking, in the back of my mind. And then he talked about being born anew. I told him that was ridiculous—no one can emerge twice from the womb! And he talked about being born of water and Spirit. And I guess he didn't mean being born again, but being born in a new way, as it were—to live life on a different level, richer, deeper, less absorbed with one's own ambitions. I think I must have seemed to him a fool, the way I kept bumbling my speech and him asking if I understood or not. How could I be a leader of the people and not know what he was talking about? he asked. But, honestly, I didn't really understand what he was saying, though I sensed that it was vitally important. And even now, I'm not sure I understand what he was saying, but it seems to me even more urgent than it did at the time. I think he was telling me that I need to think about things differently, maybe consider whether God is coming to be present with people in a new way. And people work their own judgment by not coming to the light and allowing themselves to be seen in the light. Belief in the Son of Man who will be lifted up. Having eternal life. Maybe I shouldn't have gone to him at night by myself. Maybe I shouldn't have gone to find him at all. I'm so confused. And yet, I feel as if I'm beginning on some new journey, pushed along it, almost, by a power I've never felt before. I dare not talk of this to the council.

Jesus has left the city. The rumor is that he and his followers from Galilee have gone back out into the country. There was another meeting of the council today, and a general sense of relief that he has gone. And yet, *I* don't feel that way. *I* feel strangely *empty*. It was maybe just as well for Jesus, the way some were becoming angry and even starting to voice threats. But I wanted to hear more of his teaching. It's almost as if a light were in the room, and now it's gone.

Jesus is back in town. He has been teaching in the temple. Some people are asking if he might not be the Messiah. That has upset many on the council. The chief priests and some of the Pharisees have ordered him to be arrested if he shows up at the temple again. I fear there's going to be trouble. But why? Because he's speaking the *truth* and people are *repenting*? What are we *coming* to in this country?

The fat is in the fire. Many people are speaking of Jesus as a prophet. Some are going so far as to say with certainty that he is the *Messiah*. Others are ready to believe it, except that it *can't* be so if he comes from *Galilee* and not *Bethlehem*, where *David* was born. The *council* is not going to like that any more than the *Romans* will. But something strange and surprising has happened—something that may anger the chief priests and Pharisees even more. Jesus came back to the temple to teach, and the temple police refused to arrest him. Even they have been won over by his teaching! There was another emergency meeting of the council. This time, I spoke up—I had to! There are people among us who want to have him put to death. And for *what*? For *speaking*? For making *sick* people *well*? I said, "Our law does not judge people without first giving them a hearing to find out what they are doing, does it?" Some accused me of not knowing the scriptures—that the scriptures say nothing about a prophet coming from Galilee! Many others just ignore me. The council meeting was ugly, rancorous. How can people be afraid of the truth?

Almost daily now there are reports of Jesus healing people and teaching and his followers saying he was sent from God, and the chief priests and Pharisees are getting furious. They try to trap him in his own words, but he ends up silencing them and putting them to shame—they end up being caught in their own trap. I hear he has left the city again and gone down to the Jordan. I fear for his safety if he returns to Jerusalem! What is my duty in all this? I am torn.

Word today from Bethany, spreading like flames. Jesus has brought a dead man back to life! That's the report. Impossible, of course! Or is it? The point is, many believe it. I don't know. I'm confused. Never have I known someone so—so free from public opinion or unrestrained by custom. It's almost like what he said that night I talked with him—he's like the wind, just sort of stirring things up by his presence, leaving things changed, though you can't see it, exactly, can't hold it in your hand, can't define it. He's turning things upside down. He's turning *me* upside down—or inside out.

Emergency meeting tonight. Heated debate. Fears about the Romans reacting. Caiaphas said Jesus must die, or the rest of the nation will. I was too scared to speak. Too scared. God help me!

The night before Passover, and rousted out of bed, summoned to the council. Jesus was there, apparently turned in by one of his own followers. The traitor! Caiaphas questioned him; there was a lot of confusion—it was all very rushed. Many accusations. Jesus didn't respond directly. I could not bear to look at him, turned away from him. But it felt like his eyes were fixed on me, boring into my brain. I was scared. I was confused. I don't know what to think anymore. Isn't he saying and doing exactly what the prophets said to say and do? And yet, it's upsetting so many people, seems to violate the fine points of the law. Then they sent him to Pilate, God help him. God help *me*; I'm so confused! I think I know where my duty lies, but don't I have a higher duty *still*? God is with this man. God is *in* this man. There, I've written it. Blasphemy! But how can the truth be blasphemous? O God, forgive me. O God, forgive us all.

Jesus is dead. They crucified him, treated him disgracefully. I feel such a coward. Joseph came and told me—Joseph of Arimathea. Together, we went and asked for the body, to bury it properly. I brought the spices, much more than necessary. I guess I was trying to salve my conscience as I was anointing the body. But he's dead. Nobody can change that. They may expel me from the council for this—probably will. Well, so be it. Never in my whole life have I done anything so . . . daring. Others will say "irresponsible"—befriending a criminal. What's gotten into me? What has made me so reckless? Could it be that I've become a bit like him? "If I have told you about earthly things and you do not believe . . . " (John 3:12 NRSV), he said to me when I objected that it was impossible to be born a second time. In a way, I feel that I *have* been born a second time—I mean, I seem to be seeing things differently than I did before I met him, before I heard him speak, before I saw the things that he did. I'm saying things I wouldn't have said before. "And just as Moses lifted up the serpent in the wilderness, so must the Son of Man be lifted up, that whoever believes in him may have eternal life" (3:14–15 NRSV). What, lifted up on a cross? But he's *dead* now, isn't he? No one lives *forever*, do they? At least, not in the world that we can see and touch. There's a knocking on the door, a pounding. I have been summoned by the council. I am to come immediately. God help me. And yet, I am suddenly unafraid. *This* is strange. What has come over me?

Ninth Sunday in Ordinary Time

1 Samuel 3:1–10 (11–20)
2 Corinthians 4:5–12
Mark 2:23—3:6

"Out of the Mouths . . ."

Anna Wilson sat staring at the computer screen and the email she had just received from the clerk of the Legislative Committee on Northern Development. She was both elated and anxious. For months, her organization, the Coalition for Arctic Conservation, had been petitioning to be invited to appear before the committee. Ever since the committee had announced that hearings would be conducted on a legislative proposal to open bidding for a tract of Arctic shoreline that a number of environmental groups had long identified as particularly sensitive habitat for polar bears and the seals upon which they depended, the Coalition for Arctic Conservation, or "CAC," had been debating whether their relatively small voice would be heard alongside organizations with bigger profiles, like Polar Bears International, in opposition to the well-financed mining interests. Their passion on this particular proposal, however, had convinced the grassroots CAC membership to commit the organization's resources toward making their objections known before the committee. Their resolve had been galvanized by comments of the legislative committee's chairperson, who had been openly dismissive of the environmental concerns being expressed by the opponents of the proposal, and who had a history of ridiculing and criticizing as "radical" the leading environmental organizations. And, although the Legislative Committee on Northern Development had announced the hearings several months earlier, the CAC had not had the financial resources to prepare a major presentation that might never see the light of day. In short, although the opportunity now available by way of the committee's invitation was one that Anna Wilson worried could not be met to maximum advantage, she had communicated the CAC's acceptance of the gesture. Oh, the CAC had file cabinets full of charts and figures, the results of countless studies performed by universities and environmental research organizations over the years, but pulling it all together in short order to constitute a compelling presentation, one that would garner committee support and public attention, was a task that seemed overwhelming, nearly impossible. The committee clerk had indicated that the hearings would commence in three weeks' time, although it was not yet known exactly when the CAC would be scheduled to make its presentation. Chairman Wendell Anderson's attitude was broadly thought to make opposition to the bidding process largely irrelevant anyway. What the CAC needed was a committee witness so highly respected that the chairman and others of his party could not reject their appeal outright, but would be forced to bow to public pressure rather than perfunctorily approve whatever the industry wanted to do, as was their custom.

Anna Wilson's telephone rang. Marc Delfontaine was calling. "Great news," he began, not even giving Anna a chance to share her own news about the committee's invitation. "Bill Lewis has been in touch with David Suzuki."

"*The* David Suzuki?" Anna asked.

"Yes. The one and only. And he's *very* interested in supporting us. He said he'll do whatever he can, if we can get on the committee's schedule."

"Well, I just received an email from the committee's clerk saying that we're in."

"Anna, that's great. Congratulations. You've been working so hard for this. We all have, but you were the one leading the charge."

"I've got to admit, Marc, that when the email came, I was worried. I mean, making the best possible use of our opportunity, and one that would speak to the public as well as the legislators. We've got the research on our side, but our voice is so small."

"Well, they can't just ignore David Suzuki. He'll have the public's ear even if Anderson's being supercilious or manipulative."

"At least the press should be interested now."

"When do we appear?" Marc asked.

"Our slot's not certain yet, but the hearings begin on the twelfth," Anna responded.

"The twelfth of *next* month?"

"Yes, I'm afraid so." She glanced back over the email, still on her computer screen. "They're scheduled to last for four days."

Anna heard Marc let go a discouraging whistle at the other end of the line. "Gee, I don't know. Suzuki's booked up months, years in advance, I'm sure."

"Well, we can have someone else present the facts and figures if we can just have him whiz in and out to make the philosophical appeal," Anna suggested.

"I'll get back in touch with Bill right away," Marc offered.

"Well, today's Friday. We'll already be losing the weekend. But I'll get the team working on the technical presentation. We can only do what we can do. But we've got to do our best. We can't blow this chance."

"Can we do it?" Marc asked despondently.

"God knows," Anna replied.

Normally, Anna Wilson and her husband, Tom, took their daughter Samantha to church on Sunday mornings, where Samantha eventually departed the sanctuary with other young children for Sunday school, which extended through the education hour following worship. On this Sunday, however, Anna stayed at home, working to develop a logical sequence for their allotted time in the committee hearing and hoping to hear back from Marc Delfontaine about David Suzuki's availability. She tried not to pin her hopes on the appearance of the renowned and highly respected environmentalist—his speaking on behalf of the CAC's position would certainly be a major advantage for their cause, not merely in the committee hearings but in their work overall. It was approaching noon when she heard the front door open downstairs and Tom and Samantha entering and then climbing the stairs to Anna's in-home office.

"Jim and Carla asked about you this morning," Tom said as he put his hands on his wife's shoulders, massaging them as she leaned back from the computer screen, which was filled with a table of figures that Tom could not decipher.

Anna sighed.

"I told them you were having to work under an incredibly tight schedule."

Anna, still facing the computer, reached her right hand up to his, and then, at the sound of Samantha's voice, swiveled her chair to see her daughter.

"Why didn't you come, Mommy?"

"Oh, Sam, I'm having to work on something very important. We're trying to help the polar bears and the seals and other animals up in the Arctic.

They're in danger, and Mommy and a bunch of other people are trying to keep them safe."

"Polar bears like Nook-Nook?" the little girl asked, referring to her stuffed toy polar bear that Anna and Tom had bought for her when they had visited the aquarium in Vancouver the previous summer. Tom smiled.

"Well," Anna answered, thinking of how to communicate at the level of a six-year-old, "Nook-Nook's cousins, the real polar bears. There are some people who want to take away the land where they live and where the seals live that the polar bears need to survive. We're trying very hard to keep that from happening."

"My Sunday school teacher today told us how God created all the animals and how happy God was about that, and how God told Adam that people were supposed to take care of the animals," the little girl reported. "Don't those people believe in God?"

"It's not that they don't believe in God, exactly," Tom tried to help explain. "But they want the land for other things—things that are important, too."

"But can't they use other land instead?" Samantha asked. "Somewhere that won't hurt the polar bears?"

"We're trying to get them to do that," Anna answered, and looked at Tom, appealing for more assistance. She did not want to prejudice her daughter against whole groups of people and their occupations. Tom himself was in the oil business, and the two of them had had some heated discussions about the oil and mining industries, though his was a respected voice within his company for sensitivity to environmental concerns, and he was proud that the management was scrupulous to abide by environmental regulations.

"People need what the mining companies want to dig up," Tom explained. "But the polar bears deserve to be happy, too."

"If God made them, doesn't that mean that God wants them to be OK?" Samantha reasoned.

"It certainly does," Tom agreed. "But right now, I know someone else who's probably hungry. Let's go down and have lunch."

"Yes," Anna said, looking at her watch. "Let's do that."

Anna continued to work on the strategy for the CAC's appearance before the committee. It was not until Wednesday that Marc Delfontaine called with a confirmation that David Suzuki would indeed be available to appear if the CAC's presentation was on the thirteenth or the fourteenth—the Tuesday or Wednesday of the four days of hearings. Anna told him that she could not yet confirm that the CAC would testify on either of those dates, but would forward the summary of their technical presentation to the famous environmentalist for his review as soon as it was completed. That seemed to be all they could do under the circumstances.

Again, the next Sunday, she stayed home while Tom and Samantha went to church. And again, she heard the front door open and close a few minutes before noon. Samantha bounded up the stairs ahead of her father and burst into Anna's office. "Mommy, Mommy," she ran to her mother's desk excitedly. "Guess what our teacher told us today?"

"Mommy's not very good at guessing today," Anna answered wearily, trying to smile despite her growing anxiety about the presentation. "You'll have to tell me."

"God told Noah that it was going to rain a lot and there would be a great big flood and so Noah built this great big boat and got two of every kind of animal onto it so they wouldn't drown and it rained and rained and when it stopped raining Noah and his family and all of the animals got out of the boat and were safe and God said that he loved them all so much that nothing like that would ever happen again." The little girl, almost out of breath, smiled and gave an emphatic nod, then added, "Polar bears, too."

Anna had just received an email from Marc Delfontaine confirming the inflexibility of David Suzuki's schedule and asking whether she yet had any definitive word on the date or dates of the CAC's presentation before the committee. She had had to reply that Chairman Anderson was not yet disclosing any details about the schedule, perhaps purposely trying to keep the environmental witnesses off-balance.

"That's great," she said distractedly to her daughter, and immediately addressed her husband. "You two go ahead and eat. I've got to keep working. Maybe we can eat together tonight."

More concerned about his wife than his own stomach, Tom sighed and picked up his daughter, who looked disappointed that her mother had not been more interested in her report of the Sunday school lesson. "Come down when you can," he said to his wife with resignation, then said to Samantha, "Why don't we invite Nook-Nook to join us?"

Samantha grinned.

The next Sunday was much the same. Anna's anxiety had mounted through the week. She had sent a draft summary of the CAC's technical presentation to Marc Delfontaine to forward to David Suzuki's office, but there was still no confirmation of the date or time for the group's appearance before the committee. Anna's conviction grew that this was a deliberate attempt by Wendell Anderson to make the procedure more difficult for the environmental opposition to the industry's proposal. Had he gotten word of the plan to have David Suzuki speak? she wondered. The chairman had a reputation among environmental advocates for unfairness, and it seemed that this was another case of trying to undermine the opposition.

Again, she had stayed at home working while Tom took Samantha to church and sent her on to Sunday school. When Tom and Samantha got home and came upstairs, Anna was in her chair, but had turned it away from the computer, her eyes closed and her hands clasped. Tom spoke softly, "Are you awake? Anna, are you OK?"

She opened her eyes and looked up, seemingly embarrassed. "I wasn't asleep," she answered in a quiet tone that matched Tom's. "I . . .," she began and paused before she finished her sentence, "was praying."

Tom looked concerned.

"It's only a week until the hearings begin," she continued. "And we still don't have a schedule. Mr. Suzuki's being very patient, but he's asking . . ." She broke off her sentence.

"It's not fair, is it?" Tom offered.

"Mommy." Samantha's voice was almost inaudible.

"Sam?" Anna said.

"Jesus said that God takes care of all the animals."

"Hm?" Anna asked, her mind elsewhere.

"Jesus told all the people on the mountainside that God takes care of the birds and all the other animals. God made plants and things so that they could eat and not have to worry about how they were going to live." She paused, then continued. "God wants all the animals and people to live together and not be ang, ang . . ." She looked up at her father.

"Anxious," Tom supplied. "Not be anxious."

Anna looked at her daughter and her husband and then at the computer keyboard.

"Let's go eat," Anna said quietly.

Tom had insisted that he and Samantha accompany Anna and the little delegation of CAC members to the legislative committee hearings on Thursday, the concluding day of the proceedings, when the CAC had finally been granted its ninety-minute appearance before the committee, the final slot before adjournment. Flying together across the country to attend the committee had been an unanticipated expense, but Tom knew that his support was important to Anna, and that it would be an educational adventure for their daughter. David Suzuki, of course, had been unable to attend. He had already been scheduled to speak at a United Nations climate conference in Geneva that day, and had flown to Europe overnight, apologizing profusely but unable to rearrange his long-standing commitment. Anna had been in despair ever since notice of the committee schedule had been posted, as had her colleagues. They had bravely honed their presentation, but it was blatantly dry, focused on facts gleaned from a plethora of studies but lacking any appeal for the public and for the press, much less demanding the attention of Chairman Anderson and like-minded committee members. Even the opposition members who were sympathetic to environmental concerns would likely, after nearly a week of hearings, have little capacity left to attend carefully to charts and graphs.

"As you are aware, ladies and gentlemen," Anna Wilson began her premature conclusion to the CAC presentation, "David Suzuki was planning to appear on behalf of our position during our presentation, but due to a preexisting commitment to speak at the United Nations climate conference today in Geneva, and because we had not been informed of the committee's schedule until just a few days ago, he is not available. Thus, we have concluded our—"

"Mommy!" came a voice from the audience. "Mommy! Tell them what God did."

The chairman banged his gavel. "Silence in the gallery," ordered Wendell Anderson. Anna Wilson, seated at the witness table, turned to the audience behind her and located her daughter with her gaze. She held her finger to her lips as her husband instinctively put his hand over Samantha's mouth.

"But Mommy!" came a muffled protest.

Wendell Anderson banged his gavel again, but the legislator seated beside him, the committee's ranking member of the opposition party, addressed Anna. "Do you have another witness who wishes to address the committee?" This elicited a chuckle from some of the audience, just as Samantha broke free from her father's restraint and ran through the audience to her mother, holding Nook-Nook, whom Anna and Tom had allowed their child to bring along to help keep her occupied.

"Mommy, tell them!"

"Mr. Chairman, the Coalition for Arctic Conservation still has time in its allotment," observed the ranking opposition member.

"This is improper," uttered the chairman.

"God loves the animals," Samantha said, standing beside her stunned mother and turning toward the legislators. "God made them. God wants us to take care of them."

The commotion had awakened the previously inattentive reporters and press photographers, who were now tapping on keyboards and aiming their cameras.

Flustered, the chairman was about to bang his gavel again when the ranking opposition member blurted to Anna, "Do you wish to have this witness offer more testimony on behalf of your organization?"

Anna, too stunned to speak, raised her hands in a gesture of uncertainty. Just then, Samantha began to cry. "Don't let them hurt Nook-Nook's cousins. Please don't let them."

The chairman lowered his gavel. "What's your name, little girl?" he asked in a grandfatherly tone.

"Mr. Chairman," Anna managed to sputter, "this is my daughter, Samantha."

"And who is that you've brought with you?" the chairman continued gently.

"This is my polar bear, Nook-Nook," the girl answered. "He's afraid for his cousins, that you're going to take away their home." Her little frame shuddered now with emotion. "God loves them."

There was silence in the hearing room as the legislators all sat back in their chairs, and one by one dropped their gaze to the long desk behind which they were poised. Finally, after what seemed like several minutes, Anna Wilson cleared her throat and spoke into the microphone on the table in front of her. "Mr. Chairman, our presentation is complete."

Anna stood up and took her daughter by the right hand, the little girl's left hand still clutching her stuffed polar bear, and they retreated into the audience and sat down beside Tom as cameras clicked and the sound of tapping came from a dozen laptop computers in the press gallery. Wendell Anderson raised his gavel and quietly tapped it once on the desk in front of him. "With testimony concluded," he spoke in mute dignity, "the Legislative Committee on Northern Development is adjourned, to reconvene next Monday at ten o'clock to begin our deliberations. We thank the witnesses." Then he added, "All the witnesses."

Twelfth Sunday in Ordinary Time

1 Kings 19:1–15a
Galatians 3:23–29
Luke 8:26–39

"Found"

A tear rolled down Meredith Howard's cheek as she snapped shut the clasp on her briefcase. She looked around her office. There had been amazingly few personal items in it—just a couple of photographs, and half a dozen books, plus some personal papers. Since Bill had died, she had invested her entire life in her job, but there were few of her own footprints in the carpet, so to speak. She had been very good at presenting the ideas of others, of representing the company to clients and potential clients, but had never been authorized or even asked to share her own opinions, her own vision. Then had come the lawsuit from a client who had suffered a financial loss that was being tied back to a presentation she had made a few months earlier. She had only been doing her job.

More tears rolled down her cheeks, and she blotted them with a tissue, carefully, so as not to mess her makeup. She thought about her letter of resignation, which she would leave with the receptionist. And then . . . what? Where would she go? What would she do? Her job had provided the framework for her life—her schedule, her everything. She *did* have a cottage up near Havelock, a couple of hours' drive north and east of the city. She and Bill had bought it as their getaway, but after he died, she had lost interest. She was *already* alone in their *apartment*. Why did she need to drive four hours every summer weekend to be even *more* alone?

Meredith looked out the window toward the lake. She had taken the view for granted these past couple of years of occupying that office. She had coveted it once, but when she got the promotion, all she ever had time to look at were contracts and proposals and reports. This afternoon, the lake appeared singularly uninterested in her problem, unsympathetic to her mood, unimpressed with the big corporate fish that she had landed for Bristol & Grant, Ltd. But she would miss the view. It had said something about her success. It was also lovely, she knew, even if she had so frequently taken its loveliness for granted.

Meredith took one final look around her office. There was nothing left that was hers. She sighed, took up her briefcase, opened the door, paused, then closed it behind her and headed for the reception area. Arlene was at her desk, writing something on a phone message pad. "Would you give this to Mr. Bristol, please?" Meredith asked, handing the receptionist the envelope containing her letter of resignation.

"He's still here, I think, if you want to see him," Arlene said as she reached for the telephone console to ring his office.

"No, no, that isn't necessary. Please just see that he gets it."

"All right, then. I'll see you in the morning," said the receptionist.

"No, I . . . I won't be in tomorrow."

Arlene looked at Meredith as if awaiting some word of explanation, but Meredith gave none. "Thank you," Meredith said in a murmur, and walked to the elevator.

She did not want to face Mr. Bristol—not that he was unkind or unfair, but she felt that she had let him—let the company—down, in some manner that she could not identify. And now, the company faced a serious lawsuit. He had stated it as a fact at the staff meeting on Monday afternoon. As she thought about it now, there was nothing that he had said that was critical of her or her performance. She had expected all day Tuesday to he called into his office, which did not happen. The suspense, the tension, had been too great. So, this morning, Wednesday, she had written her letter of resignation. She could not expect a letter of recommendation in return. She had some savings—actually, *substantial* savings, for she had lived rather frugally after Bill had died. The cottage and the apartment, they had been able to buy for cash, so her financial obligations were few. For the moment, she had no plans, other than to distance herself from the office and the pending lawsuit and gossip about her role in the company's troubles.

As she drove her car up out of the underground parkade, the sunlight still reached down to the street. It was not yet the rush hour, although the traffic would be building on Bloor Street. Stopped at a traffic light, she reached into her purse and turned off her cellphone. She gradually formulated in her mind a plan to drive up to the cottage and remain there through the weekend, or longer, perhaps. Then, maybe, she would go out west. She had always wanted to see the Rockies. Or perhaps east. She had a brother in Charlottetown, a professor at the university there. She had not seen him in two or three years. Perhaps he could help find her a job. Never before had she done something so irresponsible as to leave her office without saying where she was going. Well, what did it matter, after all? She had *quit*, hadn't she? What if she would be needed to testify? She didn't want to testify. What could she say anyway? As far as she was concerned, she had done the task that she had been assigned. Where it went wrong, she didn't know.

She pulled in under the canopied parking space at her apartment house and walked to the entrance of the building. On the way in, she stopped in the manager's office. "Mr. Kennedy, I'm going to be away for a few days."

"That water heater's been working all right for you, has it?" the middle-aged man asked as he stood up behind his desk. "No leaks or anything?"

"It's been fine, but I wouldn't mind your looking in once or twice to be sure, if it's not too much trouble."

"No trouble at all, Mrs. Howard. I'll be happy to."

"Thank you very much."

As she was turning to leave, he asked, "Is there anything wrong, Mrs. Howard?"

She turned back partway to look at him and shook her head.

"You look a little agitated, not your normal self, if you don't mind my saying so."

"I'm quite all right, thank you," she stammered, trying to smile. Then, she added, "My cellphone may be off, but I'll be checking for messages."

"If anything comes up, I'll let you know," the manager said. "A beautiful June day. You ought to try to get up to your cottage one of these weekends."

"As a matter of fact . . .," Meredith started, then broke off the sentence. "Yes, I suppose I should," she said after a few seconds' pause. Twenty minutes later, she passed by the manager's office wearing blue jeans and a tee-shirt, carrying a suitcase and a briefcase, now full of magazines and novels.

Meredith Howard stopped for groceries before joining the great afternoon exodus east on the 401 freeway. On her way out of the store, a woman in an apron had persuaded her to try a new cheese spread on a cracker. "You might get hungry before supper," she said cheerily. "Please remember our brand." In fact, Meredith *was* a bit hungry, and it would be a few hours before she would be able to make herself dinner. She had taken *two* crackers topped with the orange-colored stuff.

After leaving the great highway at Bowmanville and eventually passing Peterborough, the fields gave way to forest and eventually ponds and little lakes with rocky ledges along the shore. Here and there, she saw people fishing and swimming and boating, enjoying the summer evening. At Havelock, she turned off Highway 7 onto a narrower highway for a ways, then right onto a lane that eventually brought her to a driveway that she had entered only infrequently since Bill's death. They had spent happy days there, planning their life together, talking about having children someday. She pulled up in front of the little house, noticing how un-welcoming it was without any flower beds or other indications of habitation. Maybe this wasn't such a good idea after all. Bill had been gone for nearly five years now. She hadn't spent more than a dozen nights in the place since he died, instead just coming up on Saturdays occasionally to check on it and see what needed to be repaired. She *really* should have *sold* it, but Bill had delighted so much in being there, it would have seemed like dishonoring his memory.

She sighed and got out of the car, and as she walked the short distance toward the front door, she was startled to hear a crack of thunder. "Where did *that* come from?" she said to herself as she turned and looked toward the northwest. She had noticed no storm clouds building as she had driven out from the city, but a very dark cloud now had moved in front of the sun. "Is this what I'll get?" she thought to herself. "A deluge of rain, keeping me cooped up inside?"

She unlocked the door and quickly transferred the groceries, suitcase, and briefcase inside, and, batting at some cobwebs, opened the curtains. The sudden cloud cover made the interior of the little house dark, and she switched on the lights in the living room and kitchen. But as she was emptying the grocery sacks, there was a flash of light outside, followed immediately by a deafening boom, and then the lights went out. A violent wind made the house shudder and moan, and she heard a crash from outside. Meredith groped her way to the front window to see that the car was all right. A birch tree had snapped in the middle of the trunk and fallen across the gravel drive just behind the car.

Meredith's knees buckled and she sank to the dusty floor, tears pouring as freely as the rain was falling outside. "God help me!" she sobbed. "What am I doing here? What am I going to do? Oh, what am I going to do?" As she sat on the floor with her back against the wall, the time passed.

The knocking on the door finally broke into Meredith's consciousness. She opened her eyes. The interior of the cottage was in total darkness now. The lights had not come back on. Again, the knock. Who could be here? She got to her feet and looked through the window toward the porch, but could not make out the face of the shadowed figure at the door. Suddenly, she was afraid. *Very* afraid. "Is that you, Joe?" she said, coming up with the most masculine name she could think of at the moment, but barely squeaking it out. She raised her voice and tried again. "Joe, is that you back from the firing range?"

The knocking ceased. She looked again out the window. The figure had turned on a flashlight and seemed to be consulting a piece of paper. Perhaps it was someone lost in the storm. But the storm, she now noticed for the first time, had ceased. All was quiet outside. She stepped toward the door and slipped the chain lock in place, then opened it half an inch and said, "Joe?"

"Meredith?" the figure said quietly, a man's voice that she recognized. "It's me, Larry Bristol."

"M . . . Mr. Bristol," she stammered.

"May I, uh . . . ?"

"Oh, of course. Pardon me," she said, closing the door so that she could slip off the chain, and then opening it again for her boss—her former boss—to enter. He stepped from the darkness outside into the darkness inside. "The lights went off in the storm," she explained feebly.

"What are you doing *here*, Meredith?"

"Well, I messed up the Parker deal and seem to have put the company in jeopardy," she said. "Wait a minute. How did you find me? Why did you drive all the way out here?" She could not see his face, but was glad that he couldn't see hers, either.

"I read your letter, and I tried calling you, but you weren't answering your mobile phone. I went to your apartment house. The manager told me that you had just left for a few days, and that you were dressed for the cottage country. I knew that you weren't leaving town on any assignment for the company, plus your letter, of course. I asked him if he knew where your place was, and he sketched a map how to get here."

"Yes, I had him arrange for some workmen to come out and do some repairs on the roof last summer," Meredith recalled. "But, Mr. Bristol, you mean you drove all the way out here . . . ?"

"What are you doing *here*, Meredith?"

"Well, the company is being sued big-time because of me. You said at the meeting Monday that things looked bad. I'm a liability to you. I'm not up to the job. I . . ." She had run out of things to say.

"You *fulfilled* your assignment, Meredith. You did exactly what you were *asked* to do. I can't expect any more than *that*. Our analysis of the situation was incorrect. Or, rather, conditions had changed."

In the darkness, he could not tell what her silence meant.

"Meredith, you are a fine employee, a valuable asset to us, always dependable, one of the best representatives our company *has* had or ever *could* have. I want you to go to Detroit next week on the Gilbert account, and then I want you to consider managing a new office for us in Vancouver."

Meredith remained in stunned silence.

"Meredith? Did you hear what I said?"

"Yes, sir. I just . . ."

"There are opportunities out there that we must position ourselves to take advantage of, lawsuit or no lawsuit. The Palmer matter is serious, but it's not going to be our undoing. And it mustn't be the end of your career. There's too much work we need for you to accomplish for us."

The lights flickered back on just then. Larry Bristol could see that Meredith had been crying. "But before all that," he said, "I want you to take a few days off up here."

"Thank you," she said. "I guess I'll need my letter back," she added, uncertain of the protocol in such situations.

"I'm sorry," Mr. Bristol replied. "I tore it up as soon as I read it."

Meredith Howard watched the taillights of her boss's car retreat down the driveway and quickly disappear along the lane. She turned toward the kitchen, and her gaze fell on a photograph of Bill and her standing together on the little dock out behind the house, their arms around each other. She smiled, and went into the kitchen to fix a simple dinner. As she sat down to eat—she was hungry—she prayed a simple blessing, giving thanks for the meal, giving thanks for Bill, giving thanks for their cottage, giving thanks for the lights, and giving thanks that Mr. Bristol had found her.

Fourteenth Sunday in Ordinary Time

2 Samuel 5:1–5, 9–10
2 Corinthians 12:2–10
Mark 6:1–13

"Talk of the Town"

"Peace be with you," the first man said.

"And also with you," replied the second man, inviting the first man to sit down on the bench opposite him with a gesture of his hand. "Another hot day, I think."

"A spot of rain would be welcome," the first man remarked in agreement, looking toward the west, where the sky over Mount Carmel was dotted with a few small clouds blowing in off the Mediterranean. But it was not the time of year for a storm, and the clouds he saw held no promise of rain. "Ah, well," he concluded.

"Yes," said the second man, unwrapping a small cloth bundle to expose a moderate-sized chunk of bread and a large morsel of goat cheese. He held out the bread to his friend who shook his head with a smile, reaching down by his side and lifting his own small bundle to his lap. "Blessed are you, O Lord, for giving us the fruits of the earth. Blessed be your name above all names. Amen."

"Amen," echoed the first man, now unwrapping his own noontime meal. Not everyone in the hillside town ate lunch, but these two men regularly met each other in the public square to discuss current events and exchange their opinions on the affairs of the world—at least the world insofar as they knew of it from their watch-post in lower Galilee.

"Visitors in town," said the first man after a few moments of silence as they both busied themselves with taking a bite of bread.

"I saw that," the second man responded. "Heard the one in the synagogue yesterday—that craftsman, that Jesus. There were several others who came to town with him. You weren't there, I don't think."

"No, we were down in Magdala, visiting my wife's sister and her family. We came back after the sabbath. Her husband's been sick, you know. I did a few chores about the place—things that their own sons ought to be about, but—"

"Kids, these days," said the second man. They both shook their heads in agreement with the unspoken judgment upon the younger generation.

"Heard talk about this Jesus, though."

"Just such a one as you were speaking about," the second man said, rising to the theme. "His father gone now, several years, I think, and he goes off and pretty much ignores his business, abandons his mother and younger brothers and sisters."

"Carpenter, wasn't he? Or a stone mason?"

"Bit of both, I suppose. With the Romans a-building Sepphoris over there," the second one nodded toward the grand Roman town under construction on the next hilltop to the north, "you'd think there'd be more than enough work around here for a craftsman, if he tended to his trade."

"That's for sure." The first man took another bite from his loaf and chewed thoughtfully. As a modest property owner himself, he had occasion to employ skilled laborers to repair buildings and walls on a frequent basis, and now and then tended to minor physical tasks himself. "*If* a man wants to work," he said philosophically.

"Well, this Jesus certainly seems to have time on *his* hands, roaming the countryside with these other vagabonds."

"How did he presume to speak up in the synagogue, anyway? A common workman? Not that I look down on laborers." At this, the other man nodded soberly. "But where does a *workman* find the time necessary to meditate on the scriptures so that he's qualified to speak up in the synagogue?"

"You've not heard?" the second man looked at his friend in feigned surprise. "Lots of people were curious to hear him. Talk of the town, how he's been curing people with ailments of different sorts." Then he winked. "Assuming they really *were* sick."

"A charlatan?" the first man asked.

"Wouldn't be the first," the second man replied, turning back to his meal. "Nor the last. Easy to fool some people. Some claim he even raised a girl from the dead, down at Capernaum or somewhere."

"You know, I heard gossip of such a thing when we were down at Magdala. But I didn't credit it. Preposterous. Didn't connect it with this Jesus, though."

"That could have been a hoax, too," the second man mused. "Easily. Who knows but what she wasn't just sleeping?"

"So why doesn't he do such miraculous things right here, if he's truly able?" the first man asked.

"Uppity," said the second man.

"Did he look like a miracle worker?" the first man asked.

"Who? Jesus? How would *I* know? Don't know what a miracle worker's *supposed* to look like," the second man grumbled. "This Jesus looks just like anyone else. Nothing special about him, so far as I could see. No magic wand. No magic potions. Nothing like that."

"I remember his father, Joseph—if he's the one I'm thinking about," the first man reflected. "And his mother's name is Miriam, right? Mary. I think I recall him as a boy when I would pass by running around his father's shop when he was a little tyke, helping his father some when he was older."

"Large family, *needed* the help. Most likely, still *does*."

"The oldest son's place is at home," said the first man. "He's supposed to take over when the father dies. Lead the family. Assume responsibility. Make the decisions. Not travel hither and yon all over the place, getting into other people's business. It's not right. It's not decent."

"Poor Mary," the first woman said as she and her friend walked toward the market. "It must be very embarrassing."

"Everybody says she *ought* to be embarrassed," the second woman said, adding to the volume of judgment. "He certainly had chutzpah to come back home and bring more shame on his poor mother."

"She's got enough to deal with, being widowed and all," the first woman observed.

"Everyone says he's insane, or possessed by demons, or whatever you want to call it," the second woman again amplified the charges.

"The last time he was in town, Mary took her sons to try to see him and talk to him—tried to take him home quiet-like where he, well, you know, wouldn't cause a ruckus. And he barely even acknowledged that they were there. Seemed to disown them—claimed the people who had flocked to see his *spectacle* were his *true* family. Can you imagine?"

"Embarrassment and hurt. Such deep, deep hurt," the second woman said.

"'Whoever does the will of God is my brother and sister and mother' (Mark 3:35 NRSV)—that's what I hear he said. Not even acknowledging his own kin."

"You'd think she wouldn't be able to show her face in town again. Such a scandal!" the second woman augmented her indignation.

"And no wonder," said the first. "They've heard about him all the way down to Jerusalem. The scribes—I've heard that some of them came up a few weeks ago all the way from the city, convinced that the devil's in him. And they should know, shouldn't they?"

"That poor woman will never live down such a thing," the second one said.

"It's a black eye on our entire town," the first woman said, her imagination rolling. "Everyone in Galilee will be wagging their heads over it. And what must the scribes have reported when they got back to Jerusalem?"

"He's shaming us all."

"I've heard, too, that he talks rather freely with the women. Puts his hands on them sometimes, when they come complaining of aches and such."

The second woman looked shocked.

"On their heads, like," the first woman put her hands together in the shape of an upside-down bowl. "Totally improper, if you ask me."

"Somebody ought to do something," the second woman said.

In the courtyard of a house in a town along the shore of the Sea of Galilee, a man sat watching his daughter spinning wool. She was twelve years old, just on the threshold of maturity, blooming, he thought, like a rose, certainly a precious flower in *his* estimation. "Come to me, child," he said, and she got up and crossed to stand before where he sat. He stood up and drew her to him in an embrace, and she felt his tear fall on her forehead.

"O, Papa, it's all right. I'm fine now. Really, I am."

"Praise God," he said. "Praise God. I thought I'd lost you, my dear daughter. I was struck to the heart."

"I hope we see that man again someday," she said. "He was very kind."

"Yes, my child, he certainly was that." He paused, then added, speaking more to himself than to his daughter, "And to think, I almost didn't go out to find him. I nearly . . . let the opportunity go by."

His daughter drew a little away from her father and looked questioningly at him. He tried to explain. "Never judge others too quickly," he said. "Never be too proud to reach out in hope. Never forget that the Lord comes to us sometimes in surprising ways—almost in disguise, you might say, the disguise of the ordinary, the commonplace."

By her expression, the man knew that his daughter had not grasped his meaning. Perhaps, he realized, he didn't fully understand himself what it was he was trying to say. But his understanding of God had changed perceptibly that day that he cast aside his customary caution and reasonableness, frantic that his desperately sick daughter might be cured. He had heard about this man—there had been rumors, there had been criticism, but there had also been a chance. He might well have been criticized himself for seeking out such a man. After all, he was well respected, leader of the town's synagogue, upholder of the faith and the traditions of the people. But then the most precious thing in the world to him—his daughter—became sick, seriously sick, so sick that it seemed she might die. And, his servants reported, in fact she *did* die, while the teacher from Nazareth dallied along the way with some other claimant on his attention. But the man, this Jesus, had insisted on coming to his house anyway, and going into the room where his daughter was, and within moments she was well again. He had kept his own promise not to tell anyone about it, but he suspected—in fact, he was fairly certain—that his servants had *violated* his order and had spread the news about. His own position as leader of the synagogue might be in jeopardy, but what was that compared with having his daughter alive and well again? The healer had not scrupled even to touch her lifeless body, though it made *him* unclean according to the law. But neither had he been upset about that woman touching his robe—that woman with the flow of blood by which, he heard later, she had been made unclean for twelve years. The fact that she touched *his* robe had made *Jesus* unclean, too, but he only seemed to be concerned that she be made well. The man did not begrudge Jesus his concern for the woman—certainly not after Jesus restored his daughter to life. That woman could once again have a normal life—could return to her husband, if she had one, and they could again live as husband and wife for the first time in twelve years, or she could finally *become* someone's wife if she weren't yet married. And *he* would one day have the joy of seeing his own daughter taken under a man's roof as a wife, and have children of her own, and then she would know why he had been so anxious for her and how desperate he had been and so grateful for what the man had done.

He looked down at his daughter, standing before him, still with a puzzled look on her face. "Go on back to your spinning, now." He took her hand briefly and nodded toward the girl's distaff and spindle as a faint smile came to his lips.

A man was walking down the road, a small group of his followers walking along behind him, chatting, joking, in good spirits. They had been going from village to village for several weeks now, where the man had taught about the scriptures, now and then curing some who were sick, restoring soundness to some who were infirm, bringing back to right mind some who seemed possessed by demons. They were vaguely aware that what he had done had prompted rumors, had upset some of the local leaders and authorities. They approached a crossroad, and he slowed his pace, and finally stopped and looked around at the villages that crowned the neighboring hilltops and then turned to speak to them.

"It is time for you to go out and call people to repentance and silence the demons disrupting people's lives," he said. Some were apprehensive, remembering how he had been turned away from his own hometown. But others were eager to do the same things that Jesus had been doing. And he instructed the twelve whom he had called to go out in pairs, taking no provisions, but trusting in the hospitality of the people who welcomed them. They should be satisfied with whatever they were given and content with their accommodations, but were simply to *leave* anywhere that they were not welcome, shaking off the dust from their feet in sign of judgment upon such inhospitality. And when they returned to him over the next few days from their journeys amongst the villages, they told him that they had cast out many demons and had anointed many who were sick and those who had been ill became well at their touch.

Seventeenth Sunday in Ordinary Time

2 Samuel 11:1–15
Ephesians 3:14–21
John 6:1–21

"Fish, Loaves, and Faith"

"Mama!" the boy shouted as he ran into the house. "Mama! Guess what, Mama!"

"Not so loud. Slow down. Why all the fuss?" said the bedraggled woman as she looked up from her household chores, pushing a stray curl up under the scarf on her head. "You'll wake the baby!"

Indeed, there came from the back room the soft sound of rustling bunting behind a curtain drawn across a doorway.

"But Mama," the boy came over to her and started tugging at her skirt, "it was wonderful. And it wouldn't have happened without me. He said so!"

The woman stopped what she was doing and stood straight up from her bent-over position. Her hand instinctively returned to her forehead to replace the habitually unruly curl, but this time it had remained in place under the scarf, so instead, she just wiped her brow with the back of her hand. She was a woman perhaps in her mid-twenties, but prematurely middle-aged, as so many wives and mothers were in this working-class village near the Sea of Galilee. Keeping house was difficult enough in those times. But the Passover celebration was only a few days away, and the housework had increased with the anticipation of family and friends visiting. She had not even had time to go to market that day, and so had sent her young son to buy some fish and bread for supper.

He was a typical boy, affectionate and surprisingly warmhearted at times, dependable enough when there were no distractions, but scarcely conscious today of the extra burden placed upon the woman of the house by the approaching holiday. Just now, he looked up at her with big, bright eyes, and a smile which could barely contain the report of some great adventure. "Mama!" he said again. But just at that moment, she noticed that he was empty-handed.

"Where are the fish and bread that I sent you to get? And where is the basket that I gave you?" Her knitted eyebrows betrayed a vexed attitude. "Didn't you go to the market? I have too much work to do here today. Surely you could do this one thing for me that I asked you to do."

"Yes, Mama, I did just what you said. I got the fish and the bread. But let me tell you—"

"Then where are they? That was to be our dinner tonight."

"He took them, Mama. He used my fish and my bread."

"What are you talking about? Did someone steal them from you?"

"Oh, no, Mama. I offered them to him."

"What, to a beggar? We will be beggars too, if you give all of our food away."

"Mama, please listen. He's not a beggar, and he didn't steal anything from me. He needed it to feed the people. He said he couldn't have done it without me offering him my fish and my bread."

"*Our* fish and *our* bread," his mother corrected him. She had grown impatient, as adults do. "Where are they? Tell me what has happened!"

"I'm trying to, Mama. I went to the market, just like you told me. I bought two fish and five loaves of bread—the brown kind. And I was bringing them back home. But as I was coming from the market, there were a whole bunch of people walking up from the dock."

"O Lord, what shall I do with such a child?" the woman rolled her eyes upward. She closed them a few seconds in exasperation, and then looked back down at her son, sternly now. "There is work to do here to make ready for Passover, and I need your help, not to have you run off with the—"

"But Mama, I thought it must be important—so many people! There must have been a jillion! Anyway, they just went out on the hillside. It wasn't so very far. But let me tell you what happened."

"Just tell me where our dinner is," she answered dryly.

"Well, I heard some of them saying how hungry the people were, so I . . ." The boy began to sense that his mother shared none of his excitement, and he was beginning to doubt now whether she would understand the mood of generosity that had come over him and prompted him to give away their supper. "I gave them to this man."

"What man?"

"Well, he seemed to be in charge of things."

"And what did this man who seemed to be in charge of things do with *our* fish and *our* bread?"

"He used them to feed all the crowd."

"And how did he feed 'a jillion' people with two fish and five loaves of bread, eh?"

"Well, he did. He just . . . did!" The story was sounding a little implausible even to the boy now; as he remembered what had happened, it defied even his boyish logic. Why had he ever thought that his mother would share his enthusiasm? He looked up at her, the face that he knew so well that he sometimes forgot that he loved it, the dress that he knew so well that he never thought about why he had never seen her wearing any other one. "He really did," the boy muttered.

The look of bewildered disappointment in her son's down-turned face—that he had done something that *he* thought was right and proper and could not fully comprehend why *she* thought that it was foolish and wasteful—now touched the woman's heart, and she put her arms around the boy and drew him close in her embrace. "We just don't have money to throw away like that," she said gently, hoping that he would somehow understand why she was upset. "Times are hard right now," she explained, thinking to herself that times are *always* hard.

"But Mama, they were hungry!" he pleaded, and he started to cry, burying his face in her dress. "I thought—"

The woman sighed deeply, her son's tears moving her to sorrow that she had scolded him. And she even felt a little pride in her son, somehow. "It's all right. We'll manage." She knew, of course, that they *would* somehow get along. They always did.

She released her embrace when she heard a loud banging on the door of the house. "Oh, no, they'll wake the baby!" she said, half to her son and half to herself. The boy darted toward the door and opened it.

"Have you heard what happened? Have you heard about the miracle?" It was the woman who lived down the street, a typical village busybody, but today animated by some bit of news beyond any previous level of excitement. "Oh, but of course you have," she said, now noticing for the first time the boy standing in front of her, his hand still on the door handle. Remaining in the doorway, the visitor looked back into the interior of the room at the boy's mother. "It was a miracle! It was a miracle—no doubt about it! And I was there to see it—just imagine! And the bread and the fish were *real*, too; I ate some! And this dear boy of yours"—she had never spoken of him that way; in fact, she had always seemed to find much that was objectionable about any children but her own—"this dear boy of yours had a part in it all. What a good little boy. You really must come to see this man who fed all these people. I'm on my way now to find my husband to take him back out to hear the man speak." She turned and bustled toward the next house, where she pounded on the door just as loudly or more so. From the back room, mother and son could hear the baby working up to a cry, but they just looked at each other, the mother with an expression of confusion, the boy with an expression of vindication, his hand still resting on the handle of the open door.

Suddenly, the room was shadowed by the figure of a large, muscular man standing just outside the doorway. He was looking down at the boy. "They told me where you live. You forgot this," said the man to the startled lad, and the man handed him the market basket he had taken with him earlier that day. But his mother could detect from her position in the middle of the room that the basket was now obviously far from empty, for her son strained when the man handed it to him.

She walked toward the open doorway with a questioning look. The man was a Galilean, she knew from his speech, and his dress suggested that he was one of the fisherfolk.

In the dim light, the stranger had not noticed her at first, but now that she moved toward the door and put her hand on her son's shoulder, he acknowledged her presence with a smile. "I just met your son a little while ago," he explained. "He's a fine boy—and a generous one. You must be proud."

She nodded, still with a questioning look on her face, and somewhat embarrassed to be addressed by a man whom she did not know.

Suddenly, the man recognized the awkwardness of the situation. "I'm sorry, I should not have startled you. My name is Andrew. I live in Capernaum, across the lake. My people are from Bethsaida. I am traveling now with Jesus, the Nazarene. Your son did us an invaluable service today. But"—he looked back down at the boy with a kind expression—"he forgot his basket."

That drew her mind back to the basket and the burden that it seemed to contain. She glanced down and was amazed at what she saw—it was filled with morsels of bread and fish enough to last her family for days! She looked back at the Galilean fisherman, her mouth open in amazement.

"I must go now, back to Jesus and the others," he said to the mother and son. "Thank you again for your generosity," he concluded, looking down now at the boy and tousling the lad's hair with his big calloused hand. Then he turned back into the street.

The woman just stared at the fish and the bread.

"It's like I told you, Mama. And the other man—the one who was in charge—said that it was my fish and bread that made it all possible."

The woman did not go out to join the crowd, as her neighbor had urged; there was still the Passover to prepare for. But over the next few days, she heard more reports of the miraculous feeding of the crowd, and how, indeed, it had all started with her son's offer of the fish and bread which he carried in his market basket. She heard other reports, too, concerning the man about whom her son had spoken, this man Jesus—strange stories about his walking across the waves to join his companions in their boat, about how he had healed many people of their diseases and infirmities, about how he referred to himself as "bread"—the bread of life. She thought about all these things. But mostly, she thought about how she had *chided* her generous, kindhearted boy for offering their own little supper to Jesus so that "a jillion" hungry people might have something to eat.

Twenty-First Sunday in Ordinary Time

Jeremiah 1:4–10
Hebrews 12:18–29
Luke 13:22–30

"A Pilgrimage Tale: Going to the Banquet"

Three people—two men and a woman—were walking along the road, intending the same destination on a pilgrimage. They were all three dressed for a party—an older gentleman in tuxedo and tails, a middle-aged woman in an evening gown, a younger man more modestly attired in his best suit and tie.

"Perhaps we should pick up our pace," said the younger man. "We certainly wouldn't want to arrive late."

"What's the rush?" asked the middle-aged woman. "It's too hot to be in such a hurry. There's plenty of time. Besides, they ought to be grateful just to see us come at all."

"It *is* hot," said the older gentleman, "but not as hot as it will get if we don't keep walking toward our destination. However," he added, holding his head a little more erect and thrusting his chin forward, "I for one have little fear about arriving too late. I am quite sure that they will grant *me* admittance *regardless* of *when* I get there."

"A little superior, are you?" asked the woman in a clear tone of sarcasm. "It's people like you who made me wonder whether I even wanted to make this trip at all."

The older gentleman shook his head dramatically, while the younger man just tried to stare ahead at where the road met the horizon. "You just refuse to accept it, don't you, and so many others like you?" demanded the older gentleman of the woman. "If you would just spend your time wisely, pursuing the proper sorts of—"

"Look," the woman interrupted, "no lectures, please. We've come a long way today, and we still have a long way to go yet—that is, if I don't decide to turn around right here. I'm not complaining about your dedication. Just don't you condescend to me."

The older gentleman sighed audibly, and the younger man maintained an embarrassed silence.

As they walked on, the woman looked about at the scenery, what there was of it, for the green forest and verdant fields of their starting point earlier in the day had since given way to a barren landscape, dotted only here and there with a little bush providing shade barely enough for a rat to find comfort in. Ahead and behind, they could see other groups of pilgrims making the same trek on the same path, all headed toward the same destination.

Finally, to break the silence and the monotony, the younger man spoke up, but with his gaze still fixed far down the road. "I had wondered what the road would be like, but it never seemed to matter as much as making the journey to such a wonderful destination. It is really quite a privilege for all of us to be invited, don't you think?"

"Indeed, it is quite a privilege for you to have been chosen," said the older gentleman. "And you would do well always to keep that in mind. A privilege indeed for you."

"He said, 'a privilege for all of us,'" the woman corrected him. "Don't you consider it a privilege for yourself as well?"

"Well," said the older gentleman with sort of a false chuckle, "after all, I have been loyally obedient ever since I was initiated. None of us is deserving of the honor, of course, but, naturally, if *anyone* was to be invited, I would not be surprised to be included on the list. You see, he and I have had a close relationship, closer than the vast majority of people, I am sure. So, it is only to be expected."

"Well, I haven't exactly been a stranger to him myself," the woman said defensively. "I've always said that he was important, and that everyone should have faith in him and be loyal. Society would fall apart without that, and the family and everything. We celebrate his birthday—every year! I even have a cousin who's in charge of those meetings held weekly in his honor, somewhere or other."

"Strange that I've never seen you at *our* meetings, then," said the older gentleman, resuming his patronizing tone. "I never miss one, and I don't think that anyone should."

"It just so happens that I work pretty hard the rest of the time," the woman fired back, her face turning a little red. "It is more important for me to spend some time with my family at home, or having a little leisure time once in a while. Besides, I was initiated once, and if I need to, I'll come to a meeting sometime. I just don't like to be pushed."

Ignoring her outburst, the older gentleman turned to the younger man. "What about you? I don't recall seeing you at the meetings or speaking up. What are *your* qualifications for being invited?"

"Qualifications?" the younger man asked, faltering. "Why, I guess I haven't any, really."

"Hah!" interjected the older gentleman.

"As I said before, I think it's a privilege." After a pause, the younger man continued, "I have been at the meetings, almost every week, and saw you and heard you and others make speeches from time to time and say what we should do and what we shouldn't do. I used to help clean up after the meetings and take the leftover refreshments to members who were not able to attend or did not have enough food for themselves."

"Oh," said the older gentleman, "then it is no wonder that I never noticed you. My official duties of enthusiastically promoting the meetings and stringently maintaining the standards of the organization have kept me very busy, of course."

"Of course," echoed the younger man, not without respect in his voice. "I can see why *you* would be invited," he continued, again in a tone of respect, but still keeping his eyes glued to the horizon.

"Look, can't we stop for a rest?" asked the woman. "My feet are killing me. So what if we're a little late? What's the big deal?"

"I, at least, can afford the time for a little rest," said the older gentleman.

"But the invitation said that we would be able to enter the banquet hall only if we arrived on time," observed the younger man, finally turning to look at his companions who were now decelerating their pace and falling behind him. "Our journey will have been all for nothing if we are too late."

"They will surely open up for me," said the older gentleman, now stopped and brushing the dust off the sleeves of his tuxedo.

"I *dare* them to keep *me* out," said the woman, "after I've taken the time and made the effort to come all this way. Gee, it's hot," she said, looking around until her eyes met those of the older gentleman. Remembering how he responded to her previous comment about the heat, she suddenly looked like she regretted her latest reference.

But before the older gentleman could respond to the woman, the younger man said to him, "I realize that *you* must know a lot more about all this than *I* do, but even if we *could* get in despite our being late, I would not want to seem ungrateful. He has done so much for us all."

"You are quite right to be conscientious," the older gentleman said. "I commend you for your diligence. Why don't you go on ahead, and I'll catch up, or see you inside later on."

"Yeah," said the woman, "you go on ahead. I'll get there one of these days." She chuckled to hear herself repeat one of her most frequent lines, and she looked across toward the older gentleman who now was seated on a rock beside the road consulting his pocket appointment calendar. "You know," she said, "I saw him once, when he came into our city. Even went out to hear him speak. A real fine speech!"

"Indeed," said the older gentleman, resuming his condescending tone. "And yet, it seems to have left little impression on you."

"Hey," she answered, "there were plenty of people who didn't even take the time to go see him. I'm doing just fine, regardless of what people like you think."

"Hmph!" snorted the older gentleman. "People like me will be inside by the fire looking out through the window and laughing at people like you, shivering in the cold."

"I thought it was supposed to be 'burning in the flames!' You're slipping, bud."

Meanwhile, the younger man had continued walking along toward the destination, avoiding the temptation to be diverted from his stride by speculating on just what the banquet would be like. In his own way, he had developed a quiet but strong trust that his pilgrimage would be well worth any hardship, whatever exactly lay at the end. Besides, his journey seemed to him little enough effort compared to the sacrifices of other people that he knew, and especially compared with the sacrifice which his host had made for him and for everyone else.

The sun was getting low in the sky and the road was becoming more steep now, climbing out of the stark desert and promising a landscape of pleasing aspect. The heat of the day was past, and the cool of the evening was suggested by breezes that caressed him with every step. Still, he kept his face turned toward the destination. Occasionally, his mind would return to his erstwhile companions, but he refused to let himself speculate on their reception at the banquet hall, concerned only that, for himself, the generous invitation required the courtesy of a timely arrival. He had been a person who never considered himself outstanding in any particular way, except that he seemed to have a flair for art and music, and he was no less amazed than his own parents at his talents, since there had been no history of such aptitude in his family. He regarded it all as a gift, for which he was humbly thankful, and was even somewhat perplexed why anyone would compliment him on his paintings or his singing.

In company with his parents, he had attended a meeting one day near his home at which several people had spoken, including the older gentleman who had been his companion on the journey. In spite of the fact that some of those at the meeting had made him feel a little unwelcome, since he was new to the group, he had found the stories they told to be wondrous beyond measure, and they produced within him a warmth and a desire to give everything he had in the service of the one about whom the stories were told. He had been initiated and declared his trust, and had been asked if he would be willing to deliver the leftover refreshments from the meetings—there were always more than were needed—to those of the group who were ill or disabled or who for some other reason were unable to attend the meeting, or who simply could not afford to buy their own food. He appreciated the opportunity to be of service to the one who had sacrificed so much for him. He was surprised to discover how much he enjoyed his visits in the homes where he made his deliveries. He had just been getting up the courage to offer his artistic talents in making posters and his musical talents in the choir when the invitation had come, and of course he had accepted the privilege of making the journey. The fact that the road would take him through an unknown territory had not troubled him, for he was confident that the one who had already sacrificed so much for him had taken into account the hazards of the journey, and that even if misfortune befell him on the way, it was a joyful thing to know that he had been invited and that he was responding to the invitation.

Finally, just as the sun was about to set, the road led the young man over the crest of a hill, and the great banquet hall which was his destination appeared in full view. The front door was open—he could see light shining out from it and could hear the sound of singing from inside. Though he had been walking all day, in his excitement, he hastened his stride and eventually broke into a run which took him right up the steps and through the doorway and into the waiting arms of his host, whose kind face beamed with joy as the young man hugged him and buried his face in his robes.

"How good of you to come!" said the host in tender sincerity as the crowd looked on, smiling.

"It was a privilege just to be invited," replied the young man, now speaking through tears. "I don't know what I did to deserve it."

His host just smiled and said gently, "Come, let me introduce you to the others, and then I have a special place set for you at the table."

The young man looked around to see the people, obviously from every corner of the world and dressed in every sort of clothing, including many in rags, some of them dirty and unwashed, some of them diseased, some dressed well and the very picture of health. "But first," said his host, "I must close the door, for it is turning cold and stormy outside, and we must shut out the bluster and the thunder."

The young man had never known such a wonderful time as he experienced at that feast, in such congenial company and with such a kind and generous host. It was the most marvelous party anyone could have imagined. But with the sound of feasting and gaiety inside, and the storm raging outside, no one noticed later that evening the two faces pressed hard against the little window in the door of the banquet hall. If the party guests would have looked, they would have seen a rain-soaked older gentleman and a middle-aged woman in party clothes, certainly not dressed with the expectation of being caught out of doors on a stormy night. If they had been aware of it, they would have seen their host getting up from his place at the table upon finally hearing the pounding at the door, and his opening it just a crack to see who had been foolish enough to be caught outside on such a night. They might have watched the pair gesticulating wildly and appealing argumentatively as the host shook his head with a sigh and once more closed the door to them and the storm's blast. If their attention had been on the lightning and thunder rather than on their feast, they might have caught a glimpse through the windows of the hall of the older gentleman and woman now shouting, now cursing, now shaking their fists, and finally turning away and disappearing into the stormy night. But inside, the party just went on and on.

Twenty-Second Sunday in Ordinary Time

Jeremiah 2:4–13
Hebrews 13:1–8, 15–16
Luke 14:1, 7–14

"Angel in Our Midst"

It had not been a good week for Gabe Smith. There *was* the sack of apples behind the produce market that had been tossed out with the spoiled things—a mistake, he thought, which he almost drew to the manager's attention, but he was afraid that he would get into trouble for rummaging through the dumpster if he had to explain how he'd come across a sack of perfectly good fruit. He was still rather new at having to live on the streets. He had simply relied on promises too long at his job—mainly promises about paychecks that never materialized. And then the day had come when he went to work and discovered the door locked, and the owner of the company nowhere to be found. It seemed that the owner had gone back east, at least that's what the manager of the building where the office was located had heard. Wherever he was, he had left Gabe and the handful of other employees penniless and virtually powerless to pursue any private legal remedy. The public prosecutor's office had been sympathetic, but said, essentially, it's a big country, and without any more information about where to find his former employer—one Richard Johnson—they really couldn't be of much help.

The unemployment insurance had terminated three weeks ago, and Gabe, unable to find another job in a down-turning economy, without money to move to another town, and already behind on child support payments because of his employer's dishonesty, had found himself sleeping in a dingy and noisy residential hotel and without any money for food. So he had, for the first time in his life, been patrolling alleys and lanes, competing with other homeless people and drug addicts for anything edible. He had witnessed things that he had never seen before or even imagined, things that at first disgusted him, then angered him, then tugged at his heart. The people that he passed along the backside of stores and shops and flop houses had at first seemed quite alien and frightening, but during the past few days, it had occurred to him that there was no essential difference between him and them, no matter that he had attended university for two years, no matter that he had, until the divorce, lived in his own house with a lawn and a garage with two cars in it, albeit that he had bought them both used. He and his wife and two children used to go to the beach, to the park, to the movies. Now he contemplated the possibility that he might spend the rest of his life like this—earning a few dollars with a broom or a shovel, enough to pay for one week's lodging, in advance, and dining on other people's garbage. He couldn't afford to flip hamburgers—couldn't afford to wait until the end of a pay period, and nobody that he talked to among the few businesses that had taken his application was willing to make an advance on wages, and the very request seemed to prejudice them against his application. In the meantime, just finding enough to stay alive was occupying most of each day.

Gabe emerged from behind a row of industrial supply stores on Powell Street, having found nothing in the way of food, of course, and nothing in the way of junk that appeared to have a salvage value. There had been a portable stereo in the first dumpster at the opposite end of the block, but a young man with long, stringy hair and wearing a dirty tee shirt had appeared and snatched it out of his hands as soon as he had extracted it from the receptacle. The man's eyes revealed that he was on drugs; Gabe did not pursue him as he dashed out into the light of the street. Gabe had had no food all that day, and no one wanted their place swept out, and it looked like he would have to go back to his little room hungry. It was simply too dangerous to be scrounging in this neighborhood after dark. One more block, he decided, before either giving up for the day or taking his chance behind some restaurant where he would have to compete with several other hungry people.

He crossed Jackson Avenue and found himself in new territory—none of the buildings looked familiar, though, of course, very few shops and stores were remarkable from the rear. He seemed to have the block to himself, but he soon decided that he was too late to find anything of nutritional or monetary value. The dumpsters were all well picked over, and it was about five o'clock. He sat down on a concrete step at the backdoor of one of the buildings near the west end of the alley, no longer offended by the sticky stains of spilled this and that that seemed to be a standard feature of his new environment, deciding whether to wait around until the after-dinner refuse was set out behind some restaurant or another.

Down at the end of the alley, he noticed, was a building that was different from the others. It had a peaked roof, which now was in silhouette against the pinkish sky, and the rear of the building sat *in* from the alley itself. He dropped his gaze down to the street level, and noticed a picket fence. Curious, Gabe stood up and walked toward the building, which gradually came more into view around the corner of the building next to it. It was constructed of dressed stone, he noticed—different from the crumbling brick and stucco of the other buildings on the block. The picket fence, he now saw, enclosed a shallow backyard that contained a small flower garden. Drawn by the only color he had seen all day amid the grays and browns of the alleys, Gabe leaned over the fence to inspect the early autumn blossoms. What was this place that was so *different* from all the *other* buildings that someone cared even to grow flowers at the *rear* where few people would ever see them? He walked out onto the sidewalk and saw the stained glass windows that gave away its identity. Just then, the sound of bells poured out from the tower at the corner of the building that was nearest the street intersection. He looked up and noticed that the tower had a little door that opened out onto the pitched roof. Above the door was a louvered opening, matched by similar openings on the street sides, screening the chamber where the bells were located. On the whole, the building was neat and well kept, but he noticed that some of the shingles on the lower courses of the roof were loose, dangling slightly.

Gabe walked back to the flower garden to enjoy a last bit of color before the light disappeared. As he again leaned over the fence, the backdoor of the church building opened, and a woman emerged, holding a pair of shears. "Hello," she said. "How are you today?"

"Oh," Gabe said, "I was just looking at the flowers."

"They've done well this year," she said in a conversational tone very different from most of the talk Gabe had become accustomed to in the alleys. "Would you like some?" she asked, holding up the shears to indicate her purpose.

"They're very nice," he said, "but I'm not sure where I would put them. I don't have my own place just now, and I don't really have anything to keep them in—I mean, I don't have a vase or anything."

"Well," she said, "I think we could find something. I surely have some tin cans lying about. Come in," she said, holding the little wooden gate open for him.

Gabe had not experienced such friendliness at backdoors or front ones, for that matter, since he had been on the streets. "Come on," she said, not impatiently but kindly, noticing that he was hesitating to accept her first invitation. "I'm getting some flowers to put on the tables at a dinner we're having tonight. But you tell me which ones you would like first."

"I've always been partial to roses," Gabe said. "We used to have roses in our yard . . ." His voice trailed off. The woman looked at him for a moment with a slight smile, then went over to the rosebush that had the largest blooms, deep red. "But if you'd rather take them for your dinner—" he began.

"No," she said, "you take your pick, and I'll gather some other ones for the tables. There's plenty to choose from." She paused, and then said, "They'll all be fading soon, I'm afraid. But they're so nice while we have them."

"They certainly add color back here," Gabe said, watching from a respectful distance.

"Do you have plans for dinner?" the woman asked as she cut six or eight stems from the bush, her back to Gabe.

Gabe was not expecting such a question, and cleared his throat before answering. "Well, I hadn't . . . no, not exactly."

"Well, we would be honored to have you as our guest." She turned and held out the roses for his inspection and looked into his face with an expression that said she was awaiting an answer.

"Well, thank you," he said, then paused, not knowing what to do or say next. Then he recalled his situation, and said, "But I'm afraid I'm not really dressed for—"

"Nonsense," she said. "You look fine. The question is whether you would do us the honor."

"Honor?" he said. "Well, yes, of course. Thank you very much."

"By the way, I'm sorry, I forgot my manners. My name is Ruth—Ruth Groves." She transferred the roses and the shears from her right hand to her left, and held out her right hand toward him. "I'm one of the members here, and I'm in charge of the congregational dinner tonight. I hope that you like roast beef with the trimmings," she said as she turned back to cut some additional flowers.

Gabe could not believe what he was hearing. "Yes, ma'am, that would be wonderful."

"It's a fellowship meal that we have each quarter, and then we'll have just a short meeting to finish planning our fall festival for next month." She straightened up and turned back to face him, both hands now full of flowers. "Come right on in," she said, taking a step toward the backdoor from which she had come. "No, wait a minute," she said. Gabe wondered if she had changed her mind about the invitation. "Let me bring you in the *front* door. The back room is sort of a mess." She asked Gabe if he would mind closing the door, then he held the gate open for her and the two of them walked down the sidewalk and around the front of the church building and up a short flight of steps to the front door. "Thank you," she said as he held the door open for her. A stairway descended from the vestibule toward a lower level of the building. "The kitchen and refectory are downstairs," she explained, leading the way. Gabe was not sure that he had ever known what a refectory was, but when they reached the bottom of the stairs, he found himself in a large dining room with several tables and chairs, the tables covered with white lace tablecloths and set with china, crystal, and silverware.

"This is very nice," he said, as much to himself as to his hostess.

"Yes, isn't it lovely? The china was a gift from one of our dear members, and different groups within the church purchased the other things over the years."

Gabe smelled the aromas of cooking, and noticed a swinging door to what must be the kitchen. "May I help you in some way?" he asked.

"No, no, you're our guest. Besides, I think that I have everything pretty well in hand."

"Well, at least let me put the other flowers on the tables," he suggested, noticing that there were already flower vases in place.

"Well, all right," Ruth said. "Arrange them however you would like." She handed him the flowers, and walked back into the kitchen.

Before he finished, three more people came down the stairs into the room—two women and a man. The two women nodded toward him as they went to the kitchen, but the man came over to the table where he was arranging the last batch of flowers. "I'm Henry Lewis," he said, holding out his hand. "I don't think we've met."

"I'm Gabe Smith," Gabe said, wiping his hand on his pant leg before extending it toward Henry.

"Glad to meet you. Are you new to the area?"

"Not exactly," said Gabe, "but I've never been *here* before."

"Well," said Henry, "this is a very special place."

Gabe nodded in agreement.

"I suppose I'd better go see how I can help the ladies," Henry said. "I'll look forward to visiting with you at dinner."

Gabe sat down in a corner of the room, feeling a little disoriented. This evening was totally different from anything he had experienced since his unemployment benefits expired. He had seen nothing so genteel, had not been spoken to so kindly, in weeks. Four additional people descended the stairs into the dining hall but did not notice Gabe in the corner as they walked straight toward the kitchen. Then some others arrived as the helpers were filling glasses with water and setting out coffee- and teapots, found their places at the tables and, when they noticed Gabe in the corner of the room, nodded toward him and mouthed the word "Hello," to which Gabe responded with a nod. One of the men who came out of the kitchen was a young man wearing a clerical collar under his black dress coat. He looked around the room, which was now filling with people of all ages. When he saw Gabe, he walked toward him.

"Mrs. Groves said that we had a guest this evening," he said to Gabe when he reached where he was sitting. "We're happy that you're here. My name is David Burton."

He held out his hand, which Gabe reciprocated as he stood up and said, "I'm Gabe Smith."

"We're just about ready to eat," Reverend Burton said. "Won't you sit with me up front here?" he asked, gesturing toward the front of the dining hall.

"But I'm not a member of the church or anything," Gabe stammered. "I'm fine back here. I've been digging through dumpsters all day. I'm not dressed—"

"But you are our guest. We're honored to have you with us. Please . . ." The young man in the black coat put one hand on Gabe's shoulder and gestured again toward the front of the dining hall. Gabe finally yielded to his invitation. As they reached the head table, Gabe sat down alongside Reverend Burton, who welcomed everyone to the dinner, and then announced that they were very happy that evening to have a special guest, Gabe Smith, who was a church neighbor. Following the clergyman's example, everyone applauded as Gabe stood partway up from his chair and nodded sheepishly. "Let us give thanks," Reverend Burton said, and as Gabe folded his hands and bowed his head, he tried to make the words his own, praying perhaps more intensely than he had for a long time. "We thank you, O Lord, for the bounty that you have set before us, and for our ability to share it with one another. Your goodness is always more than we deserve, and is always just what we need. Bless our meal and our fellowship with the presence of your Spirit that we may serve Christ Jesus, in whose name we pray. Amen."

Gabe echoed the "Amen" audibly, with a concentration that prevented him from noticing that he was the *only* one. But following *his* speaking the word, a chorus of voices from around the room added their "Amen" to his. Within seconds, Henry Lewis appeared in front of him with a plate, covered with a thick slice of roast beef, along with Yorkshire pudding, a baked potato, and creamed spinach. "Ruth wanted to be sure that this is the way you like it," he said as he gently set the plate down in front of Gabe, "—not too rare and not too well done."

"It looks perfect," Gabe said in a voice barely audible. Then he turned to Reverend Burton, who was the next to be served. "You don't even know me. Why? How?"

Reverend Burton responded by handing him a basket of dinner rolls that had been placed on the table in front of him. "Would you like a roll?" he asked, smiling, as half a dozen people brought plates out of the kitchen and now began serving the *others* who were seated at the tables.

Gabe felt compelled to explain his present circumstances to Reverend Burton, which he did, in pieces, during the course of the meal. The minister listened, nodding in sympathetic understanding, sometimes with tears in his eyes, which then became mutual as Gabe thought of his children and the home that he had once had. "Would you be free to come and eat with my family this weekend?"

"Well, I'm not sure," Gabe said, clearing his throat and raising his napkin to his mouth.

"Why don't you think about it and let me know?" the minister asked. At one point, during the dessert of custard and fruit, Reverend Burton said, "Ruth tells me that you like flowers. Especially roses."

"I had a little rose garden," Gabe said, and looked down at his plate.

"May I get you more of anything?" Henry Lewis asked just then, standing in front of him on the opposite side of the table.

"No, thank you, but please tell Mrs. Groves that it was just wonderful."

Henry smiled and nodded.

Reverend Burton stood up. "While we're finishing our dessert," he said in a loud voice to quiet the crowd, "I wonder if we could hear some reports about preparations for the fall festival. Alex Crawford, I believe you're in charge of publicity."

A young man, about age thirty, stood up on the far side of the room. "As you know, I'm leading the youth group this year. We have made a large banner announcing the festival, which we thought we could hang from the roof on the side of the building by the bell tower, so that everyone can see it passing along on either Dunlevy Avenue or Powell Street."

"That's fine," said the minister. "But how will you get it up there?"

"The kids thought they could just go out the old roof access through the bell tower and nail it to the shingles, and then let it dangle over the edge of the roof. It's made of heavy canvas, so it shouldn't flap around too much if a breeze comes along."

Gabe's face turned white and he stood up. "No, no, don't do that," he said with urgency in his voice. "I was walking alongside the church today, and I noticed that several of those shingles by the bell tower are loose. If anyone would set foot on them, they'd give way and someone would fall."

"I sure didn't know that," Alex Crawford responded with surprise. "We don't want anyone to get hurt. I'm glad you noticed." Then he added, "Thank God you're here."

Gabe and Alex Crawford both sat down, and the room was silent for several seconds before Reverend Burton stood up again. "Bill Davis, I think the building committee ought to have a look at the roof, and put a sign up on the door in the bell tower that no one is to go out on the roof until the shingles are replaced."

"First thing tomorrow," a voice confirmed from near the middle of the room.

"We have an angel to thank," the minister said, looking down at Gabe and speaking on behalf of all those present, "—a messenger from God."

Several people spoke to Gabe when the dinner and the meeting concluded, thanking him for joining them that night, and thanking him for alerting them to the condition of the roof before a disaster had occurred. One older woman asked him to come over to a little stand in the corner of the room and sign the church guest book. "Gabe," she said, "we like to keep a record of all of our guests." The book was an old leather-bound volume with an ornate cover which she carefully opened, and then handed him a pen. Impressed by the solemnity of writing in such an elegant book, Gabe spelled out his full name, then handed the pen back to the woman. She looked down at what he had written. "Oh, but of course," she said, looking back up at him with a gleam in her eye. "You're Gabriel."

Twenty-Fifth Sunday in Ordinary Time

Proverbs 31:10–31
James 3:13—4:3, 7–8a
Mark 9:30–37

"First Things First"

Alex McClelland sat at the desk in his little office reading over the monthly sales report from the Oakville store. For some reason, the store simply wasn't showing the sales volume that it ought to for such a fast-growing, middle-class suburban area. The location was prime, on a principal thoroughfare with good visibility, and it was an attractive store. Alex had stopped in one day the previous month and talked about the figures with the store manager, who seemed competent and was certainly knowledgeable about their product lines. The sales staff seemed attentive and courteous, helpful but not pushy.

He stood up and went to the file cabinet, opened a drawer and pulled out a file folder marked "Oakville Monthly Sales" and laid it down on his desk, opened it, and flipped through the past few entries under the clasp. He sighed, slipped the clasp open, and added the latest report to the stack. Monday over lunch, he decided, he would drive back out to the store and sit down with the manager and verify the figures and try to determine why its sales profile deviated so dramatically from those of the rest of the chain. Such matters were not his responsibility, but he wanted to help the man if he could, and doing so under the guise of rechecking the figures was a plausible approach. Besides, after so many years with the company, Alex had some ideas of his own about what made a store successful or not.

"Hey, Alex, guess what?" He looked up from his desk to see the face of Amy Howell poking through his partially open doorway.

"What?" Alex replied, pushing his reading glasses up on his forehead. "You won the lottery?"

"Better," said the dark-haired woman, dressed smartly in a red blazer and plaid skirt. "Promotion. Assistant vice president of marketing." She was beaming. "And the first thing I'm going to do is move out of that cracker box in Aurora and find a place in Scarborough"—by which, Alex knew, she meant she was planning to trade her long commute from a cookie-cutter tract house in the far northern suburbs for a larger home in a more fashionable neighborhood.

Alex and Amy had joined the company at about the same time, both working in accounting. In fact, Alex was just starting to have confidence in his ability to find his space in the parking garage when she had pulled her Mazda into the space next to it that had been vacant for the two weeks or so that he had been employed by Great Buys, Ltd., a local electronics and appliance retailer with eleven outlets and soon to open its twelfth.

"That's great," Alex said, not without a genuine feeling of congratulation. Amy had seemed to be a hard worker when the two of them were in the same department. As far as he knew, she really deserved the promotion, though he was also aware of rumors that had begun after an office Christmas party. "When do you start?" Alex asked.

"First of the month," Amy answered, then looked at her watch. "Hey, it's way after five o'clock. See you next week," she said, waving as she turned to go down the hall.

Alex returned the file folder to the cabinet, looked at the stack of other file folders on his desk, and sighed. A couple of departmental crises had kept him from sifting through as much material as he had expected to this week, once again. He would try to come in Saturday evening to take care of at least some of it, after the children had gone to bed.

As Alex stood waiting for the elevator, Don Andrews joined him. "Runnin' late," the younger man said, pulling his cuff up from what appeared to be an expensive wristwatch. Alex seldom saw Don anymore since he had been promoted to be the company's purchasing manager.

"Amy Howell just told me that she's the new assistant VP of marketing," Alex shared, more to make conversation than anything.

"Replacing Pete Reynolds," Don Andrews nodded knowingly. "You know he got snapped up by Micro City." He added after a pause, "I remember when we were all down in accounting together. Wasn't that an awful bore?"

The door slid open, revealing an elevator car already filled with people from the upper floors of the office building heading home or to a cottage for the weekend. Don Andrews squeezed his way into the car, producing frowns from some of the passengers who considered the elevator to be already full. Don looked back at Alex with a sheepish expression. "Sorry, old man," he said over the heads of the people around him. "Let's do golf sometime. Not tomorrow, though—going out with the boss. Got to schmooze to get ahead, you know." He was chuckling as the elevator door closed, leaving Alex alone again to push the "Down" button and wait for the next car. After a minute or so, another elevator opened and Alex joined the four others in the compartment.

When the elevator reached the level marked "P1," Alex emerged into the subterranean garage and turned in the direction of his parking stall. Half a dozen spaces from the small elevator lobby, and much closer to it than his own parking place, he saw Don Andrews again, pounding on the roof of his Lexus and uttering a curse. Don looked up and saw Alex walking in his direction.

"Would you believe it? The battery's dead, and I'm supposed to be at the club in thirty minutes for drinks with—well, to meet someone. Do you have cables, by chance?"

"Yes, I believe so," said Alex, "unless my wife or the kids have taken them out."

Don Andrews followed him toward his beige Ford Taurus, alone at the far end of the garage. "Didn't know they let those things in here," Don said, laughing. Alex shrugged. "Seriously, man, you need something with some style."

"It gets me where I need to go," Alex replied, smarting a bit at the comment. "And the family. Plus, I carry a lot of stuff around . . ."

They reached the car and Alex opened the trunk. "We're in luck. They're here." He pulled out the twin set of battery cables and closed the trunk lid. "Why don't you go ahead and get them on your battery while I drive over there?"

"Sure," said Don, receiving them from Alex's hands as if they were snakes which he held dangling out away from his light-colored sports jacket.

Alex pulled his Ford into the empty parking space alongside Don's Lexus and pulled the release handle for his hood. Don was gingerly attaching the cables to the terminals of his battery. After checking to make certain that he was attaching positive to positive, Alex attached the remaining negative end to the chassis, then started the ignition. Don got into the Lexus, turned the ignition, and gunned the engine a few times, filling the underground chamber with a thunderous roar.

"Great, thanks," Don shouted over the noise of the engines, removing the cables from his battery and then pausing. "I sure hope I don't end up with a dead battery later tonight at the club."

"Well, feel free to take the cables with you in case," Alex said. "I shouldn't need them this weekend. We're not going out of town or anything. You can give them back on Monday."

"Right," said Don somewhat absently. "Good. Or I could bring them to you tomorrow afternoon. But I suppose you'll be out golfing or something."

"No, not golfing," Alex said.

"Great game, golf," said Don. "Great for climbing the ladder, at any rate. You know," he winked, "there's more than one game going on when you play with the boss."

Alex gave him a look showing that he didn't quite comprehend what Don had said.

"You know, getting *ahead*. *That's* what it's all about. How do you think I escaped from accounting, and then the lower echelons of purchasing? I don't know how you stand poring over numbers all day long. Maybe investing some time buttering up the boss would get you out of that closet they give you for an office and into someplace that you could see the light of day."

Alex did not respond, and still looked like he had not fully understood what Don was saying. Don shook his head dramatically and sighed, then checked his watch again. "Monday, then," he said, getting in his car and pulling the door closed. Alex stood watching the taillights on the Lexus disappear up the ramp to Sheppard Avenue.

Alex had been dimly aware that all of the people he had worked with in accounting over the years had been promoted into better-paying positions within the company, or had left for positions with more authority and higher pay in other companies. The president of Great Buys had interviewed him for other positions within the company from time to time, but, in the end, someone else had always gotten the promotion—usually someone who had been with the company for less time than Alex had. Alex did not mind being passed over for promotion—did not mind very *much*, anyway—although he had long since grown tired of some of his friends asking him if he was "still" the senior accountant for sales. The "senior" part seemed to have as much to do with his relative age as with his experience with the company; everyone else in the department was younger than he was. He had never thought of doing anything else when he was in accounting at university; his instructors never suggested that being a staff accountant was merely a stepping stone to bigger and better things. He was paid decently if not generously, and his family was comfortable, thanks of course to his wife's employment, too. Their lifestyle was not lavish, but there was always food on the table. His house was not large, but it was adequate for their needs. His automobile was not impressive, but it was safe and reliable. His children were not in private schools, but their grades were good and they each had a circle of trustworthy and well-mannered friends. It would be nice to have an office with a window, he had often thought—that much luxury would be appreciated. His superiors were pleasant enough, and generally treated their employees fairly, although as competition had sliced profit margins in retail electronics, everyone's workload, at least in accounting, had been increasing without any commensurate increase in pay.

As Alex drove up the ramp to the street, first stopping at the sidewalk and then pulling out into the traffic that was beginning to thin as the rush hour waned, he thought about the upward momentum of his colleagues. There came to mind some of his own possibilities for promotion, unfulfilled. There suddenly dawned on him a coincidence of which he had not thought before—it had to do with the occasion, just a few months previously, when he had been told that, after fourteen years with the company, he was under consideration for the position of vice president of accounting. It was shortly after that that the vice president for *sales* had called him to *his* office and complained about the way he had been classifying one category of sales figures. Alex had explained the reasoning behind what he had done, which seemed rather straightforward according to general accounting principles, but the vice president had said that the way he was doing it did not support as rosy a picture as he had been reporting to the president. It was, after all, he had said, simply a matter of interpretation. No, Alex had replied, it had to do with generally accepted accounting standards, and uniformity in reporting required classifying the entries as he had done. The meeting had ended with the vice president dismissing him rather brusquely. He had not been informed of any adverse outcome either to the vice president or to the company, but it was within a few days of that meeting that Alex had been told that he was no longer being considered for the vice presidency of accounting. When he had inquired why, the president had responded with a soliloquy about working as a team and achieving the optimum mix of people and positions. Within a few months, the vice president for sales had resigned or had been fired—it wasn't quite clear in the account that had reached Alex's ears.

The pavement was wet as he drove north toward the suburban sprawl of Markham, where his family occupied a house probably not unlike the one that Amy Howell described as her "cracker box." There had been a thunderstorm, apparently, unbeknownst to him inside his windowless cubicle. The air was heavy with midsummer humidity and the sky overhead still looked ominous, gray clouds laden with moisture that surely could not be any wetter than the atmosphere closer to the ground. The windshield wipers slapped down the water being splashed up by the car in front of him. He thought of tomorrow's schedule—as usual on Saturday, he would make the rounds of the collection boxes, then deliver what had been donated, then, after lunch, head to the community center for the game. His little fellows had been coming along pretty well this year. He had almost asked to be relieved of the weekly coaching duty, taking as much time as it did from being with his own children, but the community center director had called him in early March and had begun the conversation with how good it was to be able to rely on people like him to form the backbone of the summer sports program. So many, she said, would prefer to be on the golf course or at the beach or away at a cottage somewhere that she worried each year whether there would be enough adults to accommodate the children who had registered. Actually, the same thought had arisen in Alex's mind, and the same speech had been given by the director for about four years now.

On Saturday morning, the sky was blue and the air was clean as a front had pushed the humidity on to the south and east. As usual, for a Saturday morning, Alex left home at about ten o'clock and drove to the half-dozen collection boxes located at various strip malls around Markham, picking up the broken and bruised toys that had been left there during the week. Then he drove over to the home and workshop of Lloyd Wilson, a retired pharmacist who spent his days repairing the donated items for distribution through St. Andrew's Church to low-income children at Christmas. As usual, while they were carrying the cardboard boxes into Lloyd's workshop from the backseat and trunk of Alex's car, Alex commented on Lloyd's generous gift of time for the effort. "You do a wonderful thing," Alex said, "bringing happiness to so many children."

"*We* do a wonderful thing," Lloyd corrected him, setting a box down on his workbench. "For me, it's no great sacrifice. I enjoy working with my hands, and my days"—he waved his right hand in the air. "I've got plenty of time to do this sort of thing. I was a kid once, and we had some lean times. I'm just getting something useful out of my hobby. But *you*," he said, turning and looking Alex straight in the eyes, "I know you've got other things you could be doing. Your family, for instance." Alex had sometimes brought along one or both of his children on his Saturday morning collections and delivery. "So stop making me the hero. *You* got the permission to set up the boxes. *You* monitor them and keep them in repair. *You* do the collecting, and then *you* take the toys and make all the arrangements at Christmas."

Alex turned his eyes away momentarily, and then said, "Well, I still thank you. And I'll see you in church tomorrow."

All fifteen of Alex's team members were present when Alex arrived at the community center at one-thirty, and he was already beginning to think about how to rotate them through the nine positions and batting order. He always tried to let every child play about the same number of innings and have the same number of at-bats. He was impressed that the community center director emphasized letting the kids learn and have fun rather than stressing competition. After all, they were just children, she said. They needed to learn to trust others and develop confidence in themselves. So there were no failures, just always room for learning.

It was in the third inning, with two outs, two on base, and two strikes on the batter, that little red-haired Terry Anderson tried too hard to make an inning-ending catch of a fly ball to center field. No one quite understood how he tripped. "I'm sorry I dropped the ball," he said through the tears. "You're not mad, are you, Mr. McClelland?"

"No, of course not, Terry. Why would I be mad?" Alex asked, examining the badly skinned elbow. "Do you think you can get up?" He wasn't sure whether the child might have broken or sprained something.

"I . . . I think so," sniffed Terry, tears still rolling down his cheeks.

"We'll put a bandage on that. Then I think your folks ought to take you home to wash it off and put some disinfectant on it."

"They're not here."

"Can we call them?"

"Mom's at some seminar or something," he said, limping a little as Alex supported him under his undamaged arm.

"How about your dad?"

"He's playing golf," Terry said, "with his boss."

Thirtieth Sunday in Ordinary Time

Joel 2:23–32
2 Timothy 4:6–8, 16–18
Luke 18:9–14

"Not Like These Sinners"

Adam Foster leaned back in his chair and smiled at the telephone on his large mahogany desk. He had just set the receiver back in its cradle after a thirty-minute conversation that finally, after months of patient negotiation, had ironed out the last few sticking points in the deal that was his crowning achievement as president of New Fortune Mining Company. He had wanted one more major accomplishment before retirement. Sewing up the platinum prospect known as Bright Hope—Esperanza Clara, in the native Spanish language of the country—and finding a partner for a joint venture to develop the deposit, was it. Never had anyone connected with the company seen values like the test holes had disclosed.

His own interest in New Fortune Mining Company guaranteed an income in the tens of millions of dollars over the next twenty years of projected ore recovery. But he would not wait for that. Already, he had a buyer for his interest in the company. His family had wanted him to retire at age sixty, then sixty-five. He was now a few days short of his seventieth birthday, and he would make a present of retirement to himself and his wife, his son and his daughter, and his grandchildren. All those years of travel away from home—in the field, early on, and, later, hammering out deals and encouraging his managers in locations from northern Ontario to southern Argentina and half a dozen countries in between—were now paying off handsomely, but he had some time to make up for with those who were dearest to him. Honest, ethical, hard-working—everybody in the business described him the same way. And now, it was time for leisure travel—to see the kids, to see the sights—and to volunteer and make donations for causes he held dear—his university, medical research, his church.

Thinking of this, he picked up the phone again, checked a number in the spiral notebook that was one of the few articles atop the shiny surface of his desk, and dialed it. "Reverend Matthews, please," he said into the receiver. "This is Adam Foster." After a few seconds, he spoke again. "David, this is Adam Foster. Fine, thank you. I hope that you are. About that matter that we spoke of a couple of months ago . . . yes, yes. I am now in a position to make a major donation to start that project along." He smiled broadly as he heard words of appreciation and congratulations from the other end of the line. "Are you available to meet tomorrow for about half an hour? Maybe late afternoon on my way home? Splendid. I'll look forward to seeing you then. Yes, bye now."

He hung up the phone and swiveled his chair around. As he did, his glance passed over the photographs of his family displayed on his credenza, and photographs also of some of the New Fortune Mining Company's mine sites around the western hemisphere. Soon, there would be *another* added to the collection. His eye also passed over the small collection of popular religious books that expounded on management principles that various authors had extracted from the Bible, some of which had become bestsellers. Amongst them was nestled a copy of the Bible itself, well thumbed and underlined here and there. And, as he got up out of his chair, he also saw the framed calligraphy that spelled out the Golden Rule, hung prominently alongside the bookcase. He had scheduled a meeting with his chief geologist to receive a report on the latest test hole at Bright Hope and get an update on some other matters. After that, he would go home and deliver the news that he expected would gladden the heart of his wife—on his seventieth birthday, he would announce his retirement from the presidency of the company that he had started almost thirty years earlier after having worked his way up in the business from being a graduate mining engineer with Noranda, and that he would be selling his ownership interest to another highly reputable company, retaining only a royalty interest in the Bright Hope property, which should see him comfortably through the rest of his life. He had secured a pledge that all of his employees would keep their jobs with virtually the same responsibilities and at comparable pay. After all, they had been as much a part of New Fortune's success as he himself.

"Well, Pete, we've done the deal," Adam Foster announced to his chief geologist, Peter McCann.

The geologist returned the smile. "That's great," he said. "We're ready to go on this end."

"Now," the company president said, looking at one of the maps on the wall of the geologist's office that was punctuated with colored pins, "what did test hole BH-34 tell you?"

The next day was filled with rather routine matters for Adam Foster, but at a few minutes before four o'clock, still feeling buoyed by the Bright Hope deal, he descended to the underground parking garage, backed his car out of its assigned spot and drove up the ramp to Burrard Street, and traveled a few blocks to the modern concrete block church building on Thurlow Street where he and his family had been members for many years. The receptionist greeted him with a pleasant exchange, and waved him into the pastor's study, saying that Reverend Matthews was expecting him. The minister stood up and offered him a chair as he circled around his desk and sat down in a chair beside him.

"Good to see you, Adam. That was very good news indeed you called with yesterday. That would be a fine complement to our homeless ministry. As it happens, our community outreach and long-term planning committees are both meeting tonight. If I may, I'd like to introduce the subject this evening, and call for a joint meeting next week for you to come speak to them, if that's convenient."

"Yes, I'm in town all next week as it looks now. Would this same night next week be good?"

"I think so," the minister said, reaching for his calendar. "Yes," he confirmed, "and I think most of the committee people will be available—at least there are no conflicts on the church calendar. This could be the start of a wonderful new chapter of community service for Central Church." They stood and shook hands, and the mining executive left the church office pleased that everything seemed to be falling neatly into place, and genuinely gratified that he was in a position to be doing something positive for the church of which he was a leading member and for the city that had been so good to him.

He turned his car off of Marine Drive into the lane that led to his home, where he found his wife on the terrace that overlooked the river and the airport and suburbs beyond. "I stopped by the church and saw David Matthews. I think that this home for reforming prostitutes and drug addicts has a real chance of getting off the ground," he said, easing himself into a lounge chair that was bathed in the light of the late afternoon sun. "I'm glad that you agreed we needed to do something with our windfall that would help those poor wretches," he said. "It's a disgrace to see them on the streets."

"I think they must be pretty miserable," his wife commented.

"Well, it's not pleasant for any respectable person walking through the East End, either," he responded. "For that matter, you even see them around *our* building, sometimes."

"Anyone in that situation—" his wife began, but Adam Foster finished the sentence.

"Must be very distant from God."

"I was going to say," she said, without raising her voice in correction, "must be very unhappy in life."

Her husband, looking contentedly toward the island in the far distance, grunted softly. Both Mr. and Mrs. Foster felt confirmed in their beliefs when, on the television news that evening, there was a report of a man, known to the neighborhood as a heroin addict, who had been found dead in an alley between Hastings and Pender Streets with no signs of foul play.

"How much do you advise to the university, and how much to the church?" Mr. Foster asked his tax advisor the next day, speaking into the telephone resting on his mahogany desk. "With careful investment, I will intend to give additional similar amounts to the university from time to time. The church gift is to provide the impetus for the project, which I hope will stimulate others to donate as well. Once it gets rolling, I'll want to give from time to time to help maintain the program, but this first gift needs to be large enough to encourage others that the project is for real. If we need to delay one of the gifts 'til next year, let's delay the donation to the university— I really want the church project to get started as soon as possible."

He paused to listen to the response of the man on the other end of the line. "OK. Let me go ahead and announce the church contribution this evening when I lay the plan before the appropriate committees. Good. Thanks."

He hung up the telephone and turned to the written report of his chief geologist, confirming in writing what he had reported orally a few days before. The values from the latest test hole looked very, very promising. Everything pointed toward the Bright Hope prospect turning into the most profitable platinum mine in the western hemisphere. Adam Foster would miss shepherding its full development, but he had certainly had more than his share of handling the details of mine development at other locations over the years. It was time to let someone else bring this one to production while he took his wife on a world cruise and played with his grandchildren and turned his business expertise toward helping some nonprofit organizations, including perhaps being on the board of the halfway house he envisioned for the East End. Unlike government-run havens, this would have an unapologetic spiritual component to it; there would be mandatory Bible study and worship attendance, so that those being served could clearly distinguish between sin and righteousness, and mandatory counseling to deal with the deeper spiritual issues that lay behind the behavioral ones.

When the night of the committee meeting arrived, Adam Foster walked into the church conference room with a list of points he wanted to make during his presentation, and a dozen copies of a prospectus he had drafted for the project. He had a potential site picked out—a small apartment house on Franklin Street that a long-time business associate had purchased for investment a few years earlier, but now wanted to sell. It was structurally sound, relatively clean and well maintained, and modifications could easily be made to enhance its security. He first laid out the need, as he saw it, citing statistics he had secured from the city and statements from experts in the psychology of addiction about the sort of facility and program that would be most likely to yield positive results, plus citations to some religious magazine articles about drugs and prostitution. "Those people are in the clutches of sin," he concluded his presentation. "They need help from people like us. That, of course, means money as well as prayers. Will you join me to help redeem our streets, and to provide an example of what decent Christian folk can do in the face of such evil? Thank God we aren't in the situation they have gotten themselves into. But, with our help, perhaps *they* will come to thank God for people like *us*."

He might have tripped over the person sitting in a dark spot on the sidewalk outside the church, her back propped up against the wall, had he not heard her low agonized moaning, "Oh God! Oh God! Oh God!" As he caught himself, surprised, just before his feet would have collided with her outstretched legs, he heard her say, "He . . . , hel . . . , help . . . me." This, he chose to interpret as an appeal to God, not himself. As he continued walking, her voice dissolved into moaning sobs.

"So they've made it all the way to the church now," he thought to himself.

When he reached his car and got inside, he pulled his cellular telephone from his coat pocket and dialed "911." "I'd like to report a street person in distress on the sidewalk in the 1100 block of Thurlow." He paused, listening, and then responded. "No, nothing like that. I think she's probably an addict having withdrawal or something." He listened again. "No, there's really nothing I can do for her. But I think she needs shelter before it gets cold." Another pause. "OK, thank you." He pressed a button to terminate the call and pressed it again to turn off the cell phone so that he would not be distracted as he made his way out of downtown and along Granville Street toward home.

All in all, Adam Foster thought to himself as he drove home that night, the meeting had gone rather well. There were the skeptics of course, and one could always expect that some naysayers would delay the process, but he had a sense that the merits of his proposal would ultimately garner unanimous approval. Had the incident with the addict occurred on his way *into* the meeting, it would have been an excellent object lesson. He would call Reverend Matthews in the morning and tell him about it—he might be able to use it during conversations with committee members, maybe even work it into Sunday's sermon. Might they name the halfway house in his honor? He quickly tried to banish the thought from his mind as immodest. And yet, it would certainly be an appropriate testimony to his hard work and his reputation for integrity. Nor would it hurt to have a concrete model of civic-mindedness and an example of spiritual uprightness as an encouragement to the community for *others* to strive toward.

He pulled into his long driveway and got out of the car feeling quite satisfied. But when he entered the house, his wife told him there had been an urgent call for him a few minutes earlier. He was to call Peter McCann immediately. "What's wrong?" he said when his chief geologist answered his call.

"On the news tonight. There's been a coup down there. The mining industry has been nationalized, and all private and foreign concessions have been canceled. I called our people, and they confirmed it. Said, in fact—here's the roughest part—that news of the Bright Hope discoveries had something to do with sparking it all. They're not in any danger, but they don't see any way our plans can be salvaged. They've impounded our samples and test results. I'm afraid everything we've invested is gone."

Adam Foster hung up the phone and sat down, frowning at it. "Oh, God," he said. "Oh, God, oh God."

Some people might have said it was unfortunate, others providential, that Adam Foster, despondent as he was, did not attend worship the next Sunday, and therefore missed Reverend Matthews' sermon, which began with the words, "Two men went up to the temple to pray . . ."

Thirty-Second Sunday in Ordinary Time

Haggai 1:15b—2:9
2 Thessalonians 2:1–5, 13–17
Luke 20:27–38

"The God of the Living"

"It's just what the tornado did *here*, only even worse," Wendy Palmer explained, recounting her recent trip to the Holy Land and her tour of the Temple Mount in Jerusalem. "All that's left of the temple, really, is the wall around the Temple Mount, and all these people come to pray there every day. The mosques up on top—they're beautiful, though the people who worship up there, Muslims, have to go through all this security and are always under strict surveillance and the government shuts off their access from time to time. But it wasn't Muslims, of course, who destroyed the Jewish temple. It was the Romans, thirty or forty years after the death of Jesus. But it reminded me so much of what happened to our church."

"Well, our church *building*, anyway," Reverend Miller responded. "The *church* is still here. *We're* still here, though the building was destroyed. And that was a great loss. But the church is first and foremost the people, and, thank goodness, none of us was killed or even hurt, or other people in town, either."

"That was certainly a miracle," Wendy Palmer observed.

"A lot have moved away, though," interjected Tony Simmons. "And they won't be coming back. Left for the big cities, most of them. They'll stay where they've got jobs. And they took their money with them."

"It'll never be like it was," Anna Wilson added, sighing. "The insurance people have made that pretty clear."

"It doesn't mean that it won't be very good," Reverend Miller observed. "It will be different, yes, not as ornate perhaps, but a suitable house for worshiping God and teaching about God and just enjoying being God's people together."

"But we can't replace the memories," Tony Simmons said.

"And so many things that our parents and aunts and uncles and grandparents contributed, all gone now," Anna Wilson sighed again, her eyes starting to glisten with tears.

"We ought to put every dollar into making the new sanctuary just exactly the way it was," John Collins asserted. "That's what's important. Not all this extra stuff, like that youth center business."

"But the youth center was a part of the old building, too," observed Wendy Palmer. "We need *all* those things, and the *town* needs them, too. My children loved coming to all the activities in the youth center, and the town will need a place for wholesome youth events even more now that just about every other youth gathering spot has been damaged or destroyed. The high school gym is gone, and the auditorium. What are the kids to do, especially if the ballpark and skating rink and arts pavilion don't get rebuilt? And if they do eventually get replaced, it's not going to be soon enough to be available to *today's* youth. They will have missed out on so much of what childhood and youth should be about."

The class had obviously gotten off track. It was supposed to be an opportunity for Wendy Palmer to report on her journey to Israel and Palestine, but, like so much about Centerville, the class agenda had become dominated by the storm that had devastated much of the town a few months earlier. The church building, long a fixture in the town, both architecturally and socially, as well as spiritually, had been devastated. The sanctuary, more than a hundred years old but well maintained and an architectural gem listed on the state's register of historic places, had been utterly destroyed, as had the church's fellowship hall and youth center, which had had a basketball court and game rooms and had been a gathering place for the community's youth every weekend, not just the children of the congregation. The Christian education wing was relatively unscathed, miraculously and thanks to the caprice of the tornadic winds, but had not yet been authorized for use by local safety officials and would require some basic cosmetic repairs. After assessment by the insurance adjuster, it was clear that the entire building had been significantly underinsured for many years—the budget always seemed to require across-the-board economizing—and it was also clear that materials and builders would be at a premium for some time, limiting repairs and reconstruction not only in Centerville, but in all of the surrounding damaged communities, as well.

A portable building had been brought to the church site to accommodate worship and a couple of classes before the service, but many regular worshipers stayed away, waiting, as they said, for a "real church" before they would return. The adult class was meeting in the Simmons' living room, but one of the customary participants was confined to a wheelchair and could not gain easy access up the front stairs and through the narrow doorway, and had elected not to try to attend.

"All the beautiful stained glass and the carved wood," Anna Wilson sighed again.

"That's what drew people," John Collins added. "We have to have a beautiful sanctuary, at least as magnificent as it was before."

"But the children!" Wendy Palmer appealed. "We can worship in a youth center, but you can't play basketball in a sanctuary."

Reverend Miller was frustrated by the debate that had been going on within the congregation now for several weeks, which had also paralyzed a Session reluctant to offend any of the church members, all of whose financial support was vital to any rebuilding program, let alone maintaining the intangibles of congregational life. "Perhaps we could allow Wendy to continue with her report of her trip," he ventured. The debate ceased, but there remained a palpable mood of discontent in the room.

"You know," Wendy Palmer noted, "Judaism survived the destruction of the temple by the Romans, like it had survived the destruction of the temple of David by the Babylonians. Our tour guide talked a lot about that."

"I don't see what that has to do with our situation," John Collins said, unwilling to leave the topic of how to get on with rebuilding.

"We would be dishonoring our forebears," Anna Wilson said, "if we didn't devote every bit of our time and energy and money to rebuilding the sanctuary exactly like it was. It's like spitting on their graves."

"That's going a little far," objected Fred Morris, who up until now had kept his silence throughout the morning's discussion, as he did most Sundays. "I don't think we should hobble the future by speculating about the wishes of dead people."

"How can you say such a horrible thing?" Anna Wilson asked, obviously shocked to the core of her being.

"I mean no disrespect," Fred Morris said. "I've only been here about twelve years, and I admit I didn't know all these people you remember, people obviously important in the history of this church and of this town. But we're in danger of worshiping a structure, I think."

Reverend Miller decided it was time to intervene again. "What is it that our ancestors were building here, and why? I think that's important to think about. Yes, they sacrificed much for this church building and for this town. But what was their motive, do we think? What was their purpose? It might help, in considering all of this, to reflect on what the Bible says about rebuilding the temple in Jerusalem when the exiles returned from Babylon. Several of the books of the Old Testament address that."

"And a rebuilt temple that itself was destroyed almost two thousand years ago and has never been built again," observed Wendy Palmer.

"The sanctuary must be rebuilt," said John Collins. "It must come first. And anything else right now would delay that, maybe make it impossible."

"The Session is looking at our options, taking all of our needs into consideration," said Reverend Miller.

John Collins grumbled something unintelligible, but no one asked him to repeat it.

"You know," Fred Morris spoke again, "at this very moment, over in the portable, we have a couple of dedicated church members who are teaching a children's class and a youth class, in the same room and without tables and other things that we all took for granted in Sunday school, not ideal conditions, but trying mightily to help the younger generation to know about Jesus, and not a one of those kids knew any of the people who built and maintained the sanctuary over the decades. I think an important question is what *their* memories of this church will be when they're *our* age, making decisions about making the effort to raise their own children in the church, this one or some other one. Will it depend upon stained glass and carved wood, or upon something else?"

Wendy Palmer spoke up. "Does anyone else remember Mr. Stanton, the youth choir director back in the 1970s?" Several heads nodded. "He's the one who convinced me that I could sing. And he always used to take time in our rehearsal to talk about *what* we were singing—what the hymns and anthems were saying, both the words and the notes, and why it was important, and about the importance of helping to lead the congregation in worship. I think much of what I know about Christianity, I learned from the music we sang with him. He was always so patient with us and made us realize what an important part of the church we were."

The class fell silent, until Sherry Quincy, often a reflective and reconciling voice, said, "I don't recall noticing much about the sanctuary when I was a child, but I remember Mrs. Downing, and how she came to visit us when my mother died." She paused to wipe a tear from one eye. "Did any of you have Mrs. Downing in church school, too?"

A few heads nodded, and smiles came to lips.

"She was one of the first people to come to the house. And she just hugged me and assured me that God would take care of my mom, and would take care of us, too, my dad and my brother and me. And then, over the years, she would make a point of telling me how proud my mother would have been of me, and how she saw the Holy Spirit at work in my life—not on any particular special occasion, either—just, you know . . ."

The class fell quiet again for a few minutes. Then John Collins broke the silence. "I remember *Dr.* Downing. He came to the youth group one time, and we were divided up, the girls going off with somebody I don't remember, and Dr. Downing sat with the boys and talked about, well, I guess you would call it sex education today. Everybody was kind of nervous and embarrassed, but I guess it was something the youth leaders arranged for every few years. Anyway, I don't remember much of the specifics"—here, he broke off and chuckled self-consciously, and others in the room chuckled as well—"but I remember how he ended his talk. 'Always remember, when you're out on a date, to treat your date as a child of God, and as if Jesus was there with you. Because he is.'" John Collins shook his head meditatively. "And I remember Bill Morris—some of you might have known him before his family moved away" (at this, some heads nodded). "Anyway, I remember how Bill took me aside when we were on a double date once and things were getting, well, kind of romantic, you might say, and reminded me of what Dr. Downing had told us all about Christ being there with us. I guess that's one of the strongest memories about what this church means to me." He paused, then added, "Maybe even more than those magnificent windows. Even the one that my great-grandparents donated."

The room fell silent again. Eventually, Tony Simmons spoke. "The church is a place of memory, for sure, all the good things that went before. But I guess it really needs to dedicate its resources to what will make a positive difference for the living."

"We are assured that the faithful who have gone before us live forever with Jesus in the presence of God," Reverend Miller said after a few moments during which all were thinking about what they owed to their ancestors, and to those just starting out in life, and to those yet to come. "Thanks be to the God of the living."

John Collins clasped his hands and bowed his head.

Thirty-Third Sunday in Ordinary Time

Judges 4:1–7
1 Thessalonians 5:1–11
Matthew 25:14–30

"The Memories in the Closet"

Charlotte's mother stopped as usual at the front entrance to the gardens on her way to the ferry terminal. And, as usual, she leaned over and kissed her daughter goodbye as the girl prepared to get out the passenger-side door of the old green sedan, mostly out of habit, but also out of affection. Charlotte returned the gesture with a weak smile, as usual, and pulled the large canvas bag out of the backseat, along with the collapsible wooden stool. "Have a pleasant day," her mother said as Charlotte closed the backdoor.

A few times, in the early days of this routine, Charlotte had responded with "Pleasant crossings," but the new daily custom had quickly become a dutiful drudgery. Not that she didn't *like* to paint, but she would have preferred simply to lie on the couch in their apartment on the outskirts of the city, looking across the busy traffic on Blanshard Street toward the mountains in the distance. The doctor had said that it would be good for her to get out in the fresh air, but Charlotte suspected that it really wasn't about the fresh air at all—while she was buttoning her blouse that day in the doctor's office, she had been certain that she heard the doctor saying to her mother in the corridor outside the examining room something about "feeling sorry for herself." Well, she had a right to, didn't she? *She* didn't ask to be run into by that driver and be knocked off her bicycle, senseless, bruised, and with a dozen broken bones. It had been enough to knock her out of university, too, and to lose a semester's credit, and now that the summer was coming to an end, it didn't look like she would have the stamina yet to return for the fall semester, either. The stool and canvas bag were almost too much for her to handle, one way each in the early morning and again in the late afternoon.

She stood at the gate as still as a statue, waiting to be noticed by one of the gardeners, her canvas bag resting on the sidewalk and the stool leaning against the gatepost. By nature, she was not assertive, and her accident had made her even less so. "Pete," she finally said when she recognized a familiar figure passing through the courtyard beyond the gate. One rib had punctured her lung; her voice was still not strong, but, then, she had never talked very loudly. "Pete, can you let me in?" she asked, speaking up again when he had apparently failed to hear her the first time.

The middle-aged man with a flat green cap and full gray moustache turned his head, surprised to hear his name, but smiling as he recognized Charlotte. "Miss Charlotte," he said cheerily, bounding toward the gate and unlocking it. "Come right in," he added as he held the gate open and reached for her canvas bag. "The Sunken Garden today, or the roses, perhaps?"

"Thank you," she said, returning his smile, but not matching it either in breadth or sincerity. "The Sunken Garden, I think, since it doesn't look like rain." The Sunken Garden was the farthest from the visitor's center, which would have made it harder for her to retreat to shelter in the event of wet weather. On days when there was a mist or it was threatening rain, she preferred to work in the Italian Garden or the Rose Garden, nearer to the visitor's center.

"Oh, it's going to be a fine day," Pete said, slinging the canvas bag on his shoulder.

Charlotte's mother knew one of the managers of the famous tourist spot, and had arranged for her daughter to gain access before opening time so that she could drop her off each morning on her way to work as a steward on one of the big V-class ferries that plied their way from the island to the mainland and back again several times a day. The gardens were already busy long before most people were up for work as an army of gardeners manicured the beds and lawns, and fertilized and weeded and pruned. They had become accustomed to seeing the twenty-year-old sitting on her stool in front of the portable easel applying strokes to a canvas. But they were puzzled why, whenever any of them would come near to look at her work, she would quickly remove it from the easel or throw a cloth over it. "It's not finished," she would say if they inquired about it, or "It's not any good." People came from all over the world to paint here, but the wan face of this young woman seemed to hold none of the joy and wonder that the gardens inspired for most artists, and, at the end of the day, when she packed her paints and brushes and palette and canvas and portable easel back into her bag, there was never any indication of satisfaction or accomplishment.

There was a time when Charlotte had taken great delight in painting, had even aspired to attend art school back east. She had been painting ever since grade six, when her father surprised her one Christmas with a beginning paint set of canvas, palette, three brushes, and primary colors plus a big tube of white. That very afternoon, he had given in to her pleading, and had taken her down to the inner harbor, where she made her first effort at capturing the quay, which itself would have been filled with artists' stalls in the summertime, and the big old hotel that sat across Government Street opposite. Her parents had praised her first effort, of course, and she had gone on to paint many of the city's famous scenes until she was seventeen years old.

That was when Matthew had entered her life, or, rather, she had tried to enter *his* life. After months of hoping, Matthew had, in fact, asked her out on a date, and they had continued to date from time to time, even after the school craft fair. It was the day after she had submitted her painting of children playing in Beacon Hill Park that she saw Matthew, with two of his friends, standing in front of the picture, pointing at it and laughing. She had not picked up a brush since that day until the doctor offered his prescription about her getting out in the fresh air and her mother suggested that she take paints and a canvas to the gardens. Her father had not lived to see her set them aside, and it had taken her mother several weeks to notice that her daughter had abandoned her hobby. Charlotte had never told her about the incident with Matthew and his friends. Though they had gone to a movie together less than a month before the accident, Matthew had never since visited her or even called on the telephone. Subliminally, perhaps, that is why Charlotte did not demur when her mother made the suggestion about spending some time painting in the gardens.

Charlotte followed Pete silently along the winding path that eventually dropped into what had once been a quarry but was now a lush kaleidoscope of every sort of flower imaginable. "Where do you want to set up?" Pete asked over his shoulder. "The lupines are nice."

"All right," Charlotte responded without any hint of enthusiasm, as if she were only taking orders about how she must live life. Sensing, perhaps, that her tone might be misunderstood as rudeness, she added, "I haven't done the lupines yet."

"Sometime, I'd like to see your work," Pete said as they reached a broad grassy space between a batch of day lilies and a field of bright blue and white lupines.

"Oh," she said, "it's just something I do for myself to pass the time away. I don't think they're very good."

"Well," Pete responded, drawing the portable easel out of the bag and erecting it for her, "all of us would be interested. I'm sure your work is very good. You know, we get to see a lot of people here painting every summer. Some are probably better than others, but the point is, they enjoy it, and what they do eventually gives joy to others."

Charlotte gave no sign that she was even listening to what Pete was saying, much less heeding it, as she looked around briefly to get a sense of composition, and then turned the easel slightly and set her stool so as to get a glimpse of the water fountain playing in the pond at the far end of the garden.

"It seems to me, Miss Charlotte, that God has given you a gift." Pete's voice was gentle but full of conviction. "You mustn't waste it, and you mustn't belittle it."

Charlotte, sitting now on the stool, looked up at the gardener, squinting because of the sun breaking through the clouds behind him, then looked down again as she reached for her palette and paints. "Thank you for helping me," she said, simply. She looked back up, her hand raised to her brow in a sort of salute, but meant to keep the sun out of her eyes, her gently curled blonde hair reflecting the sunlight back into his eyes. The look of intense sincerity in Pete's face relaxed as he nodded and turned to walk away and resume his duties.

The sunshine awakened the fragrance of the flowers around Charlotte as she sketched the scene before her on the canvas. Now and then, she saw the fluttering wings of a butterfly or heard the distant buzzing of a bee, but her attention was on the lupines and the jet of water shooting up from the pond in the background. It would be a study in blue and yellow and white, but she toyed with the idea of bringing the reddish-orange cannas out from the shadow of a willow beyond the lupines and to the right of center of her picture. Or perhaps the shadow should be retained as the sun rose higher, keeping the cannas a duskier tone so they wouldn't jar the composition. That would be the safer thing to do.

Charlotte was well into painting the clouds of a late summer's morning on the island when the first tourists happened to flow into the Sunken Garden. Apparently, a tour bus had deposited a load of retirement-age Germans at the front gate. Like their Asian counterparts, these northern Europeans were polite and well mannered, remaining on the walkways and seldom, if ever, straying onto the lawn to seek a better vantage point for a photograph or investigate what Charlotte was doing. She was faintly conscious that whoever happened to climb the great stone promontory behind her could get a glimpse of her work, but she was unconcerned, so long as no one got close enough to pass critical judgment on her efforts.

By noon, as usual, she packed up her artists' equipment, for she was tired and the afternoon angle of the sun changed the scene too much to continue. And, as usual, she would find a quiet spot where she would eat the sandwich and fruit she had brought with her, and then read one of the books she had brought along until her mother returned from Swartz Bay to pick her up.

The following day, it was raining steadily when Charlotte's mother awoke. She knocked on Charlotte's bedroom door and conferred briefly with her daughter about the weather. As her mother finished dressing, Charlotte rolled over in her bed and went back to sleep. When she got up later in the morning, she decided to finish the detail on the lupines from memory so that she could start with a fresh canvas whenever the weather permitted a return to the gardens. After the lupine painting dried, it would join the others stacked in the far end of Charlotte's closet. It rained all that day, sometimes hard—rather unusual for early August—and into the night, long after her mother had returned from work. The tourist-passengers had been rather surly, her mother said, the weather keeping them from going out on deck and causing them to feel deprived of a full day of their vacation.

The next day still threatened rain, but Charlotte's mother persuaded her to hazard spending the day at the gardens; if it began raining early, she could always take the district bus back to town, since the route passed by the entrance to the parking lot at the gardens. But by the time they arrived at the gardens, the sun was out. Today, the gate was standing open long before the public opening, so Charlotte was well along the path to the Sunken Garden when Pete came up behind her. "Let me take that for you, Miss Charlotte," he said, reaching for the canvas bag and relieving it from her grip.

"Thank you, Pete," she replied, her smile still faint.

"The lawn's a soggy mess by the lupines, I'm afraid," he said. "We had so much rain last night, you know."

"Well," she replied, "I finished that yesterday while I was at home. I thought of crossing over that little stone bridge to where the hollyhocks are. I'd considered doing the delphiniums but they don't seem to be so colorful this year."

"Oh, I'm sorry, miss, but that's all shut down today. We had a sort of calamity last night."

Charlotte turned fully toward Pete and looked at him squarely for perhaps the first time, a question on her face.

"The bridge there, over the lily pond, collapsed yesterday afternoon. We guess it was the rain, softening the ground around the foundation. There was already a crack in the mortar in the middle of it, you know, and then that bad storm last winter must have weakened it. Yesterday's rain was enough to finish it off. We're just fortunate that no one was on it when it collapsed."

"That was always such a picturesque spot," Charlotte mused, starting to walk again and looking off in the direction of the lily pond, though it was not yet visible from where they were. "That's too bad."

"It fair to broke my sister's heart when I told her about it last night," Pete said.

"Oh?" Charlotte asked, not fully attentive to what he was saying.

"She used to work here, you know—was a volunteer guide for almost twenty years after her husband died and before she got sick."

Charlotte slowed her pace, listening more closely now.

"She loved these gardens. And that was her favorite place of all. Do you know, long before she began volunteering here, she and Sam, her husband, were married on that bridge? Now, if the ground can't hold a foundation, I suppose they won't try to replace it. And, of course, even if they did, it wouldn't be the same, it was so old and charming."

"I guess it's a good thing they had wedding pictures," Charlotte said, "so that she can remember it."

"There's the pity," Pete answered. "The photographs went up in smoke before Frances and Sam ever saw them, and the negatives, too. There was a fire at the photographer's studio a few days after the wedding. Since they didn't have any pictures to look at, she and Sam came back here every year on their anniversary until he died about six years after they were married."

"Well, she at least can get a postcard of the bridge. I've seen them in the gift shop."

"Yes," Pete sighed. "I suppose so."

"I guess I'll try the delphiniums, then," said Charlotte as they descended the stairs into the Sunken Garden. "Thank you for carrying my things."

"I'm happy to do it," Pete responded. "I just wish you'd let people *see* your paintings instead of keeping them *hidden*."

From where she set up her easel and stool to paint the delphiniums, back over her shoulder to her right, Charlotte could see the rubble that was once the little stone bridge over the narrow part of the lily pond. There were workmen standing inside the yellow "caution" tape that surrounded the site, pondering, she supposed, how to remove the heavy chunks of stone and mortar without tearing up the grounds around the pond with mechanized equipment.

The delphiniums, in fact, were not in full blossom this year, and the few blooms were now fading. She rearranged her easel so that, instead, she could paint the stone monolith that protruded from the garden floor and had the little observation point perched on top that delighted both children and adults. She had painted it before, of course, from a different angle, with sons and daughters and parents and grandparents squealing with delight and oohing and aahing from its height. As she thought of the visitors' enjoyment of the now-unpopulated rock, her thoughts returned to the bridge, and to Pete's sister's wedding. Slowly, another thought came to her, one that she tried to reject from her mind, but that kept reasserting itself through the course of the morning to the point that she could not concentrate on the work in front of her. Finally, but well before noon, she packed up her equipment, deposited it with an obliging sales clerk in the public nursery, and spent the remainder of the morning and early afternoon walking around the gardens, seeing them, in a sense, for the first time—through the eyes of Pete's sister, first a new bride, and then a young widow, whose love for the spot drew her back annually on the anniversary of her wedding, and then whose loss of her beloved husband drew her back as a volunteer. About two o'clock, she came across Pete, inconspicuously raking some bark in the Rose Garden.

"Where does your sister live?" she asked the gardener.

"Near Ross Bay," Pete answered, surprised at the question. "On Fairfield Road, near St. Charles Street. 1621 Fairfield Road. Why?"

"Would you be able to meet me there this evening?"

"Yes, but—"

"Would eight o'clock be all right?"

"Yes, fine, but I still—"

"Thank you," she said, turning and running, almost, back to the visitor's center.

In fact, she was out of breath when, after retrieving her book, she sat down on a bench in the Italian Garden. She tried reading, but eventually put the book down, and strolled back to the Rose Garden. Pete was no longer where she had found him half an hour earlier. A large bush with bright pink roses on it attracted her attention. She looked at it thoughtfully, then bent over it, drawing one of the blossoms up to her nose. She smelled the sweet fragrance, and she smiled.

Charlotte's mother had not asked about the noise that was emitting from her daughter's bedroom, the banging and shuffling sounds that came unevenly from her daughter's closet while she made dinner for the two of them. Neither did she ask why Charlotte asked her to drive out to Fairfield Road after dinner, nor what she had in her canvas bag that she toted along. She *had* noticed a pronounced change in Charlotte's mood, a brightening in her personality that had been missing since the accident—no, perhaps even long before that.

"Here it is, 1621," Charlotte chirped with nervous excitement. The sun had not yet set as Charlotte's mother pulled the car up to the curb, and they could see a man—Charlotte recognized him as Pete—pulling weeds out of a colorful flower bed in front of the house. "That's Pete," Charlotte said to her mother as she got out of the passenger side of the car, then put her head back in, adding, "I won't be long." Her mother watched her wave to the man when he looked up, and was heartened to think that his smile must have been returning a grin on her daughter's face which had been so lacking of joy for many months.

"Frances," Pete said as they entered the front door into the presence of a woman sitting in a stuffed flowered chair, a flowered comforter covering her lap and her legs, "you have a visitor. I'd like you to meet Charlotte . . ." He turned toward Charlotte, apologetically. "I don't know your last name."

"Ellis," Charlotte said, shifting her canvas bag to her left hand and holding her right hand out toward Pete's sister.

"How do you do?" Pete's sister answered in a voice not strong, but audible, as she shook Charlotte's hand.

"Pete told me this morning that you knew about the little stone bridge over the lily pond."

The older woman nodded, as her eyes moistened and her lower lip began to tremble.

"I'm sorry. I wish they could replace it. But I got to thinking." Charlotte reached in the canvas bag and pulled out a painting. "I thought you might like this. I did it a few weeks ago." She held it up for the woman, and Pete shifted his position to stand behind the chair, where he could see it as his sister looked at it.

"Oh, Pete," the woman said, clapping her hands together and smiling broadly now as, tears streaming down her face, she turned her head and looked up at her brother. "It's just the way I remember it."

Christ the King

Ezekiel 34:11–16, 20–24
Ephesians 1:15–23
Matthew 25:31–46

"Faces of the King"

The people of the kingdom were greatly excited. Their beloved king, known far and wide for being generous and kind to all of his subjects and concerned for their welfare, had announced the first annual good citizenship award ceremony. Although no prize had yet been announced, it seemed certain that such an important award would be accompanied by a prize of great expense and prestige—speculation centered on a new luxury automobile and dinner with the king in the palace. Of course, many people were calculating how they could win the award, although no criteria had been specified. To their credit, not a single person in the kingdom sought the award merely for the sake of the anticipated *prize*, although of course that was an added incentive. The greater motive was to show how much they loved their king, how much they appreciated his generosity and kindness.

The most prominent citizen of the kingdom was a man named Humphrey J. Limpet. So well known was he, in fact, that it would have been something of an embarrassment if he were not to receive the award. When he heard about it, he entered into the spirit of the contest with characteristic zeal. Mr. Limpet was a great planner—he was quite good at organizing his own life and the life of his family and the life of anyone else who sought his advice and counsel. So the first thing he did was to decide upon a plan. First, he would announce the formation of a Citizens' Kingdom Improvement

Committee with himself as chairperson and twelve other prominent citizens as committee members. The committee would have the task of conducting a study of all the citizens of the kingdom and making suggestions about how they could improve the quality of the moral and social life of the kingdom. Mr. Limpet was painfully aware that some of his fellow citizens were not showing adequate respect toward their king who had been so generous and kind to his subjects; some people did not keep their homes and shops neat and clean, some did not dress properly as befits people with pride in their appearance, some did not behave according to the standards of rule and custom for the kingdom; why, some more recent arrivals among the citizenry did not even speak the official language! Mr. Limpet himself had always tried to set a good example by keeping his place of business tidy, the grounds of his home neat, and himself well groomed. He went out of his way to observe the rules that the king had established and to follow the customs of the kingdom. But as for many of his fellow citizens, there was certainly much room for improvement. Surely the king would be grateful for any assistance in bringing order and maintaining the standards of hygiene in his realm.

The second part of Mr. Limpet's plan was to conduct a personal speaking tour throughout the kingdom in praise of the king, drawing to the attention of any neglectful subject the appropriate way of showing suitable homage to their monarch who was so generous and kind. Difficult as it was for Mr. Limpet to understand how some people could be so disrespectful, he was aware that a regrettably large proportion of citizens simply did not attend the weekly celebration held in the king's honor just outside the palace. He himself had *always* participated, and had not the least idea why everyone did not. Nor could he understand how anyone might fail to speak highly of such a generous and kind king at every opportunity, just as he did. Mr. Limpet was convinced that he was providing an indispensable service for his fellow citizens as well as for the king by addressing the issue.

It so happened that the day on which Mr. Limpet devised his plan was the day before the weekly celebration in front of the palace. He hit upon the happy idea of announcing the formation of the Citizens' Kingdom Improvement Committee and his speaking tour the very next day, at the celebration. What better way to demonstrate his genuine devotion to the king? As he fell asleep that night, Mr. Limpet was even entertaining the possibility that his announcement would discourage anyone *else* from even *attempting* to win the first annual good citizenship award.

Mr. Limpet awoke the next morning and dressed with extra thoughtfulness to detail; he would want to look his very best if he were going to be the center of attention at the celebration. He took his appointment book from his pocket and checked it again, to be sure that he wasn't forgetting anything. The celebration, as usual, would be at ten-thirty in the morning. On his way to the celebration, he would mail the invitations to the twelve prominent people whom he desired to serve with him on the Citizens' Kingdom Improvement Committee. After the celebration, he would drive to the airport to catch his flight to his first speaking engagement, stopping off at the police station on the way to inform the police commissioner of his absence from home for a few days and asking whether it could be patrolled extra carefully while he was away.

As Mr. Limpet started to back out of his driveway, he saw, in the rearview mirror, a poorly dressed woman sitting on the sidewalk, one hand clutching her stomach and the other outstretched to passersby who were likewise on their way to the weekly celebration. He honked his horn so that she would move out of the way of his car, but she did not budge. "Bother!" he thought as he stopped the car and got out. "I'm going to be late!"

"See here, madam, I'm afraid that you'll have to move out of the way of my car."

She turned a care-worn face up toward him and stared for a few seconds.

"I must get to the celebration, of course!"

The woman nodded slowly and shifted to a place beside the driveway. As Mr. Limpet hustled back to his automobile, he thought about the missed opportunity of telling the vagrant that *she* really ought to be at the celebration, too, but in the interest of time, he did not attempt to correct his oversight. Besides, she was hardly dressed suitably for the celebration. Driving down the street, he glanced in the rearview mirror and saw that a teenaged girl carrying a grocery bag had stopped beside the woman, and seemed to be handing the bag to her. "Hmm," Mr. Limpet said to himself, "that girl looks like Evie Cochrane," but in his preoccupation with his task, he thought nothing more about the incident.

After parking his car, Mr. Limpet got out and deposited the invitations in a nearby mailbox, then walked briskly toward the palace, where people were already gathering for the celebration. It was a warm day, and folks were lining up at the refreshment booths for soft drinks to combat the heat. Mr. Limpet would have liked a cool drink himself, but of course he was in need of getting to the speaker's platform, so he did not indulge in such a pleasure. As he neared the palace, he passed an old man seated on a bench, his face dripping with perspiration, rather shabbily dressed and showing no sign of expecting to participate in the celebration. "A disgusting way to come to the palace grounds!" thought Mr. Limpet as he surveyed the crowd.

He pressed on toward the platform. "Fellow subjects of our generous and kind king," said Mr. Limpet, "I appear before you at this glorious celebration to announce the organization of a Citizens' Kingdom Improvement Committee of twelve prominent citizens and myself who will make suggestions how the quality of the moral and social life of the kingdom can be improved. I am sure you are aware that some of our fellow citizens are not showing adequate respect toward the king who has been so generous and kind; some people do not keep their homes and shops neat and clean, some do not dress properly, some do not behave according to the standards of rule and custom for the kingdom, why, some among us do not even speak the official language! Surely our king deserves better."

As he said this, his eye caught a glimpse of the man on the bench. Barney Spencer was handing him a soft drink obviously purchased from the refreshment stand as Linda Parker walked toward him from the souvenir shop, carrying a brightly colored shirt and what looked like flowered Bermuda shorts. The sight of such attire was almost enough to cause Mr. Limpet to lose his concentration.

"Furthermore," he continued, "I want you all to know that I am leaving immediately for the airport, where I will depart on a speaking tour in praise of our king, drawing to the attention of any neglectful subject the appropriate way of showing suitable homage to our monarch who is so generous and kind."

Everyone applauded with great enthusiasm, and Mr. Limpet smiled and waved to the crowd. He pushed his way through the throng of people back toward where he had parked his automobile. "Tsk, tsk," he said under his breath, shaking his head as he passed the man on the bench, now smiling and adorned in the brightly colored shirt and flowered Bermuda shorts, sipping on a glass of lemonade.

He was surprised, when he got to his car, to discover leaning against his right front fender a young man, rather pale-looking and shivering, in spite of the heat. As Mr. Limpet approached, the young man turned his face toward him, and Mr. Limpet could see that his eyes were glassy. "Poor fellow," thought Mr. Limpet to himself, "but why did he have to choose *my* car to lean against?"

"I'm sorry, my good man," said Mr. Limpet, "but I'm afraid I must have the use of my automobile."

The young man nodded rather absentmindedly, and with great effort pushed himself away from the fender and staggered toward the curb, where he sat down.

"Thank you; I'm sorry to have had to bother you," said Mr. Limpet, not without a note of genuine concern in his voice.

"Are you all right?" asked Winnie Smith as she got out of the car parked next to Mr. Limpet's, and bent over the pale young man.

Mr. Limpet got in his car and looked at his watch. "Still time to swing by the police station on my way to the airport," he thought to himself.

"Thank you," said Mr. Limpet to the police officer who opened the door for him at the police station. "May I see the police commissioner?" he asked of the desk sergeant.

"He's not in his office right now," the desk sergeant replied. "Can I help you, Mr. Limpet?"

"Yes," said Mr. Limpet, glancing at his watch. "I am leaving on a very important speaking tour to draw the attention of our people to the appropriate way to show homage to our king, and wondered whether there could be an extra patrol around my house each day while I am gone."

"Certainly," replied the desk sergeant, "especially since you are going to perform such an important public service. You might almost ought to start over there," he said, nodding toward the iron bars across the room. A pathetic and frightened-looking man peered out of the corner of his cell at Mr. Limpet. "Caught him just this morning breaching the rules of the kingdom."

"Why do people do such things?" asked Mr. Limpet, not really expecting an answer.

"You could *ask* him," replied the desk sergeant with a shrug, "but he wouldn't understand you—doesn't even speak our language."

Mr. Limpet looked at the desk sergeant with an expression of perplexity, and then back toward the man in the cell, whose face, he now noticed, was of a different complexion than his own.

Another man had come into the police station now, Tom Murphy, a fellow who never seemed to care about his own appearance, and he asked the desk sergeant, "Do you have any prisoners today that I may visit?"

"Over there," the desk sergeant pointed without looking up from his work, "but you're wasting your time."

"It's not a waste," said Tom, walking toward the cell.

Suddenly remembering his more pressing concern, Mr. Limpet turned toward the door.

Mr. Limpet came to the weekly celebration a little earlier than usual, in spite of the fact that he was tired, having just arrived back home from his speaking tour the night before. He certainly did not want to risk being late on the very day that the first annual good citizenship award was announced. He was a little disappointed not to see a new luxury automobile or any other obvious prize on display in front of the palace, but consoled himself with the thought that the award might bring with it instead a prize trip around the world, perhaps even one on which he could serve as a sort of special goodwill ambassador, speaking in many different countries in praise of the king's generosity and kindness.

The crowd gathered in front of the palace gates, but 10:30 came and went, without any sight of the king. 10:40. 10:50. 11:00. Mr. Limpet grew impatient, as did the other people gathered around. Just then, people behind him started cheering, and the crowd parted as the king walked toward the platform, not from the direction of the *palace*, but from the *city*. The king mounted the platform.

"As you know," he said, "I am here to announce the winner of the first annual good citizenship award. Actually, there has been a tie."

Mr. Limpet's countenance fell noticeably.

"A tie between Evie Cochrane, Barney Spencer, Linda Parker, Winnie Smith, and Tom Murphy."

One by one, the people named came forward, hesitantly, it seemed, and somewhat confused. Miss Cochrane shook her head in dismay. Mr. Murphy said, "You don't mean *me*, do you?" But the king nodded. Mrs. Smith blushed.

Mr. Limpet was astounded and deeply hurt, but also curious. "Why *them* and not *me*?" he wondered.

"To you five," said the king, "I give my kingdom. From this time forth, all that is mine is yours."

"But your highness—" protested Evie.

"Why, what have *I* done to deserve *this*?" asked Barney.

"There must be some mistake," said Linda.

"Do you have the right Winnie Smith?" asked Winnie.

Tom just stood there looking dumbfounded.

"Come, inherit my kingdom, for I was hungry and you gave me food, I was thirsty and you gave me something to drink, I was a stranger and you welcomed me, I was naked and you gave me clothing, I was sick and you took care of me."

"But when—?" they started, but the king held up his hand to silence their question.

"Your highness!" shouted Mr. Limpet, in spite of his reverence for the king. "Have you perhaps not heard what *I* have been doing?"

"I am aware," answered the king. "I am aware."

He looked out over the people gathered in front of the palace. "As a good king, I must watch over all my people, must care for all my people, must be in sympathy with all my people, must identify with all my people. I *live* for my *people*, and I live *through* my people. I see myself in each of your faces; your smiles are my joy, your tears are my sorrow, your human kindness is my love, your anguish is my pain. You all saw my face this week—the face of the hungry, the face of the thirsty, the face of the stranger, the face of the naked, the face of the sick, the face of the imprisoned."

Suddenly, Mr. Limpet remembered the occasions on which he had recently seen Evie and Barney and Linda and Winnie and Tom.

"You mean that *you*—?" Mr. Limpet started to ask the king, but then broke off the question, embarrassed and not knowing what to say.

"You mean that *you*—?" asked Tom Murphy, as the king embraced the five surprised good citizens and led them into the palace.

Thanksgiving

Thanksgiving

Deuteronomy 26:1–11
1 Timothy 2:1–4
Matthew 6:25–33

"Paradise"

Martha Collins stood at the kitchen sink, looking through the back window at the clothesline and wondering whether today's weather would be a repeat of yesterday's, which, being showery, had prevented her from washing the clothes that had accumulated over the past several days in the hamper. She had gone through this process many times over the years since her husband Henry had moved her from the nation's metropolitan core to this rural valley so far away from interesting shops and fine restaurants and endless diversions. She had met him shortly after he had enrolled in university and just after she had gotten a job as a file clerk in a Bay Street law firm—they happened to share a table in a crowded diner on Yonge Street one day, and had immediately felt a mutual attraction that had progressed rather rapidly to engagement and marriage. Within weeks of their wedding, she had been promoted to a secretarial position. But just after that, Henry had received the telephone call about his father's fatal accident and the prospect that the farm that had been in the family for generations would have to be sold if Henry could not take it over. He was the lone son in the family of one boy and three girls, one of whom had married and moved to Boston, one of whom was then nearing graduation from university in Halifax and had been accepted into medical college, and the other who was just entering high school. Unexpectedly, Martha had found herself transported from the postwar promise of the big city to tiny Kemptown—from the center of the universe, as it seemed, to the remotest edge of the galaxy.

She looked at the sky and judged the clouds on the horizon of verdant hills to be neither rainmakers nor harbingers of a solid overcast. She should get on with the washing so that the clothes would have a chance to dry on the line; the day promised fair. Henry had already left the house before she had finished the morning dishes; she could hear the high-pitched chugging of an idling tractor engine from the hayfield, where Henry was beginning the second cutting of the season. Andrew, their older son, would be joining his father as soon as he had finished with the milk cows in the barn, and Laddie, whose real name was Alexander, would probably find his way down to the brook with neighbor children Billy and Annie, the MacGregor twins, to cast their lines in the water that eventually wound its way into Cobequid Bay. It was summertime, and the children of the neighborhood were living the fullness of freedom from school, enjoying the lazy days between the discipline of books and the excitement of harvest out of doors free from care. Andrew was a fine, healthy, intelligent teenager, rather obviously bound for a fine university, with the help of a scholarship—perhaps, Martha sometimes considered, like Henry had been twenty years earlier. Laddie, well, it was a little early to tell. She had dreams for both of them that had nothing to do with the Collins family farm. There had been a girl, too, but she had died at birth. Martha had also had dreams about *her*—somehow, she had just known that this baby would be a girl—and how her daughter would fulfill the expectations that she herself had never been able to realize—a fine house on a sophisticated street, travel to New York and to Europe, and so much more, so much more that, she reflected only in her most sober moments, would probably never have come about anyway for a girl from a little farm near Kemptown. Laddie had been unexpected. It would have been nice if *he* had been a girl—would have made it easier, having another child after such a gap. But he was all boy, and had worn her out until he finally reached school age. He was good, but he was active, and she did not understand how any child could dirty clothes so quickly.

Part of Martha's dissatisfaction with the way life had turned out was that she had always felt an outsider here, where families went back generations and most of them seemed to have no ambition beyond this valley. Even as she thought it, she knew that wasn't quite true—in fact, not true at all. Look at Henry's sisters, for example. Only *he* had returned to Kemptown to spend his life on the family farm. Even the youngest sister, now a teacher, had found a job in a real city. But the part about feeling an outsider was true; Martha had never grown beyond the sense of regret for the life she might have led, the places she might have gone, the things she might have seen. But even that, she knew, was as much her own attitude—was it a sense of superiority?—about having been wrenched from the constant bustle and vivacity of the city—the city that, when she had actually *lived* there, often seemed cold and gray and impersonal. And then there was also the constant worry that she had experienced about the insecurity of a life dependent upon weather and insects and commodity prices. She had never shared her feelings with Henry; she had vowed at the wedding "for better or for worse," and his immediate decision to abandon his schooling and return to the farm had seemed to leave no room for discussion. He obviously considered it the only reasonable and natural thing to do. Duty had called, and now *his* duty was *her* duty, *too*. But why did *he* not resent the change in life's plans the way *she* did? She might have been the top administrative manager of the entire law office by now.

Martha finished the dishes with a series of automatic motions that had been the same virtually every morning of her life since coming to the farm. Somehow during the procedure, she sighed involuntarily. Her thoughts about doing the wash and her thoughts about what she had missed in life were interrupted by a knock at the front door. With her mind on other things, she had not heard any car or truck drive into the yard, and thus supposed that it must be Billy or Annie calling early for Laddie, though they should know that he had morning chores to complete before he could play. She was surprised, then, to see a man about her own age, clad in pressed trousers and a white short-sleeve shirt and necktie, when she opened the door.

"Good morning, ma'am. I'm sorry if I interrupted anything."

He was an attractive man, and exuded pleasantness.

"My name is George Wilkins, and I'm with Maritime Scenics." He extracted a business card from his shirt pocket and handed it to her. She stared at it, as something unexpected and unfamiliar. The wording on the card merely confirmed the information that he had just stated, except for the italicized words "Picture Postcards, Scenic Calendars" and a Moncton address and telephone number. "I'm a photographer," he added, pointing back toward his station wagon, through whose rear windows she could see an assortment of equipment, and whose driver's door also bore the words "Maritime Scenics."

"How can I help you?" Martha mumbled, still affected by the surprise of the visit. "My husband's out in the hayfield."

"As you can see on the card," he began, "my company is in the picture postcard business, and we make scenic calendars, too. In fact, some of our photography ends up in magazines and travel brochures. I'm on assignment," here he paused a few seconds for effect, "looking for scenes to photograph for our new line of postcards and our 1965 calendar, and perhaps to sell to the railroads or the airlines."

He waited for a response from Martha, but, getting none, he continued.

"Frankly, ma'am, this valley is just about the most beautiful place I've ever seen, and the clouds to the north there are just perfect this morning for a shot of your very charming house and barn and trees and everything."

"*Our* house?" Martha finally spoke. "There's nothing special about *our* house." She might have added that she saw nothing interesting about the hills, being void of skyscrapers and department stores and clubhouses. In truth, she had never considered the landscape here as anything but a confirmation of her hidden misery.

"Ma'am, what you have here is what people in every big city in North America *dream* about. Those beautiful hills, that lush pasture, those tall, stately trees; why, I'll bet you've got children who go to a white-frame schoolhouse and spend their summer afternoons fishing down at the brook."

"A *brick* schoolhouse," she corrected him.

"Unhurried, uncomplicated, close to God," he continued, barely noticing the amendment of his description. "What you have *here*, anybody in their right mind would want," he added. "And though they can't have it, they at least feel better about their *own* lives knowing that it exists *somewhere*."

What *did* she have? A monotonous routine, she thought, life lived in pretty much one spot, predictable, ordinary, the little Eaton's mail-order store in Truro being the closest thing to civilization.

"I'd really like to capture those clouds in the background the way they are right now. I'm authorized to pay you five dollars, and then, if we publish a picture with your house or barn in it, twenty-five dollars. You just sign the release form."

"I—I think my husband should sign something like that," Martha stammered.

"And where can I find that worthy?" he asked.

"He's out in the hayfield, down that lane there," she said, pointing to the pair of tracks worn in the dirt that led east from the barn and disappeared quickly behind a grove of maple trees that were luxuriantly green now but blazed fiery red in the fall. "Alexander can show you." She walked out onto the porch, past the photographer. "*Laddie!*" she called. The eight-year-old appeared at the door of the henhouse, clad in overalls and holding a pail in his left hand. "Please take this gentleman over to the hayfield; he wants to talk to your father." Then, turning back to Mr. Wilkins, she said in an apologetic tone, "I'm afraid your car is going to get a little muddy. We had rain yesterday, and—"

"Think nothing of it," he said, smiling. "It's part of my business. If God didn't give us rain," he added, "we wouldn't have the harvest." He started down the steps to meet Laddie, who had dropped his pail and exploded through the gate in the fence that encircled the henhouse. "But isn't it just that much more wonderful that God also gives us the sunshine?"

Standing on the graveled walk now, George Wilkins stretched to his full height, and turned a smiling face toward Martha, and then to the young boy. "So you're Alexander, are you? Can you take me to your father? Jump in the car."

The boy glanced back at his mother with an expression of glee at the stranger's invitation. She nodded, and then watched them drive around the side of the house and past the barn, and she eventually went back into the house. And she thought. "Bless the rain and bless the soil," she had heard the children in the Sunday school class sing. "Bless our bread and bless our toil."

At dinner, that is, the midday meal, Henry looked up from his plate. "I think we're going to come out just fine this year, Martha. I really do. The moisture has been just right for the crops." Martha had long secretly resented living from harvest to harvest, always hoping, never knowing for sure until it was actually in. "Maybe not quite as good as last year," Henry continued, unaware of her hidden anxieties, "but where would we have been if it hadn't been for Jim?"

Martha knew that Henry was referring to his accident, falling from the roof of the hay shed and breaking his leg. A gale in late winter the year before had scattered a good number of shingles about the farmyard, and Henry had been at work replacing them just prior to the first cutting of hay. As he was starting down the ladder with the leftover shingles on his shoulder, he had lost his balance and the foot of the ladder had slipped, so that he and the shingles and the ladder all ended up on the ground—about a fifteen-foot drop. Their neighbor, Jim Carlisle, had come around as soon as he had heard about the mishap and offered to do whatever was necessary to get the hay in and anything else that he could do to help. He had then worked from dawn to dusk through the better part of the summer, caring for his own farm and, with the help of Andrew, who worked right alongside him, the Collins farm as well.

"What a good neighbor," Henry said, fork arrested in midair, gazing back over memories. "*All* of our neighbors," he added, for in fact *many* people had come to their aid on that occasion, as they had at other times of need, too, including at the death of their infant daughter, and the time Andrew sliced into his leg with an ax blade, and the time . . . well, they were too many to count.

Deep in her heart, Martha knew this was true.

"And our boys are so fine," he continued, having gotten in a reflective mood. Sitting across the table, Andrew and Laddie both reddened at the praise, but went right on with their eating.

It was the next Sunday that Reverend McDougall preached a sermon on taking seriously Jesus' words about not being anxious what might happen tomorrow, and how God provides for our needs even better than the beauty with which God clothes the field and even better than God feeds the birds. Martha Collins looked down the pew, over the head of Laddie and around the head of Andrew, at the face of her husband. And she read in his quiet expression evidence that the words of Jesus came to him as no surprise, but were the explanation of his own experience in life. She wished that she could have such a faith. And she suddenly wondered why she had never discussed such things with him. As they rose later in the service to sing "Praise God from whom all blessings flow . . . ," she looked at him again. And she saw in him something that had been there for a long time, but which she had somehow never really appreciated—a person who had learned from childhood to live in trust and therefore to be satisfied with what he had and who, therefore, could be genuinely thankful.

One day, a few weeks later, an envelope came in the mail from Moncton, with the return address of "Maritime Scenics." At first, it meant nothing to Martha, who had driven into town to collect the mail. Then, she recalled the day that the photographer had come to Kemptown. The envelope was addressed to Henry, so she did not open it, but she did hold it up to the sun to see if she could discern its contents. She couldn't.

That evening, when Henry came in from the field, before the boys came home from their adventures, he picked it up from the desk in the corner of the dining room, where the mail was always placed, and opened it. "Well, what do you know?" he said to himself. "Martha," he called through the kitchen door in a louder voice. "Guess what?"

Martha turned from the stove, with a question mark written on her face.

"It's from that photography place in Moncton. Remember that Mr. Wilkins who was here—the photographer?"

In fact, there had been little else on her mind since she had picked up the mail.

"They're publishing his picture on a postcard. They sent us a check for twenty-five dollars." He paused, looking back in the envelope. "And here's the card. Well, will you look at that? It's our house, and the barn, and isn't that a gorgeous picture with the clouds over the hills beyond?" He looked at it with an expression of pure joy—well, not *pure* joy—there was a little pride mixed in. "We really are blessed," he said, admiring the scene, and then handing it to Martha when she came up beside him. "We should be so thankful," he added, mostly to himself.

Martha turned the card over and read the one-word caption above the space allotted for the sender's message: "Paradise." Just then, Laddie bounded in through the backdoor and came up to his mother and threw his arms around her waist and pressed his cheek against her stomach. "I love you," he said, without any preface to this burst of affection. And Martha Collins smiled and began to cry.